THE EDITOR

BRIAN TREHEARNE was born in Vancouver, British Columbia, in 1957. He received his B.A. (1979), M.A. (1981), and Ph.D. (1986) from McGill University. His many publications include *Aestheticism and the Canadian Modernists: Aspects of a Poetic Influence* (1989), *The Montreal Forties: Modernist Poetry in Transition* (1999) and, as editor, *The Complete Poems of A.J.M. Smith* (2007). He is a Professor in the Department of English, McGill University, Montreal, Quebec.

CANADIAN POETRY 1920 TO 1960

CANADIAN

1920 TO 1960

POETRY

EDITED AND WITH AN AFTERWORD BY
BRIAN TREHEARNE

 McClelland & Stewart

LIBRARY AND ARCHIVES CANADA CATALOGUING IN PUBLICATION

Canadian poetry 1920 to 1960 / edited with an afterword by Brian Trehearne.

(New Canadian library)
Hardcover ed. published in a limited ed.
ISBN 978-0-7710-8631-1

1. Canadian poetry (English) – 20th century.
I. Trehearne, Brian, 1957-   II. Series: New Canadian library

PS8291.C35 2009   C811'.508   C2009-905158-3

We acknowledge the financial support of the Government of Canada through the Book
Publishing Industry Development Program and that of the Government of Ontario through
the Ontario Media Development Corporation's Ontario Book Initiative. We further
acknowledge the support of the Canada Council for the Arts and the Ontario Arts Council
for our publishing program.

ANCIENT FOREST
FRIENDLY

Typeset in Fournier by M&S, Toronto
Printed and bound in Canada

McClelland & Stewart Ltd.
75 Sherbourne Street
Toronto, Ontario
M5A 2P9
www.mcclelland.com/NCL

1 2 3 4 5   14 13 12 11 10

CONTENTS

EDITORIAL PREFACE

The present volume follows the New Canadian Library's earlier anthology *Canadian Poetry: From the Beginnings Through the First World War,* edited by Carole Gerson and Gwendolyn Davies (1994). Its period of interest therefore begins with the English-Canadian poets emerging shortly after the Great War. The selection's end-point, albeit loosely construed, is 1960, because a single volume of this convenient size could not effectively represent the rich and various Canadian poetry of the middle decades of the century *and* the great number of new poets and poetics of the 1960s, and because these four decades of exceptional Canadian poetry unquestionably deserve a dedicated anthology.

All of the poets represented here had found their mature voices and styles by 1960. Poets who only did so after 1960, by their own admission or in the critical consensus, have been left out, even if they published books before that date: among them, Leonard Cohen, Eli Mandel, and Al Purdy. These three clearly belong in an anthology that deals with the new poetry of the 1960s. On the other hand, some poets emerged in the mid-to-late 1950s who, though of distinction and note in that decade, did not continue to make a major contribution to Canadian poetry. The finest such poets are included here, for example, R.A.D. Ford, Eldon Grier, and George Johnston. Poets who had established themselves as major voices by 1960 but whose work developed and grew substantially after that year are (of course) included here – poets such as P.K. Page and Phyllis Webb – and in such cases a few of their major works between 1960 and 1970 have been included to suggest the new directions in which they moved in response to a later literary culture. Nonetheless, the anthology does not attempt to represent the full arc of their poetic development to the present day, for such an obligation could only be met in an anthology of major poets that excluded the fine minor poets of their era. The same remarks apply to the selection of Earle Birney, Louis Dudek, Irving Layton, and Dorothy Livesay.

These historical parameters interact with my reading of the period's characteristic and diverse poetic accomplishments to produce the anthology's selection. That characteristic innovation, as I suggest more extensively in the Afterword, was modernism. In one sense or another, and to differing degrees, the poets included here all understood with Virginia Woolf that "in or about December, 1910, human character changed." To be sure, some may have struggled to sustain the collapsing values of the old order while looking cautiously into the new poetic forms and ways of expressing human consciousness; others persisted in traditional forms while registering more knowingly the depth of the change that had occurred. The major voices are surely the ones we still experience as having been most courageous and exacting in both form and thought in their confrontation with the new realities. It follows that I have not included new poets of the 1920s and 1930s, no matter how acclaimed or popular they may have been at the time, who persisted wholeheartedly in the conservative literary practices of the years prior to the Great War, as if that cataclysm had enforced no necessary change in their art. The present anthology seeks to represent the modernizing period of Canadian poetry both comprehensively and with an ear for variety and dissonance, in minor as well as major voices; it welcomes poets whose modernism went tiptoe as well as those who enjoyed the production of cacophony. But Georgian poets who still wrote in the 1930s for a vanishing audience could only have their anachronism exaggerated embarrassingly were they placed in the company of this anthology's superior modern poets.

My other criteria were straightforward: I sought poetic excellence, and I hoped and looked for a comprehensive representation of poetry from the regions of Canada. Whether I was successful in the former regard only the anthology's community of readers can judge. As for the latter premise, the result has been partial. Newfoundland, the Maritimes, Quebec, Ontario, and British Columbia are represented, but the Canadian north is absent, by virtue of a lack of modern poetry in English in the period of interest. The prairie region is represented not by any poet who grew up and remained to cultivate a literary life there but by three groups of transients: those who were born or briefly raised in one of the prairie provinces (Earle Birney, Robert Finch,

Dorothy Livesay, P.K. Page) but wrote relatively little about them; those from elsewhere who nevertheless wrote intensely of prairie experience (Anne Marriott); and those poets who carried their reputations established elsewhere to the prairies for shorter or longer periods of residence (Elizabeth Brewster, James Reaney, Wilfred Watson). All this activity on the conceptual edges of the region anticipated and prepared the ground for the prairie poets emerging in numbers after 1960.

Taken together these principles of selection have led to a greatly expanded canon of Canadian modern poetry. The forty-four poets are arranged by the date of composition or publication (see below) of the earliest poem included. In all cases, the copy text of a given poem has been taken from the last version included in a volume during the author's lifetime. The volumes from which copy-texts have been taken are listed on p. 446. Editorial emendations to copy-texts are very few and only correct obvious typographical errors; they are listed on p. 450. In each poet's selection, the poems are arranged by the date of first publication in a book, whether a group publication (such as *New Provinces, Cerberus,* or *Trio*), an anthology, or an individual volume. That date appears in round brackets ({ }) below the poem. When an earlier date appears to its left in square brackets ([ ]), it indicates a known date of composition significantly earlier than the date of volume publication to the right. By "significantly earlier" I have generally meant three years earlier or more. A few exceptions have been made for a poem's first composition in a particularly significant historical context, such as A.M. Klein's composition of many of the *Rocking Chair* poems in the last months of the Second World War. These dates of composition have been arrived at variously: from critical bibliographies such as *The Annotated Bibliography of Canada's Major Authors*; from biographies such as Sandra Djwa's *The Politics of the Imagination: A Life of F.R. Scott*; from critical editions, such as Zailig Pollock's edition of A.M. Klein's *Complete Poems*; and from *The Canadian Periodical Index*. I cite these exemplary scholarly works both with gratitude and as a means of adumbrating the great number of scholars whose work I have relied on for dates yet cannot cite for reasons of space. In the majority of cases, these dates of composition are in fact based on a prior periodical publication and thus must be understood to indicate composition no later than the given year.

I am very grateful to David Staines, General Editor of the New Canadian Library, for his invitation to edit this anthology. His guidance and assistance throughout its preparation have been invaluable. I express my thanks as well to Jenny Bradshaw, my editor at McClelland and Stewart, who has been, by turns, and always at the right time, patient, helpful, and enthusiastic. In addition, I would like to thank all my teachers in this field, both those in the institution I attended and those from whom I have learnt about Canadian modernist poetry in all the other ways our profession makes possible: from colleagues, friends, and students, and from authors I may never have met whose work nevertheless has formed an essential part of my critical education: in particular, and with a sense of great luck, Louis Dudek, Desmond Cole, A.J.M. Smith, Sandra Djwa, W.J. Keith, Peter Stevens, Michael Gnarowski, D.M.R. Bentley, Irving Layton, Zailig Pollock, P.K. Page, Robert Lecker, Miranda Hickman, Astraður Eysteinsson, Dean Irvine, Medrie Purdham, and Joel Deshaye.

CANADIAN POETRY
1920 TO 1960

FRANK OLIVER CALL
1878–1956

Frank Oliver Call was born in West Brome, Quebec, and educated at Bishop's College, Lennoxville, and at McGill University. He returned to Bishop's College as a lecturer in 1907 and was made Professor of Modern Languages in 1912. He was important as a mentor and friend to Louise Morey Bowman, Ralph Gustafson, and other writers of Quebec's Eastern Townships. In his own time Call was best known for his descriptive and travel writings of French Canada, *The Spell of French Canada* (1926) and *The Spell of Acadie* (1930). Poems with Quebec settings and themes are collected in *Blue Homespun* of 1924. In the important Preface to his best-known volume of poetry, *Acanthus and Wild Grape* (1920), he articulated and defended the principles of free verse to the conservative readership of the day. The book's two sections exemplify the Preface's stance, "Acanthus" containing poems in traditional versification and "Wild Grape" those in free verse, though both sections are durably late Victorian in their materials and treatments.

THE LOON'S CRY

Outside the tent
Darkness and giant trees swaying in the wind.
The lake is moaning in its troubled sleep.
And far across the lazy lapping waves,
Above the crooning of the wind,
I hear a wild loon crying,
Like a weary soul alone on the dark water.

Inside the tent
Your gentle breathing,
Untroubled by crooning wind or wailing loon;   10
Your face is lighted by the embers of the fire.

Fainter and farther away echoes the loon's cry,
But now it is only the voice of Loneliness
Bidding me farewell,
As it passes away into the night.

You stir in your sleep softly
And turn your face to me, –
And the loon cries no more.

{1920}

To a Greek Statue

Beautiful statue of Parian marble,
Dreaming alone in the northern sunlight,
Ivory-tinted, your slender arms beckon;
I follow, I follow.

Slender and white is your beautiful body,
Gleaming against the gray walls that surround you;
Like hyacinth-flowers beneath the snow sleeping
Is the dream you emprison; –

A dream of beauty that lingers forever,
A dream of the amethyst sky of midnight,   10
A dream of the jacinth blue of still waters,
Reflecting white temples.

Your white arms beckon, I follow, I follow,
My dream goes forth with your dream to wander;
You lead me into a moonlit garden
Beside the Ægean.

White in the moonlight gleams the temple
Cutting the purple sky with its pediment;
Diamonds and sapphires fall from the fountain;
Black are the cypress trees.   20

The gods are asleep in the silent temple;
Only the lapping of waves on the sea-sand
Mingles its drowsy rhythmical beating
With the bells of the fountain.

Soft lie the panther-skins on the cool grasses,
Not in vain are your white arms lifted;
And my dream of beauty and your dream eternal
Embrace in the moonlight.

{1920}

LOUISE MOREY BOWMAN
1882–1944

Louise Morey Bowman was born in Sherbrooke, Quebec, and educated privately. Her literary friends included Frank Oliver Call and poet, journalist, and translator Florence Randal Livesay, mother of Dorothy Livesay. After her marriage in 1909 she moved to Toronto. Her work appeared in *Poetry* (Chicago) and received an approbatory review from its editor Harriet Monroe. She published three volumes of poetry; the second, *Dream Tapestries* (1924), was awarded the Quebec government's Prix David. She died in Montreal and is buried in Sherbrooke. A.J.M. Smith included Bowman's work in his *Book of Canadian Poetry* in 1943, but she was dropped from the second edition of 1948 and largely forgotten for three decades thereafter. Recently she has been reclaimed as a pioneer of Canadian modernism for her lifelong practice of free verse, but subtle experiments with voice and rich perspectives in time are her more skilful innovations.

SEA SAND

Between the rhythmical, unfathomed sea,
And the rich, warm fecundity of land
There lies the sand,
The shifting sand of beach and dune,
Pure, strange, sea dust, so alien to green earth,
With its brown furrows that the ploughman makes
Ready for sowers – and for miracle.

Here on the sand,
I lie and watch the coarse sea-grass that creeps
Like an adventurer along the dunes,   10
With wild pea-vines that bravely cling and spread
Tenacious tendrils in this sterile soil . . .
A barren mockery of useful bloom.

I let a little handful of the sand
Drift slowly through my fingers, and I see
Its myriad tiny atoms – shells and stones
That long ago the great waves tossed and ground
To starry powder on the rocky ledge.

At sunset out on the wet, shining sand
Left by the ebbing tide, rare colours fall,   20
And linger there as if they loved the sand.
Who dreams at noontide that its level ways
Can hold such colour: rose and turquoise green,
Purple and gold, and even a crimson glow
Just for a moment, till the splendour dies . . .

Then the moon, silvery and alone, shines down
Upon the sand – pure, strange, sea-dust of Time.

{1922}

THE OLD FRUIT GARDEN

MEMORY

Through tortured weeks of hospital surgery
The old fruit garden of my childhood days
Grew close about me. Through black storms of pain

Swayed joyous boughs of rosy apple-bloom;
White blossomed branches of an old plum-tree;
Old grape-vines clinging to a sunny wall;
Great bushes of red currants and raspberries.
Through hours of torturing thirst I found again
That old fruit garden – as if body and soul
Clutched at cool juicy fruits – remembering –   10
Devouring them through a parched mouth of the brain.

GRAPES

Grandfather was so courtly, wise and calm:
At times a sweet old wordling, dealing balm
Through business phrase or words of ancient psalm,
Justice and whimsical kindliness to all.
As he watched mankind, so in early Fall,
He watched his grape-vines on the stable wall.
In old Quebec the season is too brief
To ripen grapes well . . . sometimes scarlet leaf
Becomes a herald swift beyond belief.   20
The few big clusters with pale purple bloom
So slowly deepening, often met their doom
When rich October caught November's gloom.
He never lost his interest . . . every Fall
He saw his grape-vines as he'd dreamed them, all
Weighed down with purple riches, growing tall
Over the stable windows. On the way
To the rose garden where he walked each day . . .
"These grapes are riper than last year" he'd say.
In spite of all the travelling he'd done   30
He sought no changes now and thought "no sun
Could be much brighter than a Canadian one!"
Yet I knew well his grapes brought visions fair
Of mellow summer lands with temperate air.

"Grapes are like men – can't ripen everywhere . . .
Men all need sun, and right loam I suppose;
But if one strikes deep roots . . . as a rule . . . he grows!"
He smiled his smile and cut a late white rose.

RED CURRANTS

"Well! the red currants must be picked to-day.
They're ready for jelly" Grandmother would say.   40
She never wasted words yet had her way.
In cool gray cotton gown, and black straw hat
Securely tied – She made a point of that
Though no breeze stirred the lilacs where she sat
To superintend old Jock and Marie Anne
At tasks of picking. When her palm-leaf fan
Waved slowly all was well; but my blood ran
Quicker when it moved very fast . . . one knew
The hours were slipping past . . . then old Jock too
And Marie Anne, would pick with greater zest.   50
"Granny! Red currant jelly's *much* the best!"
"Black's best for colds" she'd say, as she caressed
With firm kind fingers my rough curly head.
She rarely kissed me. Deep within was bred
Acid reserve and purity . . . those red
Ripe currants, with their pleasant acid tang,
Seemed to me just *like* Grandmother! I sang
My multiplication-tables till they rang
Loud through the garden where dear Granny sat
Smiling – well-pleased – with firmly-tied black hat!   60

AMBER RASPBERRIES

Old Jock and Marie Anne could never find
Raspberries of the glowing amber kind

To fill the "ancient porcelain bowl." ('Twas lined
With amber glaze; outside a gold vine wound
In such a graceful pattern round and round.)
But if my Mother looked she always found
Enough to fill the bowl. That day we'd three
Distinguished guests. I loved to have them see
My lovely Mother as she looked at tea . . .
Her gown of creamy lace – her shining hair,   70
Her beads of old carved amber . . . all her rare
Fragile soft richness, like the berries there
With their pale amber bloom. I loved her so . . .
I wished that every body there could know . . .
"Why don't you eat your berries, Child?" . . . then low
I bent my head to hide two burning tears
Of yearning love. How strange those vague cold fears
My child heart knew that day . . . what long long years
Since those last lovely hours of ecstasy
When she made Beauty live and thrill for me.   80

{1924}

The Tea Kettle

They said, "Why yes – go walking if you like.
This is safe country all about these farms."
I felt a child, sheltered within a world
Most kindly. Round about green meadows rose
And fell like undulating wavy tides.
The long tree shadows lay like tremulous wings.
From apple tree and elm and maple stole
Invisible playmates. All the fields were sweet
And sharp with fragrance – essences distilled
And spiced from scents of cattle and new-ploughed earth.   10

Along these high hill-roads one walked alone
With new perceptions – knowing one's own soul
No longer bargained in the market place;
No longer, circumspect, kept watch and ward
Over one's body learning traffic laws;
No longer kept sharp outlook for life's thieves.

* * *

Beside the road the house stood glassy-eyed,
Lonely, discreet, reserved, and yet to me
Calling aloud: "Come home, woman, come home!"
Then all my heart beat at each dusty pane,   20
Crouched on the door stone, battered at the door,
Crept close and lifted vines of the wild grape,
Put back the thorny sweet-brier branches, found
The grassy path round to the old plum tree –
And there soft winds of peace blew on my face.
Here at this corner window one would sit
If house-bound. Hearing rhythm of long rain,
Watching the hills, arpeggios of earth
Played by a master hand eternally.
It was a most mad moment I confess   30
For never had I so possessed as now.
Mine, surely it was mine – this weathered house
In the weird pearly twilight. But I peered
Perhaps with eyes too greedy through the glass.
For the rust-rotted kettle on the stove
Emerged from out the gloom and dealt me blows –
Blow after blow resounding in my brain!
Then I remembered all that tale of death
That, in the telling, had gone in one ear
And out the other – and I turned and ran   40
In an unfathomed terror and dismay

Back – back along that unknown high hill-road.
"Why, child, you're like a ghost. What's frightened you?"
"They need a new kettle in that house," I said.

{1938}

RAYMOND KNISTER
1899–1932

In his regrettably short life Raymond Knister was a respected poet, novelist, and author of short fiction, as well as a pioneering anthologist and critic. Born in Ruscom, Ontario, Knister entered Victoria College, University of Toronto, but illness forced him to withdraw after a year. He spent the next three years working on his father's farm and writing the poetry and short fiction that would later appear in such modernist periodicals as *Poetry* and *This Quarter*. In 1923 he took up a year-long associate editorship at the avant-garde periodical *The Midland* in Iowa City, where he completed his first two novels (still unpublished). He returned to Ontario in 1924 and was living in Toronto by 1926, where he began his best-known novel, *White Narcissus* (published 1929). In 1928 Knister edited *Canadian Short Stories*, the first anthology of the form in Canada. Ill luck plagued subsequent publishing projects: a manuscript of his poetry entitled *Windfalls for Cider* was accepted by Lorne Pierce of Ryerson Press but never appeared, apparently for financial reasons, and a second novel, *My Star Predominant*, a fictionalization of the life of poet John Keats, won the Graphic Press Prize (including publication), but the Press went bankrupt before the cash award or the book was produced. Knister drowned in a boating accident off Stoney Point, Lake St Clair, in August 1932. *My Star Predominant* appeared posthumously in 1934. His *Collected Poems* finally appeared with Ryerson Press in 1949, edited by Dorothy Livesay.

CHANGE

I shall not wonder more, then,
But I shall know.

Leaves change, and birds, flowers,
And after years are still the same.

The sea's breast heaves in sighs to the moon,
But they are moon and sea forever.

As in other times the trees stand tense and lonely,
And spread a hollow moan of other times.

You will be you yourself,
I'll find you more, not else,   10
For vintage of the woeful years.

The sea breathes, or broods, or loudens,
Is bright or is mist and the end of the world;
And the sea is constant to change.

I shall not wonder more, then,
But I shall know.

[1922] {1948}

THE HAWK

Across the bristled and sallow fields,
The speckled stubble of cut clover,
Wades your shadow.

Or against a grimy and tattered
Sky
You plunge.

Or you shear a swath
From trembling tiny forests
With the steel of your wings —

Or make a row of waves   10
By the heat of your flight
Along the soundless horizon.

[1924] {1943}

THE PLOWMAN

All day I follow
Watching the swift dark furrow
That curls away before me,
And care not for skies or upturned flowers,
And at the end of the field
Look backward
Ever with discontent.
A stone, a root, a strayed thought
Has warped the line of that furrow —
And urge my horses 'round again.   10

Sometimes even before the row is finished
I must look backward;
To find, when I come to the end
That there I swerved.

Unappeased I leave the field,
Expectant, return.

The horses are very patient.
When I tell myself
This time
The ultimate unflawed turning 20
Is before my share,
They must give up their rest.

[1924] {1943}

from CORN HUSKING

VII

The early dusk is coming on, gathered in
The long pale rows of bowing corn, and from
The sky, and from the thick dark trees far off
About the country's edge, it seems to come.
Slowly it gathers in about us where we work.
The sun is going too, south-west of us,
And does not seem to want to light things up a bit
Just for a farewell shot, as he will sometimes do.
"It only seems a little while," says Bill
"Since that old sun used to go down away 10
To the north-west, but now, the rate he's going
He'll soon be setting in the south, it looks."
There is no answer, no one thinks of it,
We just keep stooping, jerking out the ears.
My father moves along, bent all the time,
Never straightening up. The sun goes down
With defiant splendour, as though he cares

Nothing for all the disregarding men
On the flat land, bent to the soil behind
Their ploughs, or husking corn, or hauling stalks,   20
Or in long rail-fenced lanes, driving cattle home.
"Soon we'll have to feel for them," for Bill
Is always anxious when night comes on
Or noon, for that matter; time cannot be
Urged on enough to suit him then.
But he looks up, and sees a long and sinuous V
Wavering toward us. Wild geese flying
Toward the south above our heads. We stop
Our rustling in the husks and look, all still
Except the horses plucking at the stalks –   30
"Just wish I had my gun," says Bill. "Oh boy!"

"You'd never reach those birds from here, oh boy."

"Oh yes I would, they're not so high!"
"Listen," I say, for there comes down a squeak,
A mellowed squeak, like a pitiful baby-cry
One and another of the great birds gives
As they cleave space, and, almost, time, across the night.

"Why, they're encouraging each other on,"
Says Father, then, "Well boys, we've got to move
Along ourselves. Jess! Jake! Get up, get up!"   40
The ears are really getting hard to see.
"How many miles does this row go, you know?"
"Ends opposite that tree along the fence,"
Says Roy.
"That big one over there, you mean? . . .
It looks as if it had no end at all.
You can't tell when you're opposite that tree,
It may be fifty yards we've got to go."

But it's nearer five, we find.
We lie upon the solid corn and pluck   50
Idly at wisps of husks, and see we have
Forgotten to take off the pegs. Then each
Recites how his hands are scarred and raw;
And Father tries to stop the team, but they
Will only rest a breath, then jerk ahead.
"They know when's suppertime," young Bill remarks.

"Well I can smell supper on the stove
From here," says Roy. We all agree to that.
Rhythmically the bent stalks click and brush
Against the axle as the wagon moves.   60

[*by 1932*] {1983}

JOE WALLACE

1890–1975

Joe Wallace was born in Toronto and grew up in Halifax. In 1922 he joined the recently founded Communist Party of Canada (CPC) and began to contribute articles, essays, and poems to party periodicals. He was briefly affiliated with the Song Fishermen, a group of Nova Scotia writers, including Kenneth Leslie and Charles Bruce, who shared his appreciation for Confederation-period poetics and, in milder forms, his politics. He left a career in advertising in 1933 to work full-time as a CPC journalist and activist. In 1940 the CPC was effectively outlawed, and Wallace was imprisoned from 1941-42. During his internment he dedicated much of his time to poetry. His first collection, *Night Is Ended* (1942), included a preface by E.J. Pratt and was well reviewed by the conservative *Saturday Night* magazine. After the war Wallace continued publication and such muted Communist activism as remained possible. Travelling in Russia and China in 1957, he found his poetry well-known and valued. His last volume, *A Radiant Sphere* (1964), including verse translations of several Russian poets, was published in Moscow in English, Russian, and Chinese, in a run of 10,000 copies per language. Wallace returned to Russia, partly for convalescence, in 1960 and stayed until 1962; he returned briefly in 1966 at the invitation of the Soviet government. He died of a heart attack in Vancouver in 1975.

The Five Point Star

Dank is the fog that dogs our steps,
    The mist that twists in siren shapes,
Edging us on to ledges dim
    Where death, expectant, grimly gapes.

Baleful the light, though beautiful,
    That leads to those seductive arms
Whose clasp is death, and burial
    Beneath the bullfrog's late alarms.

Weary of too much wandering,
    Wary of leaders who mislead,   10
We know not how to stay nor start,
    Nor to go back, nor to proceed.

Suddenly on the leaden sky,
    Bright like a bayonet afar,
Cleaving the dark, the doubt, the death,
    Rises the pilot Five Point Star.

Russia, salute! Not to your lands,
    But to your deathless working class
Who broke the spears of all the Tsars
    Upon their breasts, that we might pass   20

From haunted days and harried ways,
    (Poor hounded slaves who breathe by stealth)
Through revolution's iron gates
    Into the world-wide commonwealth.

[1922] {1942}

ALL MY BROTHERS ARE BEAUTIFUL

I am the youngest one of them all
Growing the fastest but still too small
All my brothers are straight and tall
Even when they are stooped with toil
All my brothers are beautiful.

Long ago they scattered from home
Some to settle and some to roam
What does it matter field or foam?
All my brothers are neighbours now
All my brothers are beautiful.   10

They were robbed wherever they went
Stand and deliver, profit and rent,
Eating the ashes of discontent
Still for all their bitterness
All my brothers are beautiful.

Caught in the blind man's buff of war
They died and they didn't know what for
For God and Country the gangsters swore
None of my brothers are blindfold now
All my brothers are beautiful.   20

One has the beauty of night and stars
One has the beauty of golden bars
Varying skins but the very same scars
White or red whatever the shade
All my brothers are beautiful.

I am the rainbow's radiant prism
I am its beauty and symbolism

I am the builder of socialism.
The whole world blossoms as I grow tall
Blooms for my beautiful brothers and all.   30

{1953}

E.J. PRATT

1882–1964

Edwin John Pratt was born in Western Bay in the Dominion of Newfoundland. After graduating from St John's Methodist College and three years of probationary preaching, he left for studies in Canada in 1907. At the University of Toronto he took B.A. and M.A. degrees in philosophy, psychology, and theology, and then completed a Bachelor of Divinity in 1913, after which he was ordained. He completed a doctorate in divinity in 1917, with a dissertation on the eschatology of Saint Paul; in the same year he had his first volume of poetry printed privately, to few and lukewarm notices. In 1920 he was invited to join the English department at Victoria College, University of Toronto, where he remained until his retirement in 1953. In 1923 he published the breakthrough collection *Newfoundland Verse,* with illustrations by Group of Seven painter F.H. Varley. Pratt would go on to publish eighteen more volumes of poetry and receive Governor General's Awards for *Fable of the Goats* (1937), *Brébeuf and His Brethren* (1940), and *Towards the Last Spike* (1952). In 1930 he was made a Fellow of the Royal Society of Canada; the Lorne Pierce Medal for contributions to Canadian literature followed in 1940. He was the founding editor of the new *Canadian Poetry Magazine* and notably included Dorothy Livesay's "Day and Night" in its first issue in January 1936; he held the post until 1943. Also in 1936 he joined A.J.M. Smith, F.R. Scott, A.M. Klein, Robert Finch, and Leo Kennedy in the first anthology of Canadian modern poetry, *New Provinces: Poems of Several Authors.* During the Second World War he wrote lyric and narrative poems inspired by, and hoping to inspire, the courage of Allied forces in the battle against Nazi Germany. In *Still Life and Other Verse* (1943), in which "Come Away, Death" and "The Truant" appeared, the context of global destruction gives rise to an ironic stoicism and broad humanism rather than to the patriotic certainties of the other volumes of the period. His *Collected Poems* appeared in 1944 and again, edited by Northrop Frye, in 1958.

NEWFOUNDLAND

Here the tides flow,
And here they ebb;
Not with that dull, unsinewed tread of waters
Held under bonds to move
Around unpeopled shores —
Moon-driven through a timeless circuit
Of invasion and retreat;
But with a lusty stroke of life
Pounding at stubborn gates,
That they might run   10
Within the sluices of men's hearts,
Leap under throb of pulse and nerve,
And teach the sea's strong voice
To learn the harmonies of new floods,
The peal of cataract,
And the soft wash of currents
Against resilient banks,
Or the broken rhythms from old chords
Along dark passages
That once were pathways of authentic fires.   20

Red is the sea-kelp on the beach,
Red as the heart's blood,
Nor is there power in tide or sun

To bleach its stain.
It lies there piled thick
Above the gulch-line.
It is rooted in the joints of rocks,
It is tangled around a spar,
It covers a broken rudder,
It is red as the heart's blood, 30
And salt as tears.

Here the winds blow,
And here they die,
Not with that wild, exotic rage
That vainly sweeps untrodden shores,
But with familiar breath
Holding a partnership with life,
Resonant with the hopes of spring,
Pungent with the airs of harvest.
They call with the silver fifes of the sea, 40
They breathe with the lungs of men,
They are one with the tides of the sea,
They are one with the tides of the heart,
They blow with the rising octaves of dawn,
They die with the largo of dusk,
Their hands are full to the overflow,
In their right is the bread of life,
In their left are the waters of death.

Scattered on boom
And rudder and weed 50
Are tangles of shells;
Some with backs of crusted bronze,
And faces of porcelain blue,
Some crushed by the beach stones
To chips of jade;

And some are spiral-cleft
Spreading their tracery on the sand
In the rich veining of an agate's heart;
And others remain unscarred,
To babble of the passing of the winds. 60

Here the crags
Meet with winds and tides —
Not with that blind interchange
Of blow for blow
That spills the thunder of insentient seas;
But with the mind that reads assault
In crouch and leap and the quick stealth,
Stiffening the muscles of the waves.
Here they flank the harbours,
Keeping watch 70
On thresholds, altars and the fires of home,
Or, like mastiffs,
Over-zealous,
Guard too well.

Tide and wind and crag,
Sea-weed and sea-shell
And broken rudder —
And the story is told
Of human veins and pulses,
Of eternal pathways of fire, 80
Of dreams that survive the night,
Of doors held ajar in storms.

{1923}

THE SHARK

He seemed to know the harbour,
So leisurely he swam;
His fin,
Like a piece of sheet-iron,
Three-cornered,
And with knife-edge,
Stirred not a bubble
As it moved
With its base-line on the water.

His body was tubular   10
And tapered
And smoke-blue,
And as he passed the wharf
He turned,
And snapped at a flat-fish
That was dead and floating.
And I saw the flash of a white throat,
And a double row of white teeth,
And eyes of metallic grey,
Hard and narrow and slit.   20

Then out of the harbour,
With that three-cornered fin
Shearing without a bubble the water
Lithely,
Leisurely,
He swam —
That strange fish,
Tubular, tapered, smoke-blue,

Part vulture, part wolf,
Part neither – for his blood was cold.   30

{1923}

SEA-GULLS

For one carved instant as they flew,
The language had no simile –
Silver, crystal, ivory
Were tarnished. Etched upon the horizon blue,
The frieze must go unchallenged, for the lift
And carriage of the wings would stain the drift
Of stars against a tropic indigo
Or dull the parable of snow.

Now settling one by one
Within green hollows or where curled   10
Crests caught the spectrum from the sun,
A thousand wings are furled.
No clay-born lilies of the world
Could blow as free
As those wild orchids of the sea.

[1925] {1932}

FROM STONE TO STEEL

From stone to bronze, from bronze to steel
Along the road-dust of the sun,
Two revolutions of the wheel
From Java to Geneva run.

The snarl Neanderthal is worn
Close to the smiling Aryan lips,
The civil polish of the horn
Gleams from our praying finger tips.

The evolution of desire
Has but matured a toxic wine,   10
Drunk long before its heady fire
Reddened Euphrates or the Rhine.

Between the temple and the cave
The boundary lies tissue-thin:
The yearlings still the altars crave
As satisfaction for a sin.

The road goes up, the road goes down —
Let Java or Geneva be —
But whether to the cross or crown,
The path lies through Gethsemane.

{1932}

THE HIGHWAY

What aeons passed without a count or name,
Before the cosmic seneschal,
Succeeding with a plan
Of weaving stellar patterns from a flame,
Announced at his high carnival
An orbit — with Aldebaran!

And when the drifting years had sighted land,
And hills and plains declared their birth

Amid volcanic throes,
What was the lapse before the marshal's hand   10
Had found a garden on the earth,
And led forth June with her first rose?

And what the gulf between that and the hour,
Late in the simian-human day,
When Nature kept her tryst
With the unfoldment of the star and flower –
When in her sacrificial way
Judaea blossomed with her Christ!

But what made *our* feet miss the road that brought
The world to such a golden trove,   20
In our so brief a span?
How may we grasp again the hand that wrought
Such light, such fragrance, and such love,
O star! O rose! O Son of Man?

{1932}

THE PRIZE CAT

Pure blood domestic, guaranteed,
Soft-mannered, musical in purr,
The ribbon had declared the breed,
Gentility was in the fur.

Such feline culture in the gads
No anger ever arched her back –
What distance since those velvet pads
Departed from the leopard's track!

And when I mused how Time had thinned
The jungle strains within the cells,   10
How human hands had disciplined
Those prowling optic parallels;

I saw the generations pass
Along the reflex of a spring,
A bird had rustled in the grass,
The tab had caught it on the wing:

Behind the leap so furtive-wild
Was such ignition in the gleam,
I thought an Abyssinian child
Had cried out in the whitethroat's scream.   20

[1933] {1937}

THE TITANIC

Harland
& Wolff
Works,
Belfast,
May 31, 1911

The hammers silent and the derricks still,
And high-tide in the harbour! Mind and will
In open test with time and steel had run
The first lap of a schedule and had won.
Although a shell of what was yet to be
Before another year was over, she,
Poised for the launching signal, had surpassed
The dreams of builder or of navigator.
The Primate of the Lines, she had out-classed
That rival effort to eliminate her   10
Beyond the North Sea where the air shots played
The laggard rhythms of their fusillade
Upon the rivets of the *Imperator*.
The wedges in, the shores removed, a girl's

Hand at a sign released a ribbon braid;
Glass crashed against the plates; a wine cascade,
Netting the sunlight in a shower of pearls,
Baptized the bow and gave the ship her name;
A slight push of the rams as a switch set free
The triggers in the slots, and her proud claim   20
On size – to be the first to reach the sea –
Was vindicated, for whatever fears
Stalked with her down the tallow of the slips
Were smothered under by the harbour cheers,
By flags strung to the halyards of the ships.

March 31,
1912 Completed! Waiting for her trial spin –
Levers and telegraphs and valves within
Her intercostal spaces ready to start
The power pulsing through her lungs and heart.
An ocean lifeboat in herself – so ran   30
The architectural comment on her plan.
No wave could sweep those upper decks – unthinkable!
No storm could hurt that hull – the papers said so.
The perfect ship at last – the first unsinkable,
Proved in advance – had not the folders read so?
Such was the steel strength of her double floors
Along the whole length of the keel, and such
The fine adjustment of the bulkhead doors
Geared to the rams, responsive to a touch,
That in collision with iceberg or rock   40
Or passing ship she could survive the shock,
Absorb the double impact, for despite
The bows stove in, with forward holds aleak,
Her aft compartments buoyant, watertight,
Would keep her floating steady for a week.
And this belief had reached its climax when,
Through wireless waves as yet unstaled by use,

The wonder of the ether had begun
To fold the heavens up and reinduce
That ancient *hubris* in the dreams of men,   50
Which would have slain the cattle of the sun,
And filched the lightnings from the fist of Zeus.
What mattered that her boats were but a third
Of full provision – caution was absurd:
Then let the ocean roll and the winds blow
While the risk at Lloyds remained a record low.

The Iceberg   Calved from a glacier near Godhaven coast,
It left the fiord for the sea – a host
Of white flotillas gathering in its wake,
And joined by fragments from a Behring floe,   60
Had circumnavigated it to make
It centre of an archipelago.
Its lateral motion on the Davis Strait
Was casual and indeterminate,
And each advance to southward was as blind
As each recession to the north. No smoke
Of steamships nor the hoist of mainsails broke
The polar wastes – no sounds except the grind
Of ice, the cry of curlews and the lore
Of winds from mesas of eternal snow;   70
Until caught by the western undertow,
It struck the current of the Labrador
Which swung it to its definite southern stride.
Pressure and glacial time had stratified
The berg to the consistency of flint,
And kept inviolate, through clash of tide
And gale, façade and columns with their hint
Of inward altars and of steepled bells
Ringing the passage of the parallels.
But when with months of voyaging it came   80

To where both streams – the Gulf and Polar – met,
The sun which left its crystal peaks aflame
In the sub-arctic noons, began to fret
The arches, flute the spires and deform
The features, till the batteries of storm,
Playing above the slow-eroding base,
Demolished the last temple touch of grace.
Another month, and nothing but the brute
And palaeolithic outline of a face
Fronted the transatlantic shipping route.   90
A sloping spur that tapered to a claw
And lying twenty feet below had made
It lurch and shamble like a plantigrade;
But with an impulse governed by the raw
Mechanics of its birth, it drifted where
Ambushed, fog-grey, it stumbled on its lair,
North forty-one degrees and forty-four,
Fifty and fourteen west the longitude,
Waiting a world-memorial hour, its rude
Corundum form stripped to its Greenland core.   100

Southampton, An omen struck the thousands on the shore –
Wednesday, A double accident! And as the ship
April 10,   Swung down the river on her maiden trip,
1912   Old sailors of the clipper decades, wise
To the sea's incantations, muttered fables
About careening vessels with their cables
Snapped in their harbours under peaceful skies.
Was it just suction or fatality
Which caused the *New York* at the dock to turn,
Her seven mooring ropes to break at the stern   110
And writhe like anacondas on the quay,
While tugs and fenders answered the collision
Signals with such trim margin of precision?

And was it backwash from the starboard screw
Which, tearing at the big *Teutonic,* drew
Her to the limit of her hawser strain,
And made the smaller tethered craft behave
Like frightened harbour ducks? And no one knew
For many days the reason to explain
The rise and wash of one inordinate wave,   120
When a sunken barge on the Southampton bed
Was dragged through mire eight hundred yards ahead,
As the *Titanic* passed above its grave.
But many of those sailors wise and old,
Who pondered on this weird mesmeric power,
Gathered together, lit their pipes and told
Of portents hidden in the natal hour,
Told of the launching of some square-rigged ships,
When water flowed from the inverted tips
Of a waning moon, of sun-hounds, of the shrieks   130
Of whirling shags around the mizzen peaks.
And was there not this morning's augury
For the big one now heading for the sea?
So long after she passed from landsmen's sight,
They watched her with their Mother Carey eyes
Through Spithead smoke, through mists of Isle of Wight,
Through clouds of sea-gulls following with their cries.

Wednesday evening Electric elements were glowing down
In the long galley passages where scores
Of white-capped cooks stood at the oven doors   140
To feed the population of a town.
Cauldrons of stock, purées and consommés,
Simmered with peppercorns and marjoram.
The sea-shore smells from bisque and crab and clam
Blended with odours from the fricassées.
Refrigerators, hung with a week's toll

Of the stockyards, delivered sides of lamb
And veal, beef quarters to be roasted whole,
Hundreds of capons and halibut. A shoal
Of Blue-Points waited to be served on shell.   150
The boards were loaded with pimolas, pails
Of lobster coral, jars of Béchamel,
To garnish tiers of rows of chilled timbales
And aspics. On the shelves were pyramids
Of truffles, sprigs of thyme and water-cress,
Bay leaf and parsley, savouries to dress
Shad roes and sweetbreads broiling on the grids.
And then in diamond, square, crescent and star,
Hors d'oeuvres were fashioned from the toasted bread,
With paste of anchovy and caviare,   160
Paprika sprinkled and pimento spread,
All ready, for the hour was seven!

                                             Meanwhile,
Rivalling the engines with their steady tread,
Thousands of feet were taking overhead
The fourth lap round the deck to make the mile.
Squash racquet, shuffle board and quoits; the cool
Tang of the plunge in the gymnasium pool,
The rub, the crisp air of the April night,
The salt of the breeze made by the liner's rate,
Worked with an even keel to stimulate   170
Saliva for an ocean appetite;
And like storm troops before a citadel,
At the first summons of a bugle, soon
The army massed the stairs towards the saloon,
And though twelve courses on the cards might well
Measure themselves against Falstaffian juices,
But few were found presenting their excuses,
When stewards offered on the lacquered trays
The Savoy chasers and the canapés.

The dinner gave the sense that all was well: 180
That touch of ballast in the tanks; the feel
Of peace from ramparts unassailable,
Which, added to her seven decks of steel,
Had constituted the *Titanic* less
A ship than a Gibraltar under heel.
And night had placed a lazy lusciousness
Upon a surfeit of security.
Science responded to a button press.
The three electric lifts that ran through tiers
Of decks, the reading lamps, the brilliancy   190
Of mirrors from the tungsten chandeliers,
Had driven out all phantoms which the mind
Had loosed from ocean closets, and assigned
To the dry earth the custody of fears.
The crowds poured through the sumptuous rooms and halls,
And tapped the tables of the Regency;
Smirked at the caryatids on the walls;
Talked Jacobean-wise; canvassed the range
Of taste within the Louis dynasty.
Grey-templed Caesars of the world's Exchange   200
Swallowed liqueurs and coffee as they sat
Under the Georgian carved mahogany,
Dictating wireless hieroglyphics that
Would on the opening of the Board Rooms rock
The pillared dollars of a railroad stock.

In the
gymnasium A group had gathered round a mat to watch
The pressure of a Russian hammerlock,
A Polish scissors and a German crotch,
Broken by the toe-hold of Frank Gotch;
Or listened while a young Y.M.C.A.   210
Instructor demonstrated the left-hook,
And that right upper-cut which Jeffries took

From Johnson in the polished Reno way.
By midnight in the spacious dancing hall,
Hundreds were at the Masqueraders' Ball,
The high potential of the liner's pleasures,
Where mellow lights from Chinese lanterns glowed
Upon the scene, and the *Blue Danube* flowed
In andantino rhythms through the measures.

By three the silence that proceeded from 220
The night-caps and the soporific hum
Of the engines was far deeper than a town's:
The starlight and the low wash of the sea
Against the hull bore the serenity
Of sleep at rural hearths with eiderdowns.

The quiet on the decks was scarcely less
Than in the berths: no symptoms of the toil
Down in the holds; no evidence of stress
From gears drenched in the lubricating oil.
She seemed to swim in oil, so smooth the sea. 230
And quiet on the bridge: the great machine
Called for laconic speech, close-fitting, clean,
And whittled to the ship's economy.
Even the judgment stood in little need
Of reason, for the Watch had but to read
Levels and lights, metre or card or bell
To find the pressures, temperatures, or tell
Magnetic North within a binnacle,
Or gauge the hour of docking; for the speed
Was fixed abaft where under the Ensign, 240
Like a flashing trolling spoon, the log rotator
Transmitted through a governor its fine
Gradations on a dial indicator.

Morning of Sunday promised cool and clear,
Flawless horizon, crystal atmosphere;
Not a cat's paw on the ocean, not a guy
Rope murmuring: the steamer's columned smoke
Climbed like extensions of her funnels high
Into the upper zones, then warped and broke
Through the resistance of her speed – blue sky,　　250
Blue water rifted only by the wedge
Of the bow where the double foam line ran
Diverging from the beam to join the edge
Of the stern wake like a white unfolding fan.
Her maiden voyage was being sweetly run,
Adding a half-knot here, a quarter there,
Gliding from twenty into twenty-one.
She seemed so native to her thoroughfare,
One turned from contemplation of her size,
Her sixty thousand tons of sheer flotation,　　260
To wonder at the human enterprise
That took a gamble on her navigation –
Joining the mastiff strength with whippet grace
In this head-strained, world-watched Atlantic race:
Her less than six days' passage would combine
Achievement with the architect's design.

9 a.m.　　A message from *Caronia: advice*
From ships proceeding west; sighted field ice
And growlers; forty-two north; forty-nine
To fifty-one west longitude. S.S.　　270
Mesaba *of Atlantic Transport Line*
Reports encountering solid pack; would guess
The stretch five miles in width from west to east,
And forty-five to fifty miles at least
In length.

Amerika obliged to slow
Down: warns all steamships in vicinity
Presence of bergs, especially of three
Upon the southern outskirts of the floe.

The *Baltic* warns *Titanic:* so *Touraine;*
Reports of numerous icebergs on the Banks,   280
The floe across the southern traffic lane.

The *Californian* and *Baltic* again
Present their compliments to Captain.

Titanic   *Thanks.*

Three men   "That spark's been busy all the afternoon —
talking on   Warnings! The Hydrographic charts are strewn
deck   With crosses showing bergs and pack-ice all
             Along the routes, more south than usual
             For this time of the year."
                                "She's hitting a clip
             Instead of letting up while passing through
             This belt. She's gone beyond the twenty-two."   290

             "Don't worry — Smith's an old dog, knows his ship,
             No finer in the mercantile marine
             Than Smith with thirty years of service, clean
             Record, honoured with highest of all commands,
             Majestic, then *Olympic* on his hands,
             Now the *Titanic*."
                                "Twas a lucky streak
             That at Southampton dock he didn't lose her,
             And the *Olympic* had a narrow squeak
             Some months before rammed by the British Cruiser,
             The *Hawke*."

       "Straight accident. No one to blame: 300
'Twas suction – Board absolved them both. The same
With the *Teutonic* and *New York*. No need
To fear she's trying to out-reach her speed.
There isn't a sign of fog. Besides by now
The watch is doubled at crow's nest and bow."
"People are talking of that apparition,
When we were leaving Queenstown – that head showing
Above the funnel rim, and the fires going!
A stoker's face – sounds like a superstition.
But he was there within the stack, all right;   310
Climbed up the ladder and grinned. The explanation
Was given by an engineer last night –
A dummy funnel built for ventilation."

"That's queer enough, but nothing so absurd
As the latest story two old ladies heard
At a rubber o' bridge. They nearly died with fright;
Wanted to tell the captain – of all things!
The others sneered a bit but just the same
It did the trick of breaking up the game.
A mummy from The Valley of the Kings   320
Was brought from Thebes to London. Excavators
Passed out from cholera, black plague or worse.
Egyptians understood – an ancient curse
Was visited on all the violators.
One fellow was run over, one was drowned,
And one went crazy. When in time it found
Its way to the Museum, the last man
In charge – a mothy Aberdonian –
Exploding the whole legend with a laugh,
Lost all his humour when the skeleton   330
Appeared within the family photograph,
And leered down from a corner just like one

Of his uncles."

"Holy Hades!"

"The B.M.
Authorities themselves were scared and sold
It to New York. That's how the tale is told."
"The joke is on the Yanks."

"No, not on them,
Nor on The Valley of the Kings. What's rummy
About it is — we're carrying the mummy."

7.30 p.m. *Green Turtle!*

Potage Romanoff!

"White Star

At a table in
the dining
saloon

Is out this time to press Cunarders close,   340
Got them on tonnage — fifty thousand gross.
Preferred has never paid a dividend.
The common's down to five — one hundred par.
The double ribbon — size and speed — would send
Them soaring."

"Speed is not in her design,
But comfort and security. The Line
Had never advertised it —'twould be mania
To smash the record of the *Mauretania*."

Sherry!

"The rumour's out."

"There's nothing in it."
"Bet you she docks on Tuesday night."

"I'll take it."   350
"She's hitting twenty-two this very minute."
"That's four behind — She hasn't a chance to make it."
Brook Trout!

Fried Dover Sole!

                              "Her rate will climb
From twenty-two to twenty-six in time.
The Company's known never to rush their ships
At first or try to rip the bed-bolts off.
They run them gently half-a-dozen trips,
A few work-outs around the track to let
Them find their breathing, take the boiler cough
Out of them. She's not racing for a cup."   360
Claret!
          "Steamships like sprinters have to get
Their second wind before they open up."

"That group of men around the captain's table,
Look at them, count the aggregate – the House
Of Astor, Guggenheim, and Harris, Straus,
That's Frohman, isn't it? Between them able
To halve the national debt with a cool billion!
Sir Hugh is over there, and Hays and Stead.
That woman third from captain's right, it's said,
Those diamonds round her neck – a quarter million!"   370
Mignon of Beef!
                    Quail!
                              "I heard Phillips say
He had the finest outfit on the sea;
The new Marconi valve; the range by day,
Five hundred miles, by night a thousand. Three
Sources of power. If some crash below
Should hit the engines, flood the dynamo,
He had the batteries: in emergency,
He could switch through to the auxiliary
On the boat deck."
                    Woodcock and *Burgundy!*
"Say waiter, I said *rare*, you understand."   380

Escallope of Veal!
          Roast Duckling!
                    Snipe! More *Rhine!*
"Marconi made the sea as safe as land:
Remember the *Republic* – White Star Line –
Rammed off Nantucket by the *Florida*,
One thousand saved – the *Baltic* heard the call.
Two steamers answered the *Slavonia*,
Disabled off the Azores. They got them all,
And when the *Minnehaha* ran aground
Near Bishop's Rock, they never would have found
Her – not a chance without the wireless. Same   390
Thing happened to that boat – what was her name?
The one that foundered off the Alaska Coast –
Her signals brought a steamer in the nick
Of time. Yes, sir – Marconi turned the trick."

The *Barcelona salad*; no, *Beaucaire*;
That *Russian dressing*;
                    Avocado pear!

"They wound her up at the Southampton dock,
And then the tugs gave her a push to start
Her off – as automatic as a clock."

Moselle!
          "For all the hand work there's to do   400
Aboard this liner up on deck, the crew
Might just as well have stopped ashore. Apart
From stokers and the engineers, she's run
By gadgets from the bridge – a thousand and one
Of them with a hundred miles of copper wire.
A filament glows at the first sign of fire,

A buzzer sounds, a number gives the spot,
A deck-hand makes a coupling of the hose.
That's all there's to it; not a whistle; not
A passenger upon the ship that knows   410
What's happened. The whole thing is done without
So much as calling up the fire brigade.
They don't need even the pumps – a gas is sprayed,
Carbon dioxide – and the blaze is out."

A Cherry Flan!
            Champagne!
                        Chocolate parfait!

"How about a poker crowd to-night?
Get Jones, an awful grouch – no good to play,
But has the coin. Get hold of Larry."
                                    "Right."
"You fetch Van Raalte: I'll bring in MacRae.
In Cabin D, one hundred seventy-nine.   420
In half-an-hour we start playing."
                                "Fine."

On deck   The sky was moonless but the sea flung back
           With greater brilliance half the zodiac.
           As clear below as clear above, the Lion
           Far on the eastern quarter stalked the Bear:
           Polaris off the starboard beam – and there
           Upon the port the Dog-star trailed Orion.
           Capella was so close, a hand might seize
           The sapphire with the silver Pleiades.
           And further to the south – a finger span,   430
           Swam Betelgeuse and red Aldebaran.
           Right through from east to west the ocean glassed

The billions of that snowy caravan
Ranging the highway which the Milkmaid passed.

9.05 p.m.
Californian
flashing
I say, old man, we're stuck fast in this place,
More than an hour. Field ice for miles about.

Titanic
Say, Californian, *shut up, keep out,*
You're jamming all my signals with Cape Race.

10 p.m.
A group of boys had gathered round a spot
Upon the rail where a dial registered   440
The speed, and waiting each three minutes heard
The taffrail log bell tallying off a knot.

11:20 p.m.
Behind a
deck house
First act to fifth act in a tragic plan,
Stage time, real time – a woman and a man,
Entering a play within a play, dismiss
The pageant on the ocean with a kiss.
Eleven-twenty curtain! Whether true
Or false the pantomimic vows they make
Will not be known till at the *fifth* they take
Their mutual exit twenty after two.   450

11.25 p.m.
Position half-a-mile from edge of floe,
Hove-to for many hours, bored with delay,
The *Californian* fifteen miles away,
And fearful of the pack, has now begun
To turn her engines over under slow
Bell, and the operator, his task done,
Unclamps the 'phones and ends his dullest day.

The ocean sinuous, half-past eleven;
A silence broken only by the seven

Bells and the look-out calls, the log-book showing   460
Knots forty-five within two hours – not quite
The expected best as yet – but she was going
With all her bulkheads open through the night,
For not a bridge induction light was glowing.
Over the stern zenith and nadir met
In the wash of the reciprocating set.
The foam in beveled mirrors multiplied
And shattered constellations. In between,
The pitch from the main drive of the turbine
Emerged like tuna breaches to divide   470
Against the rudder, only to unite
With the converging wake from either side.
Under the counter, blending with the spill
Of stars – the white and blue – the yellow light
Of Jupiter hung like a daffodil.

D-179   "Ace full! A long time since I had a pot."

"Good boy, Van Raalte. That's the juiciest haul
To-night. Calls for a round of roodles, what?
Let's whoop her up. Double the limit. All
In." (Jones, heard muttering as usual,   480
Demurs, but over-ruled.) "Jones sore again."

Van Raalte   "Ten dollars and all in!
(dealer)   The sea's like glass
To-night. That fin-keel keeps her steady."

Jones   "Pass."
(Not looking at his hand.)

Larry   "Pass."

Cripps   "Open for ten."
(Holding a pair of aces.) "Say, who won
The sweep to-day?"

                 "A Minnesota guy
With olive-coloured spats and a mauve tie.
Five hundred and eighty miles – Beat last day's run."

Mac   "My ten."

Harry   (Taking a gamble on his four
Spades for a flush) "I'll raise the bet ten more."   490

Van R.   (Two queens) "*And* ten."

Jones   (Discovering three kings)
"Raise you to forty" (face expressing doubt.)

Larry   (Looking hard at a pair of nines) "I'm out."

Cripps   (Flirts for a moment with his aces, flings
His thirty dollars to the pot.)

Mac   (The same.)

Harry   "My twenty. Might as well stay with the game."

Van R.   "I'm in. Draw! Jones, how bloody long you wait."

Jones   (Withholds an eight) "One." (And then draws an eight.)

Cripps   "Three." (Gets another pair.)
                     "How many, Mac?"

Mac	"Guess I'll take two, no, three." (Gets a third Jack.) 500
Harry	"One." (Draws the ace of spades.)
Van R.	"Dealer takes three."
Cripps (the opener)	(Throws in a dollar chip.)
Mac	(The same.)
Harry	"I'll raise You ten."
Van R.	"I'll see you."
Jones	(Hesitates, surveys The chips.) "Another ten."
Cripps	"I'll call you."
Mac	"See."
Harry	"White livers! Here she goes to thirty."
Van R.	"Just The devil's luck." (Throws cards down in disgust.)
Jones	"Might as well raise." (Counts twenty sluggishly, Tosses them to the centre.) "Staying, Cripps?"
Cripps	"No, and be damned to it."

Mac	"My ten." (With groans.)

Harry	(Looks at the pyramid and swears at Jones,	510
	Then calls, pitching ten dollars on the chips.)	

Jones	(Cards down.) "A full house tops the flush." (He spreads
	His arms around the whites and blues and reds.)

Mac	"As the Scotchman once said of the Sphinx,
	I'd like just to know what he thinks,
	I'll ask him, he cried,
	And the Sphinx – he replied,
	It's the hell of a time between drinks."

Cripps (watch in hand)	"Time? Eleven forty-four, to be precise."

Harry	"Jones – that will fatten up your pocket-book.	520
	My throat's like charcoal. Ring for soda and ice."	

Van R.	"Ice: God! Look – take it through the port-hole – look!"

11.45 p.m.	A signal from the crow's nest. Three bells pealed:
	The look-out telephoned – *Something ahead,*
Murdoch holding the bridge watch	*Hard to make out, sir; looks like . . . iceberg dead*
	On starboard bow!
	Starboard your helm: ship heeled
	To port. From bridge to engine-room the clang
	Of the telegraph. *Danger. Stop.* A hand sprang
	To the throttle; the valves closed, and with the churn
	Of the reverse the sea boiled at the stern. 530
	Smith hurried to the bridge and Murdoch closed
	The bulkheads of the ship as he supposed,

But could not know that with those riven floors
The electro-magnets failed upon the doors.
No shock! No more than if something alive
Had brushed her as she passed. The bow had missed.
Under the vast momentum of her drive
She went a mile. But why that ominous five
Degrees (within five minutes) of a list?

In a cabin "What was that, steward?"

                     "Seems like she hit a sea, sir." 540
"But there's no sea; calm as a landlocked bay
It is; lost a propeller blade?"

                  "Maybe, sir."
"She's stopped."

            "Just cautious like, feeling her way,
There's ice about. It's dark, no moon to-night,
Nothing to fear, I'm sure, sir."

                     For so slight
The answer of the helm, it did not break
The sleep of hundreds: some who were awake
Went up on deck, but soon were satisfied
That nothing in the shape of wind or tide
Or rock or ice could harm that huge bulk spread   550
On the Atlantic, and went back to bed.

Captain in
wireless
room "We've struck an iceberg – glancing blow: as yet
Don't know extent; looks serious; so get
Ready to sent out general call for aid;
I'll tell you when – having inspection made."

Report of
ship's
carpenter A starboard cut three hundred feet or more
From foremast to amidships. Iceberg tore
Right at the bilge turn through the double skin:

Some boiler rooms and bunkers driven in;
The forward five compartments flooded – mail   560
Bags floating. Would the engine power avail
To stem the rush?

                    Titanic, C.Q.D.
Collision: iceberg: damaged starboard side:
Distinct list forward. (Had Smith magnified
The danger? Over-anxious certainly.)
The second (joking) – "Try new call, maybe
Last chance you'll have to send it."
                                        S.O.S.
Then back to older signal of distress.

On the same instant the *Carpathia* called,
The distance sixty miles – *Putting about,*   570
And heading for you; double watch installed
In engine-room, in stokehold and look-out.
Four hours the run, should not the ice retard
The speed; but taking chances: Coming hard!

As leaning on her side to ease a pain,
The tilted ship had stopped the captain's breath:
The inconceivable had stabbed his brain,
This thing unfelt – her visceral wound of death?
Another message – this time to report her
Filling, taxing the pumps beyond their strain.   580
Had that blow rent her from the bow to quarter?
Or would the aft compartments still intact
Give buoyancy enough to counteract
The open forward holds?
                        The carpenter's
Second report had offered little chance,
And panic – heart of God – the passengers,

The fourteen hundred — seven hundred packed
In steerage — seven hundred immigrants!
Smith thought of panic clutching at their throats,
And feared that Balkan scramble for the boats.   590

No call from bridge, no whistle, no alarm
Was sounded. Have the stewards quietly
Inform the passengers: no vital harm,
Precautions merely for emergency;
Collision? Yes, but nature of the blow
Must not be told: not even the crew must know:
Yet all on deck with lifebelts, and boats ready,
The sailors at the falls, and all hands steady.

Wireless room The lilac spark was crackling at the gap,
Eight ships within the radius of the call   600
From fifteen to five hundred miles, and all
But one answering the operator's tap.
Olympic twenty hours away had heard;
The *Baltic* next and the *Virginian* third;
Frankfurt and *Burma* distant one-half day;
Mount Temple nearer, but the ice-field lay
Between the two ships like a wall of stone;
The *Californian* deaf to signals though
Supreme deliverer an hour ago:
The hope was on *Carpathia* alone.   610

On the decks So suave the fool-proof sense of life that fear
Had like the unforeseen become a mere
Illusion — vanquished by the towering height
Of funnels pouring smoke through thirty feet
Of bore; the solid deck planks and the light
From a thousand lamps as on a city street;
The feel of numbers; the security

Of wealth; the placid surface of the sea,
Reflecting on the ship the outwardness
Of calm and leisure of the passengers;   620
Deck-hands obedient to their officers;
Pearl-throated women in their evening dress
And wrapped in sables and minks; the silhouettes
Of men in dinner jackets staging an act
In which delusion passed, deriding fact
Behind the cupped flare of the cigarettes.

Women and children first! Slowly the men
Stepped backward from the rails where number ten,
Its cover off, and lifted from the chocks,
Moved outward as the Welin davits swung.   630
The new ropes creaking through the unused blocks,
The boat was lowered to B deck and hung
There while her load of sixty stepped inside,
Convinced the order was not justified.

Rockets, one, two, God! Smith – what does he mean?
The sounding of the bilges could not show
This reason for alarm – the sky serene
And not a ripple on the water – no
Collision. What report came from below?
No leak accounts for this – looks like a drill,   640
A bit of exhibition play – but still
Stopped in mid-ocean! and those rockets – *three!*
More urgent even than a tapping key
And more immediate as a protocol
To a disaster. *There!* An arrow of fire,
A fourth sped towards the sky, its bursting spire
Topping the foremast like a parasol
With fringe of fuchsia, – more a parody
Upon the tragic summons of the sea

Than the real script of unacknowledged fears   650
Known to the bridge and to the engineers.

Midnight! The Master of the ship presents
To the Master of the Band his compliments,
Desiring that the Band should play right through;
No intermission.

Conductor   "Bad?"

Officer   "Yes, bad enough,
The half not known yet even to the crew;
For God's sake, cut the sentimental stuff,
The *Blue Bells* and Kentucky lullabies.
Murdoch will have a barrel of work to do,
Holding the steerage back, once they get wise;   660
They're jumpy now under the rockets' glare;
So put the ginger in the fiddles – Zip
Her up."

Conductor   "Sure, number forty-seven:" *E-Yip
I Addy-I-A, I Ay . . . I don't care . . .*

Number ten   Full noon and midnight by a weird design
goes over   Both met and parted at the meridian line.
the side   Beyond the starboard gunwale was outspread
The jet expanse of water islanded
By fragments of the berg which struck the blow.
And further off towards the horizon lay   670
The loom of the uncharted parent floe,
Merging the black with an amorphous grey.
On the port gunwale the meridian
Shone from the terraced rows of decks that ran
Form gudgeon to the stem nine hundred feet;

And as the boat now tilted by the stern,
Or now resumed her levels with the turn
Of the controlling ropes at block and cleat,
How easy seemed the step and how secure
Back to the comfort and the warmth – the lure   680
Of sheltered promenade and sun decks starred
By hanging bulbs, amber and rose and blue,
The trellis and palms lining an avenue
With all the vista of a boulevard:
The mirror of the ceilings with festoon
Of pennants, flags and streamers – and now through
The leaded windows of the grand saloon,
Through parted curtains and the open doors
Of vestibules, glint of deserted floors
And tables, and under the sorcery   690
Of light excelling their facsimile,
The periods returning to relume
The panels of the lounge and smoking-room,
Holding the mind in its abandonment
During those sixty seconds of descent.
Lower away! The boat with its four tons
Of freight went down with jerks and stops and runs
Beyond the glare of the cabins and below
The slanting parallels of port-holes, clear
Of the exhaust from the condenser flow: 700
But with the uneven falls she canted near
The water line; the stern rose; the bow dipped;
The crew groped for the link-releasing gear;
The lever jammed; a stoker's jack-knife ripped
The aft ropes through, which on the instant brought her
With rocking keel though safe upon the water.

The
Carpathia   Fifteen, sixteen, seventeen, eighteen – three
Full knots beyond her running limit, she

Was feeling out her port and starboard points,
And testing rivets on her boiler joints.   710
The needle on the gauge beyond the red,
The blow-offs feathered at the funnel head.
The draught-fans roaring at their loudest, now
The quartermaster jams the helm hard-over,
As the revolving searchlight beams uncover
The columns of an iceberg on the bow,
Then compensates this loss by daring gains
Made by her passage through the open lanes.

The Band   *East side, West side, all around the town,*
                    The tots sang 'Ring-a-Rosie'   720
                    'London Bridge is falling down,'
                    Boy and girls together . . .

The cranks turn and the sixth and seventh swing
Over and down, the "tiller" answering
"Aye, Aye, sir" to the shouts of officers –
"Row to the cargo ports for passengers."
The water line is reached, but the ports fail
To open, and the crews of the boats hail
The decks; receiving no response they pull
Away from the ship's side, less than half full.   730
The eighth caught in the tackle foul is stuck
Half-way. With sixty-five capacity,
Yet holding twenty-four, goes number three.

The sharp unnatural deflection, struck
By the sea-level with the under row
Of dipping port-holes at the forward, show
How much she's going by the head. Behind
The bulkheads, sapping out their steel control,
Is the warp of the bunker press inclined
By many thousand tons of shifting coal.   740

The smoothest, safest passage to the sea
Is made by number one – the next to go –
Her space is forty – twelve her company:
"Pull like the devil from her – harder – row!
The minute that she founders, not a boat
Within a mile around that will not follow.
What nearly happened at Southampton? So
Pull, pull, I tell you – not a chip afloat,
God knows how far, her suction will not swallow."

Alexander's rag-time band . . . 750
It's the best band in the land . . .

"There goes the Special with the toffs. You'll make
New York to-night rowing like that. You'll take
Your death o' cold out there with all the fish
And ice around."
                    "Make sure your butlers dish
You up your toddies now, and bring hot rolls
For breakfast."
                    "Don't forget the finger bowls."

The engineering staff of thirty-five
Are at their stations: those off-duty go
Of their free will to join their mates below 760
In the grim fight for steam, more steam, to drive
The pressure through the pumps and dynamo.
Knee-deep, waist-deep in water they remain,
Not one of them seen on the decks again.
The under braces of the rudder showing,
The wing propeller blades began to rise,
And with them, through the hawse-holes, water flowing –
The angle could not but assault the eyes.
A fifteen minutes, and the fo'c'sle head

Was under. And five more, the sea had shut   770
The lower entrance to the stairs that led
From C deck to the boat deck – the short cut
For the crew. Another five, the upward flow
Had covered the wall brackets where the glow
Diffusing from the frosted bulbs turned green
Uncannily through their translucent screen.

On the
Carpathia White Star – Cunarder, forty miles apart,
Still eighteen knots! From coal to flame to steam –
Decision of a captain to redeem
Errors of brain by hazards of the heart!   780
Showers of sparks danced through the funnel smoke,
The firemen's shovels, rakes and slice-bars broke
The clinkers, fed the fires, and ceaselessly
The hoppers dumped the ashes on the sea.

As yet no panic, but none might foretell
The moment when the sight of that oblique
Breath-taking lift of the taffrail and the sleek
And foamless undulation of the swell
Might break in meaning on those diverse races,
And give them common language. As the throng   790
Came to the upper decks and moved along
The incline, the contagion struck the faces
With every lowering of a boat and backed
Them towards the stern. And twice between the hush
Of fear and utterance the gamut cracked,
When with the call for women and the flare
Of an exploding rocket, a short rush
Was made for the boats – fifteen and two.
'Twas nearly done – the sudden clutch and tear
Of canvas, a flurry of fists and curses met   800
By swift decisive action from the crew,

Supported by a quartermaster's threat
Of three revolver shots fired on the air.

But still the fifteenth went with five inside,
Who, seeking out the shadows, climbed aboard
And, lying prone and still, managed to hide
Under the thwarts long after she was lowered.

> *Jingle bells, jingle bells,*
> *Jingle all the way,*
> *O what fun . . .*   810

"Some men in number two, sir!"
                              The boat swung
Back.
        "Chuck the fellows out."
                                    Grabbed by the feet,
The lot were pulled over the gunwale and flung
Upon the deck.
                    "Hard at that forward cleat!
A hand there for that after fall. Lower
Away – port side, the second hatch, and wait."

With six hands of his watch, the bosun's mate,
Sent down to open up the gangway door,
Was trapped and lost in a flooded alley way,
And like the seventh, impatient of delay,   820
The second left with room for twenty more.

The fiddley leading from a boiler room
Lay like a tortuous exit from a tomb.
A stoker climbed it, feeling by the twist
From vertical how steep must be the list.
He reached the main deck where the cold night airs

Enswathed his flesh with steam. Taking the stairs,
He heard the babel by the davits, faced
The forward, noticed how the waters raced
To the break of the fo'c'sle and lapped
The foremast root. He climbed again and saw
The resolute manner in which Murdoch's rapped
Command put a herd instinct under law;
No life-preserver on, he stealthily
Watched Phillips in his room, bent at the key,
And thinking him alone, he sprang to tear
The jacket off. He leaped too soon. "Take that!"
The second stove him with a wrench. "Lie there,
Till hell begins to singe your lids – you rat!"

But set against those scenes where order failed,
Was the fine muster at the fourteenth where,
Like a zone of calm along a thoroughfare,
The discipline of sea-worn laws prevailed.
No women answering the repeated calls,
The men filled up the vacant seats: the falls
Were slipping through the sailors' hands,
When a steerage group of women, having fought
Their way over five flights of stairs, were brought
Bewildered to the rails. Without commands
Barked from the lips of officers; without
A protest registered in voice or face,
The boat was drawn up and the men stepped out
Back to the crowded stations with that free
Barter of life for life done with the grace
And air of a Castilian courtesy.

> *I've just got here through Paris,*
> *From the sunny Southern shore,*
> *I to Monte Carlo went . . .*

Isidor and
Ida Straus At the sixteenth — a woman wrapped her coat
Around her maid and placed her in the boat;   860
Was ordered in but seen to hesitate
At the gunwale, and more conscious of her pride
Than of her danger swiftly took her fate
With open hands, and without show of tears
Returned unmurmuring to her husband's side;
"We've been together now for forty years,
Whither you go, I go."

                 A boy of ten,
Ranking himself within the class of men,
Though given a seat, made up his mind to waive
The privilege of his youth and size, and piled   870
The inches on his stature as he gave
Place to a Magyar woman and her child.

And men who had in the world's run of trade,
Or in pursuit of the professions, made
Their reputation, looked upon the scene
Merely as drama in a life's routine:
Millet was studying eyes as he would draw them
Upon a canvas; Butt, as though he saw them
In the ranks; Astor, social, debonair,
Waved "Good-bye" to his bride — "See you to-morrow," 880
And tapped a cigarette on a silver case;
Men came to Guggenheim as he stood there
In evening suit, coming this time to borrow
Nothing but courage from his calm, cool face.

And others unobserved, of unknown name
And race, just stood behind, pressing no claim
Upon priority but rendering proof
Of their oblation, quiet and aloof

Within the maelstrom towards the rails. And some
Wavered a moment with the panic urge,   890
But rallied to attention on the verge
Of flight as if the rattle of a drum
From quarters faint but unmistakable
Had put the stiffening in the blood to check
The impulse of the feet, leaving the will
No choice between the lifeboats and the deck.

The four collapsibles, their lashings ripped,
Half-dragged, half-lifted by the hooks, were slipped
Over the side. The first two luckily
Had but the forward distance to the sea.   900
Its canvas edges crumpled up, the third
Began to fill with water and transferred
Its cargo to the twelfth, while number four,
Abaft and higher, nose-dived and swamped its score.

The wireless cabin – Phillips in his place,
Guessing the knots of the Cunarder's race.
Water was swirling up the slanted floor
Around the chair and sucking at his feet.
Carpathia's call – the last one heard complete –
Expect to reach position half-past four.   910
The operators turned – Smith at the door
With drawn incredulous face. "Men, you have done
Your duty. I release you. Everyone
Now for himself." They stayed ten minutes yet,
The power growing fainter with each blue
Crackle of flame. Another stammering jet –
Virginian heard "a tattering C.Q."
Again a try for contact but the code's
Last jest had died between the electrodes.

Even yet the spell was on the ship: although   920
The last lifeboat had vanished, there was no
Besieging of the heavens with a crescendo
Of fears passing through terror into riot –
But on all lips the strange narcotic quiet
Of an unruffled ocean's innuendo.
In spite of her deformity of line,
Emergent like a crag out of the sea,
She had the semblance of stability,
Moment by moment furnishing no sign,
So far as visible, of that decline   930
Made up of inches crawling into feet.
Then, with the electric circuit still complete,
The miracle of day displacing night
Had worked its fascination to beguile
Direction of the hours and cheat the sight.
Inside the recreation rooms the gold
From Arab lamps shone on the burnished tile.
What hindered the return to shelter while
The ship clothed in that irony of light
Offered her berths and cabins as a fold?   940
And, was there not the *Californian*?
Many had seen her smoke just over there,
But two hours past – it seemed a harbour span –
So big, so close, she could be hailed, they said;
She must have heard the signals, seen the flare
Of those white stars and changed at once her course.
There under the *Titanic*'s foremast head,
A lamp from the look-out cage was flashing Morse.
No ship afloat unless deaf, blind and dumb
To those three sets of signals but would come.   950
And when the whiz of a rocket bade men turn
Their faces to each other in concern
At shattering facts upon the deck, they found

Their hearts take reassurance with the sound
Of the violins from the gymnasium, where
The bandsmen in their blithe insouciance
Discharged the sudden tension of the air
With the fox-trot's sublime irrelevance.

The fo'c'sle had gone under the creep
Of the water. Though without a wind, a lop   960
Was forming on the wells now fathoms deep.
The seventy feet – the boat deck's normal drop –
Was down to ten. Rising, falling, and waiting,
Rising again, the swell that edged and curled
Around the second bridge, over the top
Of the air-shafts, backed, resurged and whirled
Into the stokehold through the fiddley grating.

Under the final strain the two wire guys
Of the forward funnel tugged and broke at the eyes:
With buckled plates the stack leaned, fell and smashed 970
The starboard wing of the flying bridge, went through
The lower, then tilting at the davits crashed
Over, driving a wave aboard that drew
Back to the sea some fifty sailors and
The captain with the last of the bridge command.

Out on the water was the same display
Of fear and self-control as on the deck –
Challenge and hesitation and delay,
The quick return, the will to save, the race
Of snapping oars to put the realm of space   980
Between the half-filled lifeboats and the wreck.
The swimmers whom the waters did not take
With their instant death-chill struck out for the wake
Of the nearer boats, gained on them, hailed

The steersmen and were saved: the weaker failed
And fagged and sank. A man clutched at the rim
Of a gunwale, and a woman's jewelled fist
Struck at his face: two others seized his wrist,
As he released his hold, and gathering him
Over the side, they staunched the cut from the ring.   990
And there were many deeds envisaging
Volitions where self-preservation fought
Its red primordial struggle with the "ought,"
In those high moments when the gambler tossed
Upon the chance and uncomplaining lost.

Aboard the ship, whatever hope of dawn
Gleamed from the *Carpathia*'s riding lights was gone,
For every knot was matched by each degree
Of list. The stern was lifted bodily
When the bow had sunk three hundred feet, and set   1000
Against the horizon stars in silhouette
Were the blade curves of the screws, hump of the rudder.
The downward pull and after buoyancy
Held her a minute poised but for a shudder
That caught her frame as with the upward stroke
Of the sea a boiler or a bulkhead broke.

Climbing the ladders, gripping shroud and stay,
Storm-rail, ringbolt or fairlead, every place
That might befriend the clutch of hand or brace
Of foot, the fourteen hundred made their way   1010
To the heights of the aft decks, crowding the inches
Around the docking bridge and cargo winches.
And now that last salt tonic which had kept
The valour of the heart alive – the bows
Of the immortal seven that had swept
The strings to outplay, outdie their orders – ceased.

Five minutes more, the angle had increased
From eighty on to ninety when the rows
Of deck and port-hole lights went out, flashed back
A brilliant second and again went black.   1020
Another bulkhead crashed, then following
The passage of the engines as they tore
From their foundations, taking everything
Clean through the bows from 'midships with a roar
Which drowned all cries upon the deck and shook
The watchers in the boats, the liner took
Her thousand fathoms journey to her grave.

*

And out there in the starlight, with no trace
Upon it of its deed but the last wave
From the *Titanic* fretting at its base,   1030
Silent, composed, ringed by its icy broods,
The grey shape with the palaeolithic face
Was still the master of the longitudes.

{1935}

COME AWAY, DEATH

Willy-nilly, he comes or goes, with the clown's logic,
Comic in epitaph, tragic in epithalamium,
And unseduced by any mused rhyme.
However blow the winds over the pollen,
Whatever the course of the garden variables,
He remains the constant,
Ever flowering from the poppy seeds.

There was a time he came in formal dress,
Announced by Silence tapping at the panels
In deep apology. 10
A touch of chivalry in his approach,
He offered sacramental wine,
And with acanthus leaf
And petals of the hyacinth
He took the fever from the temples
And closed the eyelids,
Then led the way to his cool longitudes
In the dignity of the candles.

His mediaeval grace is gone –
Gone with the flame of the capitals 20
And the leisured turn of the thumb
Leafing the manuscripts,
Gone with the marbles
And the Venetian mosaics,
With the bend of the knee
Before the rose-strewn feet of the Virgin.
The *paternosters* of his priests,
Committing clay to clay,
Have rattled in their throats
Under the gride of his traction tread. 30

One night we heard his footfall – one September night –
In the outskirts of a village near the sea.
There was a moment when the storm
Delayed its fist, when the surf fell
Like velvet on the rocks – a moment only;
The strangest lull we ever knew!
A sudden truce among the oaks
Released their fratricidal arms;
The poplars straightened to attention

As the winds stopped to listen
To the sound of a motor drone –
And then the drone was still.
We heard the tick-tock on the shelf,
And the leak of valves in our hearts.
A calm condensed and lidded
As at the core of a cyclone ended breathing.
This was the monologue of Silence
Grave and unequivocal.

What followed was a bolt
Outside the range and target of the thunder,
And human speech curved back upon itself
Through Druid runways and the Piltdown scarps,
Beyond the stammers of the Java caves,
To find its origins in hieroglyphs
On mouths and eyes and cheeks
Etched by a foreign stylus never used
On the outmoded page of the Apocalypse.

[1940] {1943}

The Truant

"What have you there?" the great Panjandrum said
To the Master of the Revels who had led
A bucking truant with a stiff backbone
Close to the foot of the Almighty's throne.

"Right Reverend, most adored,
And forcibly acknowledged Lord
By the keen logic of your two-edged sword!
This creature has presumed to classify

Himself — a biped, rational, six feet high
And two feet wide; weighs fourteen stone;   10
Is guilty of a multitude of sins.
He has abjured his choric origins,
And like an undomesticated slattern,
Walks with tangential step unknown
Within the weave of the atomic pattern.
He has developed concepts, grins
Obscenely at your Royal bulletins,
Possesses what he calls a will
Which challenges your power to kill."

"What is his pedigree?"   20

"The base is guaranteed, your Majesty —
Calcium, carbon, phosphorus, vapour
And other fundamentals spun
From the umbilicus of the sun,
And yet he says he will not caper
Around your throne, nor toe the rules
For the ballet of the fiery molecules."

"His concepts and denials — scrap them, burn them —
To the chemists with them promptly."

                                        "Sire,
The stuff is not amenable to fire.   30
Nothing but their own kind can overturn them.
The chemists have sent back the same old story —
'With our extreme gelatinous apology,
We beg to inform your Imperial Majesty,
Unto whom be dominion and power and glory,
There still remains that strange precipitate
Which has the quality to resist

Our oldest and most trusted catalyst.
It is a substance we cannot cremate
By temperatures known to our Laboratory.'"   40

And the great Panjandrum's face grew dark –
"I'll put those chemists to their annual purge,
And I myself shall be the thaumaturge
To find the nature of this fellow's spark.
Come, bring him nearer by yon halter rope:
I'll analyse him with the cosmoscope."

Pulled forward with his neck awry,
The little fellow six feet short,
Aware he was about to die,
Committed grave contempt of court   50
By answering with a flinchless stare
The Awful Presence seated there.

The ALL HIGH swore until his face was black.
He called him a coprophagite,
A genus *homo*, egomaniac,
Third cousin to the family of worms,
A sporozoan from the ooze of night,
Spawn of a spavined troglodyte:
He swore by all the catalogue of terms
Known since the slang of carboniferous Time.   60
He said that he could trace him back
To pollywogs and earwigs in the slime.
And in his shrillest tenor he began
Reciting his indictment of the man,
Until he closed upon this capital crime –
"You are accused of singing out of key,
(A foul unmitigated dissonance)
Of shuffling in the measures of the dance,

Then walking out with that defiant, free
Toss of your head, banging the doors, 70
Leaving a stench upon the jacinth floors.
You have fallen like a curse
On the mechanics of my Universe.

"Herewith I measure out your penalty —
Hearken while you hear, look while you see:
I send you now upon your homeward route
Where you shall find
Humiliation for your pride of mind.
I shall make deaf the ear, and dim the eye,
Put palsy in your touch, make mute 80
Your speech, intoxicate your cells and dry
Your blood and marrow, shoot
Arthritic needles through your cartilage,
And having parched you with old age,
I'll pass you wormwise through the mire;
And when your rebel will
Is mouldered, all desire
Shrivelled, all your concepts broken,
Backward in dust I'll blow you till
You join my spiral festival of fire. 90
Go, Master of the Revels — I have spoken."

And the little genus *homo,* six feet high,
Standing erect, countered with this reply —
"You dumb insouciant invertebrate,
You rule a lower than a feudal state —
A realm of flunkey decimals that run,
Return; return and run; again return,
Each group around its little sun,
And every sun a satellite.
There they go by day and night, 100

Nothing to do but run and burn,
Taking turn and turn about,
Light-year in and light-year out,
Dancing, dancing in quadrillions,
Never leaving their pavilions.

"Your astronomical conceit
Of bulk and power is anserine.
Your ignorance so thick,
You did not know your own arithmetic.
We flung the graphs about your flying feet; 110
We measured your diameter —
Merely a line
Of zeros prefaced by an integer.
Before we came
You had no name.
You did not know direction or your pace;
We taught you all you ever knew
Of motion, time and space.
We healed you of your vertigo
And put you in our kindergarten show, 120
Perambulated you through prisms, drew
Your mileage through the Milky Way,
Lassoed your comets when they ran astray,
Yoked Leo, Taurus, and your team of Bears
To pull our kiddy cars of inverse squares.

"Boast not about your harmony,
Your perfect curves, your rings
Of *pure and endless light* — 'Twas we
Who pinned upon your Seraphim their wings,
And when your brassy heavens rang 130
With joy that morning while the planets sang
Their choruses of archangelic lore,

'Twas we who ordered the notes upon their score
Out of our winds and strings.
Yes! all your shapely forms
Are ours – parabolas of silver light,
Those blueprints of your spiral stairs
From nadir depth to zenith height,
Coronas, rainbows after storms,
Auroras on your eastern tapestries   140
And constellations over western seas.

"And when, one day, grown conscious of your age,
While pondering an eolith,
We turned a human page
And blotted out a cosmic myth
With all its baby symbols to explain
The sunlight in Apollo's eyes,
Our rising pulses and the birth of pain,
Fear, and that fern-and-fungus breath
Stalking our nostrils to our caves of death –   150
That day we learned how to anatomize
Your body, calibrate your size
And set a mirror up before your face
To show you what you really were – a rain
Of dull Lucretian atoms crowding space,
A series of concentric waves which any fool
Might make by dropping stones within a pool,
Or an exploding bomb forever in flight
Bursting like hell through Chaos and Old Night.

"You oldest of the hierarchs   160
Composed of electronic sparks,
We grant you speed,
We grant you power, and fire
That ends in ash, but we concede

To you no pain nor joy nor love nor hate,
No final tableau of desire,
No causes won or lost, no free
Adventure at the outposts – only
The degradation of your energy
When at some late   170
Slow number of your dance your sergeant-major Fate
Will catch you blind and groping and will send
You reeling on that long and lonely
Lockstep of your wave-lengths towards your end.

"We who have met
With stubborn calm the dawn's hot fusillades;
Who have seen the forehead sweat
Under the tug of pulleys on the joints,
Under the liquidating tally
Of the cat-and-truncheon bastinades;   180
Who have taught our souls to rally
To mountain horns and the sea's rockets
When the needle ran demented through the points;
We who have learned to clench
Our fists and raise our lightless sockets
To morning skies after the midnight raids,
Yet cocked our ears to bugles on the barricades,
And in cathedral rubble found a way to quench
A dying thirst within a Galilean valley –
No! by the Rood, we will not join your ballet."   190

{1943}

W.W.E. ROSS
1894–1966

William Wrightson Eustace Ross is recognized as the exemplary
Canadian Imagist, although his practice in the manner was rela-
tively brief. He was born in Peterborough and grew up in
Pembroke, Ontario. He supported his B.Sc. studies at the University
of Toronto with summer work on geological surveys in regions of
northern Ontario later made famous by the paintings of the Group
of Seven. He served in the Canadian Expeditionary Force in World
War One and was employed as a geophysicist in the Dominion
Magnetic Observatory in Agincourt, Ontario, from 1924. He began
to write poetry in the early 1920s and found his work readily
accepted for publication in Marianne Moore's *The Dial* and in
Poetry. A volume of this Imagist work, including a few classical
adaptations, was published as *Laconics* in 1930. Strikingly, this
ground-breaking publication was followed by the *Sonnets* of 1932,
only a few of which are of interest, usually for mirroring the subject
matter and imagery of the modernist poems. In the 1930s Ross
translated the writings of Max Jacob, the experimental French poet,
and penned the earliest prose poems in English in Canada. Ross's
correspondence with A.J.M. Smith and Ralph Gustafson has been
published. In 1968 Raymond Souster and John Robert Colombo
edited the comprehensive selection *Shapes & Sounds: Poems of
W.W.E. Ross*.

RECIPROCAL

The shuttle swinging
to and fro;
the piston
of the locomotive
moving smoothly,
powerfully,
into the cylinder,
out of the cylinder;

dancers swaying
in one place;   10
crows' wings
in lazy flight;
waves on the ocean
up to the shore
and back swiftly
broken and foaming.

[1925] {1968}

THE DIVER

I would like to dive
Down
Into this still pool
Where the rocks at the bottom are safely deep,

Into the green
Of the water seen from within,
A strange light
Streaming past my eyes —

Things hostile;
You cannot stay here, they seem to say;   10
The rocks, slime-covered, the undulating
Fronds of weeds —

And drift slowly
Among the cooler zones;
Then, upward turning,
Break from the green glimmer

Into the light,
White and ordinary of the day,
And the mild air,
With the breeze and the comfortable shore.   20

[1927] {1968}

IF ICE

                              If
ice shall melt
                         if
thinly the fresh
cold clear   water
running   shall make
grooves in the sides
of the ice;
if life return
                    after death   10
or depart not at death,
then shall buds
burst into   May-
leafing, the blooms of May

appear like stars
on the brown dry
            forest-bed.

[1927] {1968}

SPRING SONG

One day   in the spring
walking   walking
along   the railroad track
the track   near the town
I passed   looking at
a pond   a pond
slimy   of greenish water
greenish   a large pond
From it came incessantly
sounds   sounds   10
of frogs   frogs piping
piping   frogs in the water
I picked up   I could not see
a stone   any frogs
and threw it   I threw a stone
into the pond into the pond
The stone   it splashed
splashed   a big splash
and the piping and the sounds
of the frogs   the frogs' piping   20
stopped

[1928] {1968}

One Leaf

One leaf is
floating on
ripples in
shallow
shore-side
water

over the
sand at the
bottom that
shimmers in   10
sunlight

where the leaf's
shadow lies
motionless
almost
there on the
flat sand

among the
swift-moving
bright   20
refractions of
sunlight.

[1929] {1968}

PINE GUM

The white gum showing
in the gloom
along the massive
trunk of a great
pine-tree standing
on the hill,
with a deep bed
of needles below; –

scarcely a breeze
along the hill;   10
scarcely a current
of morning air
to make the pine's
old melody,
for it is evening;
the air has ceased

its daily stirring;
the light grows dimmer
within the shadow
of the pine,   20
but ever appears
through the darkness
the ghostly glimmering
of the gum.

[1929] {1930}

F.R. SCOTT

1899–1985

Francis Reginald Scott was born in Quebec City, where his father, the Confederation-period poet F.G. Scott, was rector of St Matthew's Church. He studied at Bishop's College and in 1920 went as a Rhodes Scholar to Oxford University, where he took a second B.A. and a B.Litt. (1922, 1923) in history. He returned to Montreal for legal studies at McGill. There he began a lifelong collaboration with A.J.M. Smith by co-editing the *McGill Fortnightly Review.* In 1928 Scott married painter Marian Dale and began to teach in McGill's law faculty. During the Depression he helped to found the League for Social Reconstruction (1932), co-wrote the Regina Manifesto that established the Co-operative Commonwealth Federation party (1933), and served a year's term as party president (1935–36). In 1936 he and Smith co-edited *New Provinces: Poems of Several Authors,* the first anthology of modern poetry published in Canada. In 1942, Scott joined Patrick Anderson, P.K. Page, and others in editing *Preview,* a mimeographed little magazine that ran until 1945. Scott's first solo volume, *Overture: Poems,* appeared in 1945; *Events and Signals,* arguably his finest, followed in 1954. Scott returned to legal practise for two landmark civil liberties cases: in 1956 he argued successfully in the Supreme Court against a Quebec law allowing police to shut down premises they claimed to be affiliated with Communist sedition, and in 1962 he convinced the Court to overturn a ruling banning importation of D.H. Lawrence's *Lady Chatterley's Lover.* In the 1950s Scott began to translate the francophone poets of Quebec and the Maritimes; eventually collected as *Poems of French Canada* in 1977, these works would win the Canada

Council's Translation Prize. Scott won Governor General's awards for non-fiction, for his *Essays on the Constitution* (1977), and for poetry, for his *Collected Poems* (1981). He is buried in Montreal's Mount Royal Cemetery, under the epitaph "the dance is one," the title of one of his last volumes.

NEW PATHS

Child of the North,
Yearn no more after old playthings,
Temples and towers and gates
Memory-haunted thoroughfares and rich palaces
And all the burdensome inheritance, the binding legacies,
Of the Old World and the East.

Here is a new soil and a sharp sun.

Turn from the past,
Walk with me among these indigent firs,
Climb these rough crags   10
And let winds that have swept lone cityless plains,
Gathering no sad tales of past endeavour,
Tell you of fresh beauty and full growth.

[1926] {1981}

THE CANADIAN AUTHORS MEET

Expansive puppets percolate self-unction
Beneath a portrait of the Prince of Wales.
Miss Crotchet's muse has somehow failed to function,
Yet she's a poetess. Beaming, she sails

From group to chattering group, with such a dear
Victorian saintliness, as is her fashion,
Greeting the other unknowns with a cheer –
Virgins of sixty who still write of passion.

The air is heavy with Canadian topics,
And Carman, Lampman, Roberts, Campbell, Scott,   10
Are measured for their faith and philanthropics,
Their zeal for God and King, their earnest thought.

The cakes are sweet, but sweeter is the feeling
That one is mixing with the *literati*;
It warms the old, and melts the most congealing.
Really, it is a most delightful party.

Shall we go round the mulberry bush, or shall
We gather at the river, or shall we
Appoint a Poet Laureate this fall,
Or shall we have another cup of tea?   20

O Canada, O Canada, O can
A day go by without new authors springing
To paint the native maple, and to plan
More ways to set the selfsame welkin ringing?

[1927] {1945}

OVERTURE

In the dark room, under a cone of light,
You precisely play the Mozart sonata. The bright
Clear notes fly like sparks through the air
And trace a flickering pattern of music there.

Your hands dart in the light, your fingers flow.
They are ten careful operatives in a row
That pick their packets of sound from steel bars
Constructing harmonies as sharp as stars.

But how shall I hear old music? This is an hour
Of new beginnings, concepts warring for power,   10
Decay of systems – the tissue of art is torn
With overtures of an era being born.

And this perfection which is less yourself
Than Mozart, seems a trinket on a shelf,
A pretty octave played before a window
Beyond whose curtain grows a world crescendo.

[1934] {1945}

LAURENTIAN SHIELD

Hidden in wonder and snow, or sudden with summer,
This land stares at the sun in a huge silence
Endlessly repeating something we cannot hear.
Inarticulate, arctic,
Not written on by history, empty as paper,
It leans away from the world with songs in its lakes
Older than love, and lost in the miles.

This waiting is wanting.
It will choose its language
When it has chosen its technic,   10
A tongue to shape the vowels of its productivity.

A language of flesh and roses.

Now there are pre-words,
Cabin syllables,
Nouns of settlement
Slowly forming, with steel syntax,
The long sentence of its exploitation.

The first cry was the hunter, hungry for fur,
And the digger for gold, nomad, no-man, a particle;
Then the bold command of monopolies, big with machines, 20
Carving their kingdoms out of the public wealth;
And now the drone of the plane, scouting the ice,
Fills all the emptiness with neighbourhood
And links our future over the vanished pole.

But a deeper note is sounding, heard in the mines,
The scattered camps and the mills, a language of life,
And what will be written in the full culture of occupation
Will come, presently, tomorrow,
From millions whose hands can turn this rock into children.

[1945] {1954}

Spain 1937

For these we too are bleeding: the homes burning,
The schools broken and ended, the vision thwarted,
The youths, their backs to the wall, awaiting the volley,
The child staring at a huddled form.

And Guernica, more real than our daily bread.

For these our hurt and hate, sharp couriers,
Arouse a waking world: the black crusade,
Pious brutality, mass massacre,
Sudden cohesion of class, wealth and creed,
Behind the gilded cross, the swastika,   10
Behind neutrality, the will to kill.

And Lorca, rising godlike from fascist guns.

In the spring of ideas they were, the rare spring
That breaks historic winters. Street and field
Stirring with hope and green with new endeavour,
The cracking husks copious with sprouting seed.
Here was destruction before flowering,
Here freedom was cut in its first tendrils.

This issue is not ended with defeat.

{1945}

WILL TO WIN

Your tall French legs, my V for victory,
My sign and symphony, Eroica,
Uphold me in these days of my occupation
And stir my underground resistance.

Crushed by the insidious infiltration of routine
I was wholly overrun and quite cut off.
The secret agents of my daily detail
Had my capital city under their rule and thumb.

Only a handful of me escaped to the hillside,
Your side, my sweet and holy inside,   10
And cowering there for a moment I drew breath,
Grew solid as trees, took root in a fertile soil.

Here by my hidden fires, drop your supplies –
Love, insight, sensibility, and myth –
Thousands of fragments rally to my cause,
I ride like Joan to conquer my whole man.

[1948] {1954}

LAKESHORE

The lake is sharp along the shore
Trimming the bevelled edge of land
To level curves; the fretted sands
Go slanting down through liquid air
Till stones below shift here and there
Floating upon their broken sky
All netted by the prism wave
And rippled where the currents are.

I stare through windows at this cave
Where fish, like planes, slow-motioned, fly.   10
Poised in a still of gravity
The narrow minnow, flicking fin,
Hangs in a paler, ochre sun,
His doorways open everywhere.

And I am a tall frond that waves
Its head below its rooted feet

Seeking the light that draws it down
To forest floors beyond its reach
Vivid with gloom and eerie dreams.

The water's deepest colonnades
Contract the blood, and to this home
That stirs the dark amphibian
With me the naked swimmers come
Drawn to their prehistoric womb.

They too are liquid as they fall
Like tumbled water loosed above
Until they lie, diagonal,
Within the cool and sheltered grove
Stroked by the fingertips of love.

Silent, our sport is drowned in fact
Too virginal for speech or sound
And each is personal and laned
Along his private aqueduct.

Too soon the tether of the lungs
Is taut and straining, and we rise
Upon our undeveloped wings
Toward the prison of our ground
A secret anguish in our thighs
And mermaids in our memories.

This is our talent, to have grown
Upright in posture, false-erect,
A landed gentry, circumspect,
Tied to a horizontal soil
The floor and ceiling of the soul;

20

30

40

Striving, with cold and fishy care
To make an ocean of the air.

Sometimes, upon a crowded street,
I feel the sudden rain come down
And in the old, magnetic sound
I hear the opening of a gate   50
That loosens all the seven seas.
Watching the whole creation drown
I muse, alone, on Ararat.

[1950] {1954}

CREED

The world is my country
The human race is my race
The spirit of man is my God
The future of man is my heaven

[1952] {1964}

A GRAIN OF RICE

Such majestic rhythms, such tiny disturbances.
The rain of the monsoon falls, an inescapable treasure,
Hundreds of millions live
Only because of the certainty of this season,
        The turn of the wind.

The frame of our human house rests on the motion
Of earth and of moon, the rise of continents,

Invasion of deserts, erosion of hills,
            The capping of ice.

Today, while Europe tilted, drying the Baltic,   10
I read of a battle between brothers in anguish.
            A flag moved a mile.

And today, from a curled leaf cocoon, in the course of its rhythm,
I saw the break of a shell, the creation
Of a great Asian moth, radiant, fragile,
Incapable of not being born, and trembling
            To live its brief moment.

Religions build walls round our love, and science
Is equal of truth and of error. Yet always we find
Such ordered purpose in cell and in galaxy,   20
So great a glory in life-thrust and mind-range,
Such widening frontiers to draw out our longings,
            We grow to one world
            Through enlargement of wonder.

{1954}

DEGENERATION

The first to go are the niceties,
The little minor conformities
That suddenly seem absurdities.

Soon kindling animosities
Surmount the old civilities
And start the first brutalities.

Then come the bold extremities,
The justified enormities,
The unrestrained ferocities.

{1964}

ECLIPSE

I looked the sun straight in the eye.
He put on dark glasses.

{1964}

MOUNT ROYAL

No things sit, set, hold. All swim,
Whether through space or cycle, rock or sea.
This mountain of Mount Royal marks the hours
On earth's sprung clock. Look how where
This once was island, lapped by salty waves,
And now seems fixed with sloping roads and homes.
Where flowers march, I dig these tiny shells
Once deep-down fishes safe, it seemed, on sand.
What! Sand, mud, silt, where now commuters go
About their civic clatter! Boulevards   10
Where crept the shiny mollusc! Time is big
With aeon seconds now, its pendulum
Swung back to ice-pressed pole-cap, that drove down
This chest of earth, until the melting came
And left a hollow cavity for seas
To make into a water waiting-room.
But sea-bed floated slowly, surely up

As weight released brought in-breath back to earth
And ground uprising drove the water back
In one more tick of clock. Pay taxes now,   20
Elect your boys, lay out your pleasant parks,
You gill-lunged, quarrelsome ephemera!
The tension tightens yearly, underneath,
A folding continent shifts silently
And oceans wait their turn for ice or streets.

{1964}

WINTER SPARROWS

Feathered leaves
    on a leafless bush.
Dropping to feed
    they fly back to the stems.

{1973}

A.J.M. SMITH
1902–1980

Arthur James Marshall Smith was born in Westmount, Quebec, to British parents. The family lived in London, England, from 1918 to 1920, where Smith frequented Harold Monro's Poetry Bookshop and first encountered modernist poetry. His M.A. thesis at McGill University was on the writings of William Butler Yeats (1926). With F.R. Scott and Leon Edel, later the biographer of Henry James, he founded and edited the *McGill Fortnightly Review* from 1925-27. Smith contributed not only his poems but also ground-breaking essays on modern poetry, including Canada's first critical study of the poetry of T.S. Eliot. Smith left for Edinburgh in 1927 for doctoral studies on the Metaphysical poets; he returned to Montreal in 1929. After a year of high-school teaching he held a series of short-term academic positions in the mid-western United States; from 1933 to 1934 he was unemployed. In 1936 he joined the English Department at Michigan State College in East Lansing. In the same year he and Scott published *New Provinces: Poems of Several Authors*, a landmark anthology containing their work and that of Leo Kennedy, A.M. Klein, E.J. Pratt, and Robert Finch. Smith's preface to the volume – to the radicalism of which Pratt objected so strenuously that it was withdrawn – demands the contemporary Canadian poet's commitment, at a time of global crisis, to practical social action. Although through the 1930s Smith had been publishing in major British, American, and Canadian periodicals, his first volume, *News of the Phoenix and Other Poems*, would not appear until 1943. It won a Governor General's Award. In the same year Smith published a definitive new anthology of English Canadian poetry, *The Book of Canadian Poetry*. It provoked vociferous debate, chiefly for Smith's favouring a cosmopolitan modernism in his introduction and selections. His poetic output thereafter dwindled until the late 1950s, when his growing awareness of mortality and outrage at nuclear proliferation and global conflict generated new work in the vernacular style of later modernism. Smith's *Poems New and Collected* was published in 1967; his essays, prefaces, and introductions were collected in *Towards a View of Canadian Letters* in 1973. Brian Trehearne edited *The Complete Poems of A.J.M. Smith* in 2007.

THE LONELY LAND

Cedar and jagged fir
uplift sharp barbs
against the gray
and cloud-piled sky;
and in the bay
blown spume and windrift
and thin, bitter spray
snap
at the whirling sky;
and the pine trees   10
lean one way.

A wild duck calls
to her mate,
and the ragged
and passionate tones
stagger and fall,
and recover,
and stagger and fall,
on these stones —

are lost

20

in the lapping of water
on smooth, flat stones.

This is a beauty
of dissonance,
this resonance
of stony strand,
this smoky cry
curled over a black pine
like a broken
and wind-battered branch   30
when the wind
bends the tops of the pines
and curdles the sky
from the north.

This is the beauty
of strength
broken by strength
and still strong.

[1926] {1943}

LIKE AN OLD PROUD KING IN A PARABLE

A bitter king in anger to be gone
From fawning courtier and doting queen
Flung hollow sceptre and gilt crown away,
And breaking bound of all his counties green
He made a meadow in the northern stone
And breathed a palace of inviolable air
To cage a heart that carolled like a swan,

94   A.J.M. SMITH

And slept alone, immaculate and gay,
With only his pride for a paramour.

O who is that bitter king? It is not I.   10

Let me, I beseech thee, Father, die
From this fat royal life, and lie
As naked as a bridegroom by his bride,
And let that girl be the cold goddess Pride:

And I will sing to the barren rock
Your difficult, lonely music, heart,
Like an old proud king in a parable.

[1928] {1943}

PROTHALAMIUM

Here in this narrow room there is no light;
The dead tree sings against the window pane;
Sand shifts a little, easily; the wall
Responds a little, inchmeal, slowly, down.

My sister, whom my dust shall marry, sleeps
Alone, yet knows what bitter root it is
That stirs within her; see, it splits the heart –
Warm hands grown cold, grown nerveless as a fin,
And lips enamelled to a hardness –
Consummation ushered in   10
By wind in sundry corners.

This holy sacrament was solemnized
In harsh poetics a good while ago –

At Malfy and the Danish battlements,
And by that preacher from a cloud in Paul's.

No matter: each must read the truth himself,
Or, reading it, reads nothing to the point.
Now these are me, whose thought is mine, and hers,
Who are alone here in this narrow room —
Tree fumbling pane, bell tolling,   20
Ceiling dripping and the plaster falling,
And Death, the voluptuous, calling.

[1928] {1943}

NOCTAMBULE

Under the flag of this pneumatic moon,
— Blown up to bursting, whitewashed white,
And painted like the moon — the piracies of day
Scuttle the crank hulk of witless night.
The great black innocent Othello of a thing
Is undone by the nice clean pockethandkerchief
Of 6 a.m., and though the moon is only an old
Wetwash snotrag — horsemeat for good *rosbif* —
Perhaps to utilize substitutes is what
The age has to teach us,

                             wherefore let the loud   10
Unmeaning warcry of treacherous daytime
Issue like whispers of love in the moonlight,
— Poxy old cheat!
                 So mewed the lion,
Until mouse roared once and after lashed
His tail: Shellshock came on again, his skin
Twitched in the rancid margarine, his eye

Like a lake isle in a florist's window:
Reality at two removes, and mouse and moon
Successful.

[1932] {1943}

NEWS OF THE PHOENIX

They say the Phoenix is dying, some say dead.
Dead without issue is what one message said,
But that has been suppressed, officially denied.

I think myself the man who sent it lied.
In any case, I'm told, he has been shot,
As a precautionary measure, whether he did or not.

[1933] {1943}

A SOLDIER'S GHOST

How shall I speak
To the regiment of young
Whose throats break
Saluting the god

Descending onto the drumhead
— Stalled
Each in his proper stance
Upholding the service?

Bones
Distilled in the frontier sand

10

Fumble
The natty chevron.

Can a memberless ghost
Tell?
These lost
Are so many brother bones.

The hieroglyph
Of ash
Concedes an anagram
Of love.   20

[1933] {1943}

To a Young Poet

FOR C.A.M.

Tread the metallic nave
Of this windless day with
A pace designed and grave:
— Iphigenia in her myth

Creating for stony eyes
An elegant, fatal dance
Was signed with no device
More alien to romance

Than I would have you find
In the stern, autumnal face   10
Of Artemis, whose kind
Cruelty makes duty grace,

Whose votary alone
Seals the affrighted air
With the worth of a hard thing done
Perfectly, as though without care.

[1933] {1943}

RESURRECTION OF ARP

On the third day rose Arp
out of the black sleeve of the tomb:
he could see like a cat in the dark,
but the light left him dumb.

He stood up to testify,
and his tongue wouldn't work
in the old groove; he had to try
other tongues, including the Scandinavian.

The saints were all well pleased;
his periods rattled and rolled;   10
heresies scattered like ninepins;
all the tickets were sold.

When they turned down the gas
everybody could see there was
a halo of tongues of pale fire
licking the grease off his hair,

and a white bird
fluttered away in the rafters;
people heard
the breaking of a mysterious wind (laughter).   20

He spoke another language
majestic beautiful wild
holy superlative believable
and undefiled

by any comprehensible
syllable
to provoke dissent
or found a schism . . .

After the gratifying large
number of converts had been given receipts
the meeting adjourned to the social hall
for sexual intercourse (dancing) and eats.

Arp talked to the reporters:
on the whole, was glad to have cheated the tomb,
though the angels had been "extremely courteous,"
and death, after all, was only "another room."

[1934] {1954}

SON-AND-HEIR

1930

The nine-months-long-awaited heir is born,
And the parents are pretty proud of the thing.
Instinct censors any real, as too forlorn,
Preview of coming attractions. Angels sing

Like press agents the praises of their lamb
In minds as polite as a mezzanine floor.
They do concoct a brave, politic sham
To ravel the plot, feature the smirking star.

They see him innocency's Jaeger pelt
Hide in the wolf's coat of angry youth,   10
Striding over the very veldtlike veldt
In a bandolier full of Kodak films.

They make him up in the attractive role
Of a he-god in the next episode,
Bringing his woman dividends to roll
A cigarette with, giving his old dad

Market tips, and cigars on Father's Day,
And his Mother telegrams and roses,
Walking in rightwiseness, always *au fait*,
Always sure of the thing he supposes.   20

Who will turn the lights up on this show?
You will find something has gone wrong with the switch,
Or their eyes, used to horse opera, cannot grow
Used to an ordinary sonofabitch

Like you or me for a son, or the doom
We discern – the empty years, the hand to mouth,
The moving cog, the unattended loom,
The breastless street, and lolling summer's drouth,

Or zero's shears at paper window pane . . .
And so forth and so forth and so forth.   30
Let us keep melodrama out of this scene,
Eye open to daylight, foot on the firm earth.

[1935] {1943}

POLITICAL INTELLIGENCE

Nobody said Apples for nearly a minute –
I thought I should die.
Finally, though, the second sardine
from the end, on the left,
converted a try.
(It brought down the house.
The noise was terrific.
I dropped my glass eye.)

Meanwhile the P.M.
managed to make himself heard.   10
He looked sad
but with characteristic aplomb said
Keep calm there is no cause for alarm.

Two soldiers' crutches
crossed up a little bit of fluff
from a lint bandage
in the firing chamber of a 12-inch gun.
People agreed not to notice.
The band played a little bit louder.
It was all very British.   20

[1936] {1954}

FAR WEST

Among the cigarettes and the peppermint creams
Came the flowers of fingers, luxurious and bland,
Incredibly blossoming in the little breast.
And in the Far West

The tremendous cowboys in goatskin pants
Shot up the town of her ignorant wish.

In the gun flash she saw the long light shake
Across the lake, repeating that poem
At Finsbury Park.
But the echo was drowned in the roll of the trams –   10
Anyway, who would have heard? Not a soul.
Not one noble and toxic like Buffalo Bill.

In the holy name *bang! bang!* the flowers came
With the marvellous touch of fingers
Gentler than the fuzzy goats
Moving up and down up and down as if in ecstasy
As the cowboys rode their skintight stallions
Over the barbarous hills of California.

[1939] {1943}

ODE: THE EUMENIDES

I

If we could go again
To the innocent wood
Where the crisp floor
Muffles the tread,
And the classic shade
Of cedar and pine
Soothes the depraved head
In the children's glen,
It might be that the casual dead

In their stained shrouds
Would not find us there.

These times indeed
Breed anguish.

Betrayed by the cold front
And the bright line
How shall we return
To the significant dark
Of piety and fear
Where holiness smoothed our hair
And honour kissed us goodbye?

II

How shall we ask for
What we need whose need
Is less, not more?

Now that the dragon seed
Grows tall and red, we
Harvest in the field
Sharp sheaves, and see
The reaper felled
By what we took such care
To sow so straight.

Our secular prayer,
Sincere and passionate,
Created its own
Power and instrument
And will. There is none,
However innocent

In heart or head,
That shall escape
The stench of the dead
Emptied and butchered hope   40
In lives and deaths made
Meaningless froth.

How shall we ask for
What we need whose need
Is less, not more?

III

Where foreheads bleed
The cry is blood!

We have a date in another wood,
In the stifling dark,
Where the Furies are.   50

The unravelled implacable host
With accurate eyes levelled
Wait in the enchanted shade.

Where we spilled our bloodshot seed
They wait, each patient ghost
My ruined son.

The Furies lift the veil —
I know that face!

[1941–1944] {1954}

The Common Man

I

Somewhere his number must have been betrayed,
Caught in the dazzle that the goldfish made
Or lost in the gas of the first mock raid.

A jittery clerk with a slippery pen
Condemned him to limbo, a headless hen
Gyrating about in a bloodstained pen.

He lived by luck and a sense of touch.
These were his two gifts and they were not too much.
One was a black patch and the other a crutch.

He lived at last on scraps of a food card   10
Chewed up and torn and found in the yard
Beside a corpse the death ray only charred.

II

To survive, at first an escapist's whim,
Became with time, as his trim grew slim,
Less a point of honour than a duty grim.

He was the only man in the world
Not registered. He was a node, a furled
Forgotten flag, a still point still unwhirled.

His function was to stand outside.
At first he thought this helped him when he tried   20
To tell who told the truth, who plainly lied.

He was the unseen watcher standing there
By the sweating statue in Parliament Square,
The one who could not care and had to care.

III

His job was to listen in on the queues,
To decode the official releases, and fuse
The cheers on parade with the jeers in the mews.

The diminishing pressure of hands
Gave him a valuable clue. Mourning bands
Were not worn, but he noticed that sands   30

Were much sought after for building castles on.
(The castles might crumble but not burn down.
Incendiaries fizzle in sand and soon are done.)

The dead were not mentioned, though each was planted.
Even the stricken areas were not haunted.
The dead, being of spirit, were not wanted.

IV

At last his "amour-propre" became "the public weal":
He was the common man, Platonic and ideal,
Mercurial and elusive, yet alive and real.

He was the public good, the target one   40
At whom each sugar-coated poison-spraying gun
Was levelled. Whatever was done was done

To him. He was the ear communiqués
Addressed, the simple mind for which the maze
Of policy was clarified. His praise

Was what the leaders said was their reward.
To pierce his heart the patriotic sword
Was dipped in ink and gall and flourished hard.

v

He fell, of course. An abstract man
Who ended much as he began –   50
An exile in a universal plan.

Not to let the leaders down became his mission.
To ascertain their will was his obsession.
His hope, somehow to wangle their permission

To speak and be himself and have a name,
And shake abstraction's disembodied shame,
And play, not overlook, the murderous game . . .

He boils a soiled shard of his purloined card
And bends where the lamplight ends over the hard
Significant puzzle. The ignorant policeman walks the yard.   60

[1942] {1954}

THE WISDOM OF OLD JELLY ROLL

How all men wrongly death to dignify
Conspire, I tell. Parson, poetaster, pimp,
Each acts or acquiesces. They prettify,

Dress up, deodorize, embellish, primp,
And make a show of Nothing. Ah, but met-
aphysics laughs; she touches, tastes, and smells
– Hence knows – the diamond holes that make a net.
Silence resettled testifies to bells.
"Nothing" depends on "Thing," which is or was:
So death makes life or makes life's worth, a worth   10
Beyond all highfalutin' woes or shows
To publish and confess. "Cry at the birth,
Rejoice at the death," old Jelly Roll said,
Being on whiskey, ragtime, chicken, and the scriptures fed.

[1958] {1962}

CHARLES BRUCE

1906–1971

Charles Bruce was the youngest of the Song Fishermen, an informal group of Maritime writers including Kenneth Leslie, Robert Norwood, and Charles G.D. Roberts. Bruce was born the descendant of Loyalists in Port Shoreham on Chedabucto Bay, Nova Scotia. In 1927 he joined the Halifax *Chronicle,* then moved to the Halifax offices of the Canadian Press. He published his first hand-stitched chapbook, *Wild Apples,* in 1927. Though much of the verse is derivative, he was already a gifted portraitist of Maritime landscapes and seasonal life. *Tomorrow's Tide* appeared with Macmillan in 1932. In 1933 the Canadian Press transferred him to Toronto; he became its general superintendent in 1945. He was a war correspondent in Europe and was briefly missing after the airplane in which he was travelling was shot down. He published two volumes of poetry in the Allied cause, *Personal Note* (1941) and *Grey Ship Moving* (1945). The long poem *The Flowing Summer* (1947) returns to his original inspiration by showing a Toronto child's awakening to the enduring pleasures of Maritime farming life. Bruce's best-known collection was *The Mulgrave Road* (1951), which won a Governor General's Award. After its publication he concentrated on fiction; his pastoral family saga *The Channel Shore* was published in 1954.

Sea Sense

These we have known: the light spruce needles sifting
Through dried brown arms; ridged reefs by tides enthralled;
And all the long lone beaches, robed and shawled
In wind whipped mist; the boom of torn surf lifting;
Austere October hills; the blown sky shifting;
Towers and towns, and gardens, squared and walled;
Dark dreams, too deep in sleep to be recalled;
And shadowy clouds, across the cool grass sifting.

These, to the spruce clad hill and golden hollow
Blow on the wistful wind, and linger there.   10
Down the dim rocks, with these for grace, we follow
A still strange dream, most gloriously rare,
And careless flaring with the skyward swallow:
A splendour, fugitive and frail and fair.

{1927}

Armistice Day

We are the ranks who were too young to go;
We saw the summer fade, the spring return,
Found in the golden fall, the winter snow,
Armies to battle with and towns to burn.
The whittled rifle at our shoulder set,
Beyond the years' impenetrable door
We heard the bugles of our own regret.
We are the ranks who were too young for war.

Now we are told the ringing words were lies,
The flag a blind across the eyes of youth,   10

The sharp adventure but a grim surprise
Of brutish pain. We cannot guess the truth.
  Still when the Legion's marching men go by
  Far bugles call across the autumn sky.

{1932}

TOMORROW'S TIDE

Not yet, behind the bluffs of Ragged Head,
Red light has lifted, nor the wind astir
Made the bay quick with breath. The beach is still.
Night lies with us and we are wed to her.
But the pulse beats; and a relentless will
Forswears the velvet lover. In her stead
Slow tides of grey set the sharp dark ablur,
Before the morning swell is ringed with red.

Not now the sleep encircled night may drown
This early lamplight pale against the pane,   10
Nor woodsmoke drowsing in the tranquil dusk.
Now stubborn kinsmen of the viking strain
Join crisp and thrifty greeting with a brusque
Brief scraping, as the weathered boats go down
To meet dark water in the need to gain
This day the daily bread of no renown.

Caught from the common rasp of stem and strake
Through furrowed gravel, and the guttural hiss
Of water streaming in the shoreward wake,
The word they leave you in the sand is this: 20

"Tomorrow's tide is deaf to call,
Without recourse the daylight dies;
No treaty binds the shifting squall,
With wind there is no compromise."

Life's urge exploited, statesmen shape the truss
Of ribboned foolscap in a distant room,
And wait new wars behind the terms of peace.
Here on the beach the seeds of struggle bloom
Beyond the need for militant release;
Hazard is never second-hand to us —   30
Though millions ache to wear its crimson plume,
Here on the beach we are not troubled thus.

While simple strength and rugged beauty live,
Unmarked of splendour crowned or glory sped,
The faith we leave you and the word we give
Beats in the surf that breaks on Ragged Head:

"Let go the signed and sealed excuse
That nourishes maturing spoil;
And turn your thirsting millions loose
On hill and forest, sea and soil.   40

Unchecked, the rainwet troopers ride,
The sunlight-feathered arrow flies;
Implacable as creeping tide,
With wind there is no compromise."

{1932}

EARLE BIRNEY

1904–1995

Although he dedicated himself fully to poetry only in his mid-thir-
ties, Earle Birney won Governor General's Awards for his first two
collections and went on to publish over twenty more. Birney was
born in Calgary, Alberta, and grew up near Lacombe, in Banff, and
in the Kootenay Valley, where he worked briefly as a labourer in
the region's national parks. He graduated from the University of
British Columbia in 1926 and took M.A. and Ph.D. degrees from the
University of Toronto in Old English and medieval studies. In the
early 1930s he was active in the Trotskyite wing of the Communist
Party of Canada. He taught at the University of Toronto and was
the literary editor of the *Canadian Forum* (1938–40). His first
volume, *David, and Other Poems,* appeared in 1942. From 1942–45
Birney served in the Canadian army overseeing troop allocations in
Holland and Belgium. After being invalided back to Canada, he
worked for a year in the Canadian Broadcasting Corporation's
International Service before joining the English department at the
University of British Columbia (1946–65) and inheriting the edi-
torship of the *Canadian Poetry Magazine* from E.J. Pratt. The
achievements and frustrations of this period (1946-48) are recorded
in his memoir *Spreading Time* (1980). His satiric war novel *Turvey*
appeared in 1949 and scandalized many readers with its profanity;
it was banned from a number of schools and public libraries. At
U.B.C. he championed and pioneered teaching and programs in
creative writing. Frequent world travel in the 1950s inspired
renewed poetic activity: Birney helped to popularize the lyric travel
poem in *Ice Cod Bell or Stone* (1962) and *November Walk near False*

Creek Mouth (1964). In 1965 he resigned from U.B.C. and took up a series of writer-in-residence positions at several Canadian universities. During the 1960s he revised the layout and punctuation of many of his earlier poems, such as "Vancouver Lights," to accord with the typographical fashions of the sixties and in later volumes both anticipated and imitated the innovations of younger poets. Birney suffered a debilitating stroke in 1987 and passed away in 1995.

SLUG IN WOODS

For eyes he waves greentipped
taut horns of slime   They dipped
hours back   across a reef
a salmonberry leaf
then strained to grope past fin
of spruce   Now eyes suck in
as through the hemlock butts
of his day's ledge there cuts
a vixen chipmunk   Stilled
is he – green mucus chilled   10
or blotched and soapy stone
pinguid in moss   alone
Hours on   he will resume
his silver scrawl   illume
his palimpsest   emboss
his diver's line across
that waving green illim-
itable seafloor   Slim
young jay his sudden shark
The wrecks he skirts are dark   20
and fungussed firlogs   whom
spirea sprays emplume

encoral   Dew his shell
while mounting boles foretell
of isles in dappled air
fathoms above his care
Azygous muted life
himself his viscid wife
foodward he noses cold beneath his sea
So spends a summer's jasper century   30

Crescent Beach, B.C. 1928

[1928] {1942}

ANGLOSAXON STREET

Dawndrizzle ended   dampness steams from
blotching brick and   blank plasterwaste
Faded housepatterns   hoary and finicky
unfold stuttering   stick like a phonograph

Here is a ghetto   gotten for goyim
O with care denuded   of nigger and kike
No coonsmell rankles   reeks only cellarrot
attar of carexhaust   catcorpse and cookinggrease
Imperial hearts   heave in this haven
Cracks across windows   are welded with slogans   10
There'll Always Be An England   enhances geraniums
and V's for Victory   vanquish the housefly

Ho! with climbing sun   march the bleached beldames
festooned with shopping bags   farded flatarched
bigthewed Saxonwives   stepping over buttrivers
waddling back wienerladen   to suckle smallfry

Hoy! with sunslope   shrieking over hydrants
flood from learninghall   the lean fingerlings
Nordic nobblecheeked   not all clean of nose
leaping Commandowise   into leprous lanes   20

What! after whistleblow!   spewed from wheelboat
after daylong doughtiness   dire handplay
in sewertrench or sandpit   come Saxonthegns
Junebrown Jutekings   jawslack for meat

Sit after supper   on smeared doorsteps
not humbly swearing   hatedeeds on Huns
profiteers politicians   pacifists Jews

Then by twobit magic   to muse in movie
unlock picturehoard   or lope to alehall
soaking bleakly   in beer skittleless   30

Home again to hotbox   and humid husbandhood
in slumbertrough adding   sleepily to Anglekin
Alongside in lanenooks   carling and leman
caterwaul and clip   careless of Saxonry
with moonglow and haste   and a higher heartbeat

Slumbers now slumtrack   unstinks cooling
waiting brief for milkmaid   mornstar and worldrise

Toronto 1942

{1942}

DAVID

I

David and I that summer cut trails on the Survey,
All week in the valley for wages, in air that was steeped
In the wail of mosquitoes, but over the sunalive week-ends
We climbed, to get from the ruck of the camp, the surly

Poker, the wrangling, the snoring under the fetid
Tents, and because we had joy in our lengthening coltish
Muscles, and mountains for David were made to see over,
Stairs from the valleys and steps to the sun's retreats.

II

Our first was Mount Gleam. We hiked in the long afternoon
To a curling lake and lost the lure of the faceted   10
Cone in the swell of its sprawling shoulders. Past
The inlet we grilled our bacon, the strips festooned

On a poplar prong, in the hurrying slant of the sunset.
Then the two of us rolled in the blanket while round us the cold
Pines thrust at the stars. The dawn was a floating
Of mists till we reached to the slopes above timber, and won

To snow like fire in the sunlight. The peak was upthrust
Like a fist in a frozen ocean of rock that swirled
Into valleys the moon could be rolled in. Remotely unfurling
Eastward the alien prairie glittered. Down through the dusty   20

Skree on the west we descended, and David showed me
How to use the give of shale for giant incredible
Strides. I remember, before the larches' edge,
That I jumped a long green surf of juniper flowing

Away from the wind, and landed in gentian and saxifrage
Spilled on the moss. Then the darkening firs
And the sudden whirring of water that knifed down a fern-hidden
Cliff and splashed unseen into mist in the shadows.

III

One Sunday on Rampart's arête a rainsquall caught us,
And passed, and we clung by our blueing fingers and bootnails 30
An endless hour in the sun, not daring to move
Till the ice had steamed from the slate. And David taught me

How time on a knife-edge can pass with the guessing of fragments
Remembered from poets, the naming of strata beside one,
And matching of stories from schooldays. . . . We crawled astride
The peak to feast on the marching ranges flagged

By the fading shreds of the shattered stormcloud. Lingering
There it was David who spied to the south, remote,
And unmapped, a sunlit spire on Sawback, an overhang
Crooked like a talon. David named it the Finger.   40

That day we chanced on the skull and the splayed white ribs
Of a mountain goat underneath a cliff-face, caught
On a rock. Around were the silken feathers of hawks.
And that was the first I knew that a goat could slip.

IV

And then Inglismaldie. Now I remember only
The long ascent of the lonely valley, the live
Pine spirally scarred by lightning, the slicing pipe
Of invisible pika, and great prints, by the lowest

Snow, of a grizzly. There it was too that David
Taught me to read the scroll of coral in limestone   50
And the beetle-seal in the shale of ghostly trilobites,
Letters delivered to man from the Cambrian waves.

V

On Sundance we tried from the col and the going was hard.
The air howled from our feet to the smudged rocks
And the papery lake below. At an outthrust we baulked
Till David clung with his left to a dint in the scarp,

Lobbed the iceaxe over the rocky lip,
Slipped from his holds and hung by the quivering pick,
Twisted his long legs up into space and kicked
To the crest. Then grinning, he reached with his freckled wrist   60

And drew me up after. We set a new time for that climb.
That day returning we found a robin gyrating
In grass, wing-broken. I caught it to tame but David
Took and killed it, and said, "Could you teach it to fly?"

VI

In August, the second attempt, we ascended The Fortress,
By the forks of the Spray we caught five trout and fried them
Over a balsam fire. The woods were alive
With the vaulting of mule-deer and drenched with clouds all the
    morning,

Till we burst at noon to the flashing and floating round
Of the peaks. Coming down we picked in our hats the bright   70
And sunhot raspberries, eating them under a mighty
Spruce, while a marten moving like quicksilver scouted us.

But always we talked of the Finger on Sawback, unknown
And hooked, till the first afternoon in September we slogged
Through the musky woods, past a swamp that quivered with
   frog-song,
And camped by a bottle-green lake. But under the cold

Breath of the glacier sleep would not come, the moon-light
Etching the Finger. We rose and trod past the feathery
Larch, while the stars went out, and the quiet heather
Flushed, and the skyline pulsed with the surging bloom   80

Of incredible dawn in the Rockies. David spotted
Bighorns across the moraine and sent them leaping
With yodels the ramparts redoubled and rolled to the peaks,
And the peaks to the sun. The ice in the morning thaw

Was a gurgling world of crystal and cold blue chasms,
And seracs that shone like frozen saltgreen waves.
At the base of the Finger we tried once and failed. Then David
Edged to the west and discovered the chimney; the last

Hundred feet we fought the rock and shouldered and kneed
Our way for an hour and made it. Unroping we formed   90
A cairn on the rotting tip. Then I turned to look north
At the glistening wedge of giant Assiniboine, heedless

Of handhold. And one foot gave. I swayed and shouted.
David turned sharp and reached out his arm and steadied me,
Turning again with a grin and his lips ready
To jest. But the strain crumbled his foothold. Without

A gasp he was gone. I froze to the sound of grating
Edge-nails and fingers, the slither of stones, the lone
Second of silence, the nightmare thud. Then only
The wind and the muted beat of unknowing cascades.   100

VIII

Somehow I worked down the fifty impossible feet
To the ledge, calling and getting no answer but echoes
Released in the cirque, and trying not to reflect
What an answer would mean. He lay still, with his lean

Young face upturned and strangely unmarred, but his legs
Splayed beneath him, beside the final drop,
Six hundred feet sheer to the ice. My throat stopped
When I reached him, for he was alive. He opened his gray

Straight eyes and brokenly murmured "over. . . . over."
And I, feeling beneath him a cruel fang   110
Of the ledge thrust in his back, but not understanding,
Mumbled stupidly, "Best not to move," and spoke

Of his pain. But he said, "I can't move . . . If only I felt
Some pain." Then my shame stung the tears to my eyes
As I crouched, and I cursed myself, but he cried,
Louder, "No, Bobbie! Don't ever blame yourself.

I didn't test my foothold." He shut the lids
Of his eyes to the stare of the sky, while I moistened his lips
From our water flask and tearing my shirt into strips
I swabbed the shredded hands. But the blood slid   120

From his side and stained the stone and the thirsting lichens,
And yet I dared not lift him up from the gore

Of the rock. Then he whispered, "Bob, I want to go over!"
This time I knew what he meant and I grasped for a lie

And said, "I'll be back here by midnight with ropes
And men from the camp and we'll cradle you out." But I knew
That the day and the night must pass and the cold dews
Of another morning before such men unknowing

The ways of mountains could win to the chimney's top.
And then, how long? And he knew. . . . and the hell of hours   130
After that, if he lived till we came, roping him out.
But I curled beside him and whispered, "The bleeding will stop.

You can last." He said only, "Perhaps. . . . For what? A wheelchair,
Bob?" His eyes brightening with fever upbraided me.
I could not look at him more and said, "Then I'll stay
With you." But he did not speak, for the clouding fever.

I lay dazed and stared at the long valley,
The glistening hair of a creek on the rug stretched
By the firs, while the sun leaned round and flooded the ledge,
The moss, and David still as a broken doll.   140

I hunched to my knees to leave, but he called and his voice
Now was sharpened with fear. "For Christ's sake push me over!
If I could move. . . . Or die. . . ." The sweat ran from his forehead,
But only his eyes moved. A hawk was buoying

Blackly its wings over the wrinkled ice.
The purr of a waterfall rose and sank with the wind.
Above us climbed the last joint of the Finger
Beckoning bleakly the wide indifferent sky.

Even then in the sun it grew cold lying there. . . . And I knew
He had tested his holds. It was I who had not. . . . I looked   150
At the blood on the ledge, and the far valley. I looked
At last in his eyes. He breathed, "I'd do it for you, Bob."

IX

I will not remember how nor why I could twist
Up the wind-devilled peak, and down through the chimney's empty
Horror, and over the traverse alone. I remember
Only the pounding fear I would stumble on It

When I came to the grave-cold maw of the bergschrund. . . . reeling
Over the sun-cankered snowbridge, shying the caves
In the névé. . . . the fear, and the need to make sure It was there
On the ice, the running and falling and running, leaping   160

Of gaping greenthroated crevasses, alone and pursued
By the Finger's lengthening shadow. At last through the fanged
And blinding seracs I slid to the milky wrangling
Falls at the glacier's snout, through the rocks piled huge

On the humped moraine, and into the spectral larches,
Alone. By the glooming lake I sank and chilled
My mouth but I could not rest and stumbled still
To the valley, losing my way in the ragged marsh.

I was glad of the mire that covered the stains, on my ripped
Boots, of his blood, but panic was on me, the reek   170
Of the bog, the purple glimmer of toadstools obscene
In the twilight. I staggered clear to a firewaste, tripped

And fell with a shriek on my shoulder. It somehow eased
My heart to know I was hurt, but I did not faint

And I could not stop while over me hung the range
Of the Sawback. In blackness I searched for the trail by the creek

And found it. . . . My feet squelched a slug and horror
Rose again in my nostrils. I hurled myself
Down the path. In the woods behind some animal yelped.
Then I saw the glimmer of tents and babbled my story.   180

I said that he fell straight to the ice where they found him,
And none but the sun and incurious clouds have lingered
Around the marks of that day on the ledge of the Finger,
That day, the last of my youth, on the last of our mountains.

Toronto 1940

{1942}

VANCOUVER LIGHTS

About me the night   moonless   wimples the mountains
wraps ocean   land   air   and mounting
sucks at the stars   The city   throbbing below
webs the sable peninsula   The golden
strands overleap the seajet   by bridge and buoy
vault the shears of the inlet   climb the woods
toward me   falter   and halt   Across to the firefly
haze of a ship on the gulf's erased horizon
roll the lambent spokes of a lighthouse

Through the feckless years we have come to the time   10
when to look on this quilt of lamps is a troubling delight
Welling from Europe's bog   through Africa flowing
and Asia   drowning the lonely lumes on the oceans

tiding up over Halifax   ·   now to this winking
outpost comes flooding the primal ink

On this mountain's brutish forehead with terror of space
I stir   of the changeless night and the stark ranges
of nothing   pulsing down from beyond and between
the fragile planets   We are a spark beleaguered
by darkness   this twinkle we make in a corner of emptiness   20
how shall we utter our fear that the black Experimentress
will never in the range of her microscope find it?   Our Phoebus
himself is a bubble that dries on Her slide   while the Nubian
wears for an evening's whim a necklace of nebulae

Yet we must speak   we the unique glowworms
Out of the waters and rocks of our little world
we conjured these flames   hooped these sparks
by our will   From blankness and cold we fashioned stars
to our size   and signalled Aldebaran
This must we say   whoever may be to hear us   30
if murk devour   and none weave again in gossamer:

                                    These rays were ours
we made and unmade them   Not the shudder of continents
doused us   the moon's passion   nor crash of comets
In the fathomless heat of our dwarfdom   our dream's combustion
we contrived the power   the blast that snuffed us
No one bound Prometheus   Himself he chained
and consumed his own bright liver   O stranger
Plutonian   descendant   or beast in the stretching night –
there was light   40

{1942}

The Road to Nijmegen

December my dear on the road to Nijmegen
between the stones and the bitten sky
was your face

Not yours at first
but only the countenance of lank canals
and gathered stares
(too rapt to note my passing)
of graves with frosted billy-tins for epitaphs
bones of tanks beside the stoven bridges

and old men in the mist   10
hacking the last chips
from a boulevard of stumps

These for miles and the fangs of homes
where women wheeled in the wind
on the tireless rims of their cycles
like tattered sailboats,
tossing over the cobbles

and the children
groping in gravel for knobs of coal
or clustered like wintered flies   20
at the back of messhuts
their legs standing like dead stems out of their clogs

Numbed on the long road to mangled Nijmegen
I thought that only the living of others assures us
the gentle and true we remember as trees walking
Their arms reach down from the light of kindness
into this Lazarus tomb

So peering through sleet as we neared Nijmegen
I glimpsed the rainbow arch of your eyes
Over the clank of the jeep   30
your quick grave laughter
outrising at last the rockets
brought me what spells I repeat
as I travel this road
that arrives at no future
and what creed I can bring
to our daily crimes
to this guilt
in the griefs of the old
and the graves of the young   40

{1945}

BUSHED

He invented a rainbow but lightning struck it
shattered it into the lake-lap of a mountain
so big his mind slowed when he looked at it

Yet he built a shack on the shore
learned to roast porcupine belly and
wore the quills on his hatband

At first he was out with the dawn
whether it yellowed bright as wood-columbine
or was only a fuzzed moth in a flannel of storm
But he found the mountain was clearly alive   10
sent messages whizzing down every hot morning
boomed proclamations at noon and spread out

a white guard of goat
before falling asleep on its feet at sundown

When he tried his eyes on the lake   ospreys
would fall like valkyries
choosing the cut-throat
He took then to waiting
till the night smoke rose from the boil of the sunset

But the moon carved unknown totems   20
out of the lakeshore
owls in the beardusky woods derided him
moosehorned cedars circled his swamps and tossed
their antlers up to the stars
then he knew   though the mountain slept   the winds
were shaping its peak to an arrowhead
poised

And now he could only
bar himself in and wait
for the great flint to come singing into his heart   30

Wreck Beach 1951

{1952}

The Bear on the Delhi Road

Unreal   tall as a myth
by the road the Himalayan bear
is beating the brilliant air
with his crooked arms

About him two men   bare
spindly as locusts   leap

One pulls on a ring
in the great soft nose   His mate
flicks   flicks with a stick
up at the rolling eyes   10

They have not led him here
down from the fabulous hills
to this bald alien plain
and the clamorous world   to kill
but simply to teach him to dance

They are peaceful both   these spare
men of Kashmir   and the bear
alive is their living   too
If   far on the Delhi way
around him galvanic they dance   20
it is merely to wear   wear
from his shaggy body the tranced
wish forever to stay
only an ambling bear
four-footed in berries

It is no more joyous for them
in this hot dust to prance
out of reach of the praying claws
sharpened to paw for ants
in the shadows of deodars   30
It is not easy to free
myth from reality
or rear this fellow up

to lurch   lurch with them
in the tranced dancing of men

Srinagar 1958 / Île des Porquerolles 1959

{1962}

EL GRECO: *ESPOLIO*

The carpenter is intent on the pressure of his hand

on the awl   and the trick of pinpointing his strength
through the awl to the wood   which is tough
He has no effort to spare for despoilings
or to worry if he'll be cut in on the dice
His skill is vital to the scene   and the safety of the state
Anyone can perform the indignities   It's his hard arms
and craft that hold the eyes of the convict's women
There is the problem of getting the holes exact
(in the middle of this elbowing crowd)   10
and deep enough to hold the spikes
after they've sunk through those bared feet
and inadequate wrists he knows are waiting behind him

He doesn't sense perhaps that one of the hands
is held in a curious gesture over him —
giving   or asking   forgiveness? —
but he'd scarcely take time to be puzzled by poses
Criminals come in all sorts
as anyone knows who makes crosses
are as mad or sane as those who decide on their killings   20
Our one at least has been quiet so far

though they say he talked himself into this trouble
a carpenter's son who got notions of preaching

Well here's a carpenter's son who'll have carpenter sons
God willing   and build what's wanted
temples or tables   mangers or crosses
and shape them decently
working alone in that firm and profound abstraction
which blots out the bawling of rag-snatchers
To construct with hands   knee-weight   braced thigh   30
keeps the back turned from death

But it's too late now for the other carpenter's boy
to return to this peace before the nails are hammered

Point Grey 1960

{1962}

A.M. KLEIN

1909–1972

Abraham Moses Klein was born in Ratno, Ukraine; his family moved to Montreal in 1910. He had an orthodox Jewish education and briefly considered the rabbinate. At McGill University he began lasting friendships with Leon Edel, Leo Kennedy, and A.J.M. Smith of the *McGill Fortnightly Review,* though he never published in the periodical. After graduation from McGill in 1930 he entered law school at the Université de Montréal. In 1934 he started a desultory law practice; his contact with the socio-economic realities of the Depression deepened the political consciousness of his poetry, as had the rise of Fascism and anti-Semitism in Europe. In 1936 he appeared in *New Provinces: Poems of Several Authors. Hath Not a Jew* appeared in 1940 with an American publisher specializing in Jewish writing, as would his next collection, *Poems* (1944). *The Hitleriad* (1944), though bearing the modernist imprimatur of New Directions Press, was severely reviewed for lacking a profound representation of Hitler's evil. Klein's involvement in the early 1940s with the Montreal little magazines *Preview* and *First Statement* gave new impetus to his poetry. By mid-decade he launched a series of poems on modern Quebec's scenes, persons, and themes that he would collect in *The Rocking Chair, and Other Poems* (1948), for which he received the Governor General's Award. "Portrait of the Poet as Landscape," his acknowledged masterpiece, conveys both the ambition and the bleaker undertones of the *Rocking Chair* project. Klein was twice a candidate for the Co-operative Commonwealth Federation: he withdrew abruptly in 1944 and was humiliatingly trounced in 1949. From 1945 to 1948 he taught English at McGill. The Canadian Jewish Congress sent him on a 1949 fact-finding tour of the new state of Israel; he represented his journey in fictional form in his only published novel, *The Second Scroll* (1951). Shortly after its appearance, Klein suffered a series of nervous breakdowns, attempted suicide more than once, and was institutionalized. After his recovery, he lived more and more reclusively; he would write no new poems after the age of 46. He died in his sleep in 1972. His *Complete Poems* were edited by Zailig Pollock in 1990.

OUT OF THE PULVER AND THE POLISHED LENS

I

The paunchy sons of Abraham
Spit on the maculate streets of Amsterdam,
Showing Spinoza, Baruch *alias* Benedict,
He and his God are under interdict.

Ah, what theology there is in spatted spittle,
And in anathema what sacred prose
Winnowing the fact from the suppose!
Indeed, what better than these two things can whittle
The scabrous heresies of Yahweh's foes,
Informing the breast where Satan gloats and crows   10
That saving it leave false doctrine, jot and tittle,
No vigilant thumb will leave its orthodox nose?
What better than ram's horn blown,
And candles blown out by maledictory breath,
Can bring the wanderer back to his very own,
The infidel back to his faith?

Nothing, unless it be that from the ghetto
A soldier of God advance to teach the creed,
Using as rod the irrefutable stiletto.

II

Uriel da Costa   20
Flightily ranted
Heresies one day,
Next day recanted.

Rabbi and bishop
Each vies to smuggle
Soul of da Costa
Out of its struggle.

Confessional hears his
Glib paternoster;
Synagogue sees his   30
Penitent posture.

What is the end of
This catechism?
Bullet brings dogma
That suffers no schism.

III

Malevolent scorpions befoul thy chambers,
O my heart; they scurry across its floor,
Leaving the slimy vestiges of doubt.

Banish memento of the vermin; let
No scripture on the wall affright you; no   40

Ghost of da Costa; no, nor any threat.
Ignore, O heart, even as didst ignore
The bribe of florins jingling in the purse.

IV

Jehovah is factotum of the rabbis;
And Christ endures diurnal Calvary;
Polyglot God is exiled to the churches;
Synods tell God to be or not to be.

The Lord within his vacuum of heaven
Discourses his domestic policies,
With angels who break off their loud hosannas   50
To help him phrase infallible decrees.

Soul of Spinoza, Baruch Spinoza bids you
Forsake the god suspended in mid-air,
Seek you that other Law, and let Jehovah
Play his game of celestial solitaire.

V

   Reducing providence to theorems, the horrible atheist com-
piled such lore that proved, like proving two and two make four,
that in the crown of God we all are gems. From glass and dust of
glass he brought to light, out of the pulver and the polished lens,
the prism and the flying mote; and hence the infinitesimal   60
and infinite.
   Is it a marvel, then, that he forsook the abracadabra of the
synagogue, and holding with timelessness a duologue, deciphered
a new scripture in the book? Is it a marvel that he left old fraud
for passion intellectual of God?

Unto the crown of bone cry *Suzerain!*
Do genuflect before the jewelled brain!
Lavish the homage of the vassal; let
The blood grow heady with strong epithet;
O cirque of the Cabbalist! O proud skull!   70
Of alchemy O crucible!
Sanctum sanctorum; grottoed hermitage
Where sits the bearded sage!
O golden bowl of Koheleth! and of fate
O hourglass within the pate!
Circling, O planet in the occiput!
O Macrocosm, sinew-shut!
Yea, and having uttered this loud *Te Deum*
Ye have been singularly dumb.

VII

I am weak before the wind; before the sun   80
    I faint; I lose my strength;
I am utterly vanquished by a star;
    I go to my knees, at length

Before the song of a bird; before
    The breath of spring or fall
I am lost; before these miracles
    I am nothing at all.

VIII

Lord, accept my hallelujahs; look not askance at these my
petty words; unto perfection a fragment makes its prayer.

For thou art the world, and I am part thereof; thou art 90
the blossom and I its fluttering petal.

I behold thee in all things, and in all things: lo, it is myself;
I look into the pupil of thine eye, it is my very countenance
I see.

Thy glory fills the earth; it is the earth; the noise of the deep,
the moving of many waters, is it not thy voice aloud, O Lord,
aloud that all may hear?

The wind through the almond-trees spreads the fragrance
of thy robes; the turtle-dove twittering utters diminutives of
thy love; at the rising of the sun I behold thy countenance. 100

Yea, and in the crescent moon, thy little finger's finger-nail.

If I ascend up into heaven, thou art there; If I make my bed
in hell, behold thou art there.

Thou art everywhere; a pillar to thy sanctuary is every blade
of grass.

Wherefore I said to the wicked, Go to the ant, thou sluggard,
seek thou an audience with God.

On the swift wings of a star, even on the numb legs of a snail,
thou dost move, O Lord.

A babe in swaddling clothes laughs at the sunbeams on 110
the door's lintel; the sucklings play with thee; with thee
Kopernik holds communion through a lens.

I am thy son, O Lord, and brother to all that lives am I.

The flowers of the field, they are kith and kin to me; the lily
my sister, the rose is my blood and flesh.

Even as the stars in the firmament move, so does my inward
heart, and even as the moon draws the tides in the bay, so does
it the blood in my veins.

For thou art the world, and I am part thereof;

Howbeit, even in dust I am resurrected; and even in 120
decay I live again.

IX ·

Think of Spinoza, then, not as you think
Of Shabbathai Zvi who for a time of life
Took to himself the Torah for a wife,
And underneath the silken canopy
Made public: Thou art hallowed unto me.

Think of Spinoza, rather, plucking tulips
Within the garden of Mynheer, forgetting
Dutchmen and Rabbins, and consumptive fretting,
Plucking his tulips in the Holland sun,   130
Remembering the thought of the Adored,
Spinoza, gathering flowers for the One,
The ever-unwedded lover of the Lord.

[1931] {1940}

HEIRLOOM

My father bequeathed me no wide estates;
No keys and ledgers were my heritage;
Only some holy books with *yahrzeit* dates
Writ mournfully upon a blank front page –

Books of the Baal Shem Tov, and of his wonders;
Pamphlets upon the devil and his crew;
Prayers against road demons, witches, thunders;
And sundry other tomes for a good Jew.

Beautiful: though no pictures on them, save
The scorpion crawling on a printed track;   10

The Virgin floating on a scriptural wave,
Square letters twinkling in the Zodiac.

The snuff left on this page, now brown and old,
The tallow stains of midnight liturgy –
These are my coat of arms, and these unfold
My noble lineage, my proud ancestry!

And my tears, too, have stained this heirloomed ground,
When reading in these treatises some weird
Miracle, I turned a leaf and found
A white hair fallen from my father's beard.   20

[1934] {1940}

A PRAYER OF ABRAHAM, AGAINST MADNESS

Lord, for the days allotted me,
Preserve me whole, preserve me hale!
Spare me the scourge of surgery.
Let not my blood nor members fail.

But if Thy will is otherwise,
And I am chosen such an one
For maiming and for maladies –
So be it; and Thy will be done.

Palsy the keepers of the house;
And of the strongmen take Thy toll.   10
Break down the twigs; break down the boughs.
But touch not, Lord, the golden bowl!

O, I have seen these touched ones –
Their fallow looks, their barren eyes –
For whom have perished all the suns
And vanished all fertilities;

Who, docile, sit within their cells
Like weeds, within a stagnant pool.
I have seen also their fierce hells,
Their flight from echo, their fight with ghoul.   20

Behold him scrabbling on the door!
His spittle falls upon his beard,
As, cowering, he whines before
The voices and the visions, feared.

Not these can serve Thee. Lord, if such
The stumbling that awaits my path –
Grant me Thy grace, Thy mortal touch,
The full death-quiver of Thy wrath!

[1940–41] {1944}

A Psalm of Abraham, Concerning That Which He
Beheld Upon the Heavenly Scarp

1

And on that day, upon the heavenly scarp,
The hosannahs ceased, the hallelujahs died,
And music trembled on the silenced harp.
An angel, doffing his seraphic pride,
Wept; and his tears so bitter were, and sharp,
That where they fell, the blossoms shrivelled and died.

2

Another with such voice intoned his psalm
It sang forth blasphemy against the Lord.
Oh, that was a very imp in angeldom,
Who, thinking evil, said no evil word –   10
But only pointed, at each *Te Deum*
Down to the earth, and its abhorrèd horde.

3

The Lord looked down, and saw the cattle-cars:
Men ululating to a frozen land.
He saw a man tear at his flogged scars,
And saw a babe look for its blown-off hand.
Scholars, he saw, sniffing their bottled wars,
And doctors who had geniuses unmanned.

4

The gentle violinist whose fingers played
Such godly music, washing a gutter, with lye,   20
He saw. He heard the priest who called His aid.
He heard the agnostic's undirected cry.
Unto Him came the odour Hunger made,
And the odour of blood before it is quite dry.

5

The angel who wept looked into the eyes of God.
The angel who sang ceased pointing to the earth.
A little cherub, now glimpsing God's work flaw'd,
Went mad, and flapped his wings in crazy mirth.
And the good Lord said nothing, but with a nod
Summoned the angels of Sodom down to earth.   30

[1941] {1944}

MONTREAL

1

O city metropole, isle riverain!
Your ancient pavages and sainted routs
Traverse my spirit's conjured avenues!
Splendor erablic of your promenades
Foliates there, and there your maisonry
Of pendent balcon and escalier'd march,
Unique midst English habitat,
Is vivid Normandy!

2

You populate the pupils of my eyes:
Thus, does the Indian, plumèd, furtivate   10
Still through your painted autumns, Ville-Marie!
Though palisades have passed, though calumet
With tabac of your peace enfumes the air,
Still do I spy the phantom, aquiline,
Genuflect, moccasin'd, behind
His statue in the square!

3

Thus, costumed images before me pass,
Haunting your archives architectural:
Coureur de bois, in posts where pelts were portaged;
Seigneur within his candled manoir; Scot   20
Ambulant through his bank, pillar'd and vast.
Within your chapels, voyaged mariners
Still pray, and personage departed,
All present from your past!

4

Grand port of navigations, multiple
The lexicons uncargo'd at your quays,
Sonnant though strange to me; but chiefest, I,
Auditor of your music, cherish the
Joined double-melodied vocabulaire
Where English vocable and roll Ecossic,   30
Mollified by the parle of French
Bilinguefact your air!

5

Such your suaver voice, hushed Hochelaga!
But for me also sound your potencies,
Fortissimos of sirens fluvial,
Bruit of manufactory, and thunder
From foundry issuant, all puissant tone
Implenishing your hebdomad; and then
Sanct silence, and your argent belfries
Clamant in orison!   40

6

You are a part of me, O all your quartiers –
And of dire pauvreté and of richesse –
To finished time my homage loyal claim;
You are locale of infancy, milieu
Vital of institutes that formed my fate;
And you above the city, scintillant,
Mount Royal, are my spirit's mother,
Almative, poitrinate!

7

Never do I sojourn in alien place
But I do languish for your scenes and sounds,   50
City of reverie, nostalgic isle,

Pendant most brilliant on Laurentian cord!
The coigns of your boulevards – my signiory –
Your suburbs are my exile's verdure fresh,
Yours parks, your fountain'd parks –
Pasture of memory!

8
City, O city, you are vision'd as
A parchemin roll of saecular exploit
Inked with the script of eterne souvenir!
You are in sound, chanson and instrument!
Mental, you rest forever edified
With tower and dome; and in these beating valves,
Here in these beating valves, you will
For all my mortal time reside!

60

[1944] {1948}

A PSALM TOUCHING GENEALOGY

Not sole was I born, but entire genesis:
For to the fathers that begat me, this
Body is residence. Corpuscular,
They dwell in my veins, they eavesdrop at my ear,
They circle, as with Torahs, round my skull,
In exit and in entrance all day pull
The latches of my heart, descend, and rise –
And there look generations through my eyes.

{1944}

Portrait of the Poet as Landscape

I

Not an editorial-writer, bereaved with bartlett,
mourns him, the shelved Lycidas.
No actress squeezes a glycerine tear for him.
The radio broadcast lets his passing pass.
And with the police, no record. Nobody, it appears,
either under his real name or his alias,
missed him enough to report.

It is possible that he is dead, and not discovered.
It is possible that he can be found some place
in a narrow closet, like the corpse in a detective story,   10
standing, his eyes staring, and ready to fall on his face.
It is also possible that he is alive
and amnesiac, or mad, or in retired disgrace,
or beyond recognition lost in love.

We are sure only that from our real society
he has disappeared; he simply does not count,
except in the pullulation of vital statistics –
somebody's vote, perhaps, an anonymous taunt
of the Gallup poll, a dot in a government table –
but not felt, and certainly far from eminent –   20
in a shouting mob, somebody's sigh.

O, he who unrolled our culture from his scroll –
the prince's quote, the rostrum-rounding roar –
who under one name made articulate
heaven, and under another the seven-circled air,
is, if he is at all, a number, an x,

a Mr. Smith in a hotel register, –
incognito, lost, lacunal.

II

The truth is he's not dead, but only ignored –
like the mirroring lenses forgotten on a brow   30
that shine with the guilt of their unnoticed world.
The truth is he lives among neighbours, who, though they will
    allow
him a passable fellow, think him eccentric, not solid,
a type that one can forgive, and for that matter, forego.

Himself he has his moods, just like a poet.
Sometimes, depressed to nadir, he will think all lost,
will see himself as throwback, relict, freak,
his mother's miscarriage, his great-grandfather's ghost,
and he will curse his quintuplet senses, and their tutors
in whom he put, as he should not have put, his trust.   40

Then he will remember his travels over that body –
the torso verb, the beautiful face of the noun,
and all those shaped and warm auxiliaries!
A first love it was, the recognition of his own.
Dear limbs adverbial, complexion of adjective,
dimple and dip of conjugation!

And then remember how this made a change in him
affecting for always the glow and growth of his being;
how suddenly was aware of the air, like shaken tinfoil,
of the patents of nature, the shock of belated seeing,   50
the lonelinesses peering from the eyes of crowds;
the integers of thought; the cube-roots of feeling.

Thus, zoomed to zenith, sometimes he hopes again,
and sees himself as a character, with a rehearsed role:
the Count of Monte Cristo, come for his revenges;
the unsuspected heir, with papers; the risen soul;
or the chloroformed prince awaking from his flowers;
or – deflated again – the convict on parole.

III

He is alone; yet not completely alone.
Pins on a map of a colour similar to his,   60
each city has one, sometimes more than one:
here, caretakers of art, in colleges;
in offices, there, with arm-bands, and green-shaded;
and there, pounding their catalogued beats in libraries, –

everywhere menial, a shadow's shadow.
And always for their egos – their outmoded art.
Thus, having lost the bevel in the ear,
they know neither up nor down, mistake the part
for the whole, curl themselves in a comma,
talk technics, make a colon their eyes. They distort –   70

such is the pain of their frustration – truth
to something convolute and cerebral.
How they do fear the slap of the flat of the platitude!
Now Pavlov's victims, their mouths water at bell,
the platter empty.
                    See they set twenty-one jewels
into their watches; the time they do not tell!

Some, patagonian in their own esteem,
and longing for the multiplying word,
join party and wear pins, now have a message,

an ear, and the convention-hall's regard.
Upon the knees of ventriloquists, they own,
of their dandled brightness, only the paint and board.

And some go mystical, and some go mad.
One stares at a mirror all day long, as if
to recognize himself; another courts
angels, – for here he does not fear rebuff;
and a third, alone, and sick with sex, and rapt,
doodles him symbols convex and concave.

O schizoid solitudes! O purities
curdling upon themselves! Who live for themselves,   90
or for each other, but for nobody else;
desire affection, private and public loves;
are friendly, and then quarrel and surmise
the secret perversions of each other's lives.

IV

He suspects that something has happened, a law
been passed, a nightmare ordered. Set apart,
he finds himself, with special haircut and dress,
as on a reservation. Introvert.
He does not understand this; sad conjecture
muscles and palls thrombotic on his heart.   100

He thinks an impostor, having studied his personal biography,
his gestures, his moods, now has come forward to pose
in the shivering vacuums his absence leaves.
Wigged with his laurel, that other, and faked with his face,
he pats the heads of his children, pecks his wife,
and is at home, and slippered, in his house.

So he guesses at the impertinent silhouette
that talks to his phone-piece and slits open his mail.
Is it the local tycoon who for a hobby
plays poet, he so epical in steel?   110
The orator, making a pause? Or is that man
he who blows his flash of brass in the jittering hall?

Or is he cuckolded by the troubadour
rich and successful out of celluloid?
Or by the don who unrhymes atoms? Or
the chemist death built up? Pride, lost impostor'd pride,
it is another, another, whoever he is,
who rides where he should ride.

V

Fame, the adrenalin: to be talked about;
to be a verb; to be introduced as *The;*   120
to smile with endorsement from slick paper; make
caprices anecdotal; to nod to the world; to see
one's name like a song upon the marquees played;
to be forgotten with embarrassment; to be –
to be.

It has its attractions, but is not the thing;
nor is it the ape mimesis who speaks from the tree
ancestral; nor the merkin joy . . .
Rather it is stark infelicity
which stirs him from his sleep, undressed, asleep   130
to walk upon roofs and window-sills and defy
the gape of gravity.

VI

Therefore he seeds illusions. Look, he is
the nth Adam taking a green inventory
in world but scarcely uttered, naming, praising,
the flowering fiats in the meadow, the
syllabled fur, stars aspirate, the pollen
whose sweet collision sounds eternally.
For to praise

the world – he, solitary man – is breath   140
to him. Until it has been praised, that part
has not been. Item by exciting item –
air to his lungs, and pressured blood to his heart. –
they are pulsated, and breathed, until they map,
not the world's, but his own body's chart!

And now in imagination he has climbed
another planet, the better to look
with single camera view upon this earth –
its total scope, and each afflated tick,
its talk, its trick, its tracklessness – and this,   150
this he would like to write down in a book!

To find a new function for the déclassé craft
archaic like the fletcher's; to make a new thing;
to say the word that will become sixth sense;
perhaps by necessity and indirection bring
new forms to life, anonymously, new creeds –
O, somehow pay back the daily larcenies of the lung!

These are not mean ambitions. It is already something
merely to entertain them. Meanwhile, he
makes of his status as zero a rich garland,   160

a halo of his anonymity,
and lives alone, and in his secret shines
like phosphorus. At the bottom of the sea.

[1944–45] {1948}

INDIAN RESERVATION: CAUGHNAWAGA

Where are the braves, the faces like autumn fruit,
who stared at the child from the coloured frontispiece?
And the monosyllabic chief who spoke with his throat?
Where are the tribes, the feathered bestiaries? –
Rank Aesop's animals erect and red,
with fur on their names to make all live things kin! –
Chief Running Deer, Black Bear, Old Buffalo Head?

Childhood, that wished me Indian, hoped that
one afterschool I'd leave the classroom chalk,
the varnish smell, the watered dust of the street,   10
to join the clean outdoors and the Iroquois track.
Childhood; but always, – as on a calendar, –
there stood that chief, with arms akimbo, waiting
the runaway mascot paddling to his shore.

With what strange moccasin stealth that scene is changed!
With French names, without paint, in overalls,
their bronze, like their nobility expunged, –
the men. Beneath their alimentary shawls
sit like black tents their squaws; while for the tourist's
brown pennies scattered at the old church door,   20
the ragged papooses jump, and bite the dust.

Their past is sold in a shop: the beaded shoes,
the sweetgrass basket, the curio Indian,
burnt wood and gaudy cloth and inch-canoes —
trophies and scalpings for a traveller's den.
Sometimes, it's true, they dance, but for a bribe;
after a deal don the bedraggled feather
and welcome a white mayor to the tribe.

This is a grassy ghetto, and no home.
And these are fauna in a museum kept.   30
The better hunters have prevailed. The game,
losing its blood, now makes these grounds its crypt.
The animals pale, the shine of the fur is lost,
bleached are their living bones. About them watch
as through a mist, the pious prosperous ghosts.

[1945] {1948}

THE ROCKING CHAIR

It seconds the crickets of the province. Heard
in the clean lamplit farmhouses of Quebec, —
wooden, — it is no less a national bird;
and rivals, in its cage, the mere stuttering clock.
To its time, the evenings are rolled away;
and in its peace the pensive mother knits
contentment to be worn by her family,
grown-up, but still cradled by the chair in which she sits.

It is also the old man's pet, pair to his pipe,
the two aids of his arithmetic and plans,   10
plans rocking and puffing into market-shape;

and it is the toddler's game and dangerous dance.
Moved to the verandah, on summer Sundays, it is,
among the hanging plants, the girls, the boy-friends,
sabbatical and clumsy, like the white haloes
dangling above the blue serge suits of the young men.

It has a personality of its own;
is a character (like that old drunk Lacoste,
exhaling amber, and toppling on his pins);
it is alive; individual; and no less   20
an identity than those about it. And
it is tradition. Centuries have been flicked
from its arcs, alternately flicked and pinned.
It rolls with the gait of St. Malo. It is act

and symbol, symbol of this static folk
which moves in segments, and returns to base, –
a sunken pendulum: *invoke, revoke*;
loosed yon, leashed hither, motion on no space.
O, like some Anjou ballad, all refrain,
which turns about its longing, and seems to move   30
to make a pleasure out of repeated pain,
its music moves, as if always back to a first love.

[1945] {1948}

SONNET UNRHYMED

When, on the frustral summit of *extase*,
– the leaven of my loins to no life spent,
yet vision, as all senses, sharper, – I
peer the vague forward and flawed prism of Time,

many the bodies, my own birthmark bearing,
and many the faces, like my face, I see:
shadows of generation looking backward
and crying *Abba* in the muffled night.

They beg creation. From the far centuries
they move against the vacuum of their murder,   10
yes, and their eyes are full of such reproach
that although tired, I do wake, and watch
upon the entangled branches of the dark
my sons, my sons, my hanging Absaloms.

[1945] {1974}

THE BREAK-UP

They suck and whisper it in mercury,
the thermometers. It is shouted red
from all the Aprils hanging on the walls.
In the dockyard stalls
the stevedores, their hooks rusty, wonder; the
wintering sailors in the taverns bet.

A week, and it will crack! Here's money that
a fortnight sees the floes, the smokestacks red!
Outside *The Anchor*'s glass, St. Lawrence lies
rigid and white and wise,   10
nor ripple and dip, but fathom-frozen flat.
There are no hammers will break that granite lid.

But it will come! Some dead of night with boom
to wake the wagering city, it will break,

will crack, will melt its muscle-bound tides
and raise from their iced tomb
the pyramided fish, the unlockered ships,
and last year's blue and bloated suicides.

[1945–46] {1948}

GRAIN ELEVATOR

Up from the low-roofed dockyard warehouses
it rises blind and babylonian
like something out of legend. Something seen
in a children's coloured book. Leviathan
swamped on our shore? The cliffs of some other river?
The blind ark lost and petrified? A cave
built to look innocent, by pirates? Or
some eastern tomb a travelled patron here makes local?

But even when known, it's more than what it is:
for here, as in a Josephdream, bow down   10
the sheaves, the grains, the scruples of the sun
garnered for darkness; and Saskatchewan
is rolled like a rug of a thick and golden thread.
O prison of prairies, ship in whose galleys roll
sunshines like so many shaven heads,
waiting the bushel-burst out of the beached bastille!

Sometimes, it makes me think Arabian,
the grain picked up, like tic-tacs out of time:
first one; an other; singly; one by one; –
to save life. Sometimes, some other races claim   20
the twinship of my thought, – as the river stirs
restless in a white Caucasian sleep,

or, as in the steerage of the elevators,
the grains, Mongolian and crowded, dream.

A box: cement, hugeness, and rightangles –
merely the sight of it leaning in my eyes
mixes up continents and makes a montage
of inconsequent time and uncontiguous space.
It's because it's bread. It's because
bread is its theme, an absolute. Because   30
always this great box flowers over us
with all the coloured faces of mankind . . .

[1945–46] {1948}

MEDITATION UPON SURVIVAL

At times, sensing that the golgotha'd dead
run plasma through my veins, and that I must live
their unexpired six million circuits, giving
to each of their nightmares my body for a bed –
inspirited, dispirited –
those times that I feel their death-wish bubbling the
channels of my blood –
I grow bitter at my false felicity –
the spared one –and would almost add my wish
for the centigrade furnace and the cyanide flood.   10

However, one continues to live, though mortally.
O, like some frightened, tattered, hysterical man
run to a place of safety – the whole way run –
whose lips, now frenzy-foamed, now delirium-dry,
cry out the tenses of the verb to die,
cry love, cry loss, being asked: *And yet unspilled*

your own blood? weeps, and makes
his stuttering innocence a kind of guilt –
O, like that man am I, bereaved and suspect,
convicted with the news my mourning breaks.   20

Us they have made the monster, made that thing
that lives though cut in three: the severed head
which breathes, looks on, hears, thinks, weeps, and is bled
continuously with a drop by drop longing
for its members' re-membering!
And, the torn torso, spilling heart and lights
and the cathartic dregs!
These, for the pit! Upon the roads, the flights –
– O how are you reduced, my people, cut down to a limb! –
upon the roads the flights of the bodiless legs.   30

Myself to recognize: a curio;
the atavism of some old coin's face;
one who, though watched and isolate, does go –
the last point of a diminished race –
the way of the fletched buffalo.
Gerundive of extinct. An original.
What else, therefore, to do
but leave these bones that are not ash to fill –
O not my father's vault – but the glass-case
some proud museum catalogues *Last Jew*.   40

[1946] {1974}

POLITICAL MEETING

FOR CAMILLIEN HOUDE

On the school platform, draping the folding seats,
they wait the chairman's praise and glass of water.
Upon the wall the agonized Y initials their faith.

Here all are laic; the skirted brothers have gone.
Still, their equivocal absence is felt, like a breeze
that gives curtains the sounds of surplices.

The hall is yellow with light, and jocular;
suddenly some one lets loose upon the air
the ritual bird which the crowd in snares of singing

catches and plucks, throat, wings, and little limbs.   10
Fall the feathers of sound, like *alouette's.*
The chairman, now, is charming, full of asides and wit,

building his orators, and chipping off
the heckling gargoyles popping in the hall.
(Outside, in the dark, the street is body-tall,

flowered with faces intent on the scarecrow thing
that shouts to thousands the echoing
of their own wishes.) The Orator has risen!

Worshipped and loved, their favourite visitor,
a country uncle with sunflower seeds in his pockets,   20
full of wonderful moods, tricks, imitative talk,

he is their idol: like themselves, not handsome,
not snobbish, not of the *Grande Allée! Un homme!*
Intimate, informal, he makes bear's compliments

to the ladies; is gallant; and grins;
goes for the balloon, his opposition, with pins;
jokes also on himself, speaks of himself

in the third person, slings slang, and winks with folklore;
and knows now that he has them, kith and kin.
Calmly, therefore, he begins to speak of war,   30

praises the virtue of being *Canadien,*
of being at peace, of faith, of family,
and suddenly his other voice: *Where are your sons?*

He is tearful, choking tears; but not he
would blame the clever English; in their place
he'd do the same; maybe.

Where *are* your sons ?
                    The whole street wears one face,
shadowed and grim; and in the darkness rises
the body-odour of race.

[1946] {1948}

DOROTHY LIVESAY

1909–1996

Dorothy Livesay was born in Winnipeg to J.F.B. Livesay, a founder and later general manager of the Canadian Press, and Florence Randal Livesay, a poet and translator. She received a B.A. from the University of Toronto in 1926. Her parents encouraged her early writing and its publication: *Green Pitcher* appeared, to favourable notices from Charles Bruce and Raymond Knister, in 1928. *Signpost* appeared in 1932, but by the time of its publication Livesay was critical of its lyric orientation. From 1931-32 she had studied at the Sorbonne and been radicalized by the conditions and political activists of Depression-era Paris. Upon her return to Canada she joined the Communist Party and completed a diploma in social work. She moved to Vancouver in 1936. During the Depression Livesay was a Party propagandist and organizer; she wrote agit-prop dramas and mass chants for assemblies and demonstrations. She documented this period of intense political commitment in *Right Hand Left Hand* (1977). As for many on the Canadian left, disillusionment followed Stalin's 1939 non-aggression pact with Hitler and the outbreak of world war. She helped to establish a new Vancouver poetry quarterly, *Contemporary Verse*, in 1941 and contributed to the magazine throughout the decade. Her next two collections, *Day and Night* (1944) and *Poems for People* (1947), won Governor General's Awards. In 1949 she wrote a radio verse drama condemning the wartime internment of Japanese Canadians, *Call My People Home*. *Contemporary Verse* dedicated an entire issue to its publication. During the 1950s she taught, raised her two children, and wrote comparatively little. In 1958 she travelled to London on a Canada Council fellowship; while there she learned of her husband's death in 1959. From 1960-63 she taught for UNESCO in Zambia (then Northern Rhodesia). The experience of African cultures and persons was liberating for Livesay's writing, as was an affair with a younger man upon her return to Canada, which she embodied in the passionate free verse of *The Unquiet Bed* (1967). In later years she anthologized Canadian women poets, wrote a memoir of her Winnipeg childhood, and served as writer-in-residence at a number of Canadian universities. Her *Collected Poems: The Two Seasons* was published in 1972.

GREEN RAIN

I remember long veils of green rain
Feathered like the shawl of my grandmother –
Green from the half-green of the spring trees
Waving in the valley.

I remember the road
Like the one which leads to my grandmother's house,
A warm house, with green carpets,
Geraniums, a trilling canary
And shining horse-hair chairs;
And the silence, full of the rain's falling   10
Was like my grandmother's parlour
Alive with herself and her voice, rising and falling –
Rain and wind intermingled.

I remember on that day
I was thinking only of my love
And of my love's house.
But now I remember the day

As I remember my grandmother.
I remember the rain as the feathery fringe of her shawl.

{1932}

TESTAMENT

We moved this way before; observed the leaves
Of restless poplars merging with bulrush spikes
The sun a haze drawing warm sweet odour
From the marsh and the marsh-wet ground.
Clothes without thinking we took off
To be free and relieved of thought
And after caressing, bodies together moving
We could withdraw released as the tree from the wind
Yet not divided, quiet in our escape
For a moment only: days folded away   10
Between hot asphalt and the tap, tap, tap
Of offices, their files, their rubber stamps
Days for a moment only remembered, held
In the mind while the nose was pressed
Against hot glass, the wary eyes aware
Of flat black roofs, a city's offering
To the sun and the far planets.

Business of living crushing us, until
We come out from between the rollers
Flat as newspapers, with a few headlines   20
For recognition, someone's photograph, and a "lost" column.

In the beginning, in the folded away
It was all sensation. Feel it, the air sings
The sun burns in exaltation.

Or here is dirt, ugliness, squalor
Children in rags with tear-smudged faces –
We recoil, at all costs brush out the memory.

When thought began to push a shy root
Into our consciousness, our sensitive crust,
Sensation took on new form –   30
An illustration of the indictment.
We know nothing, we haven't touched anything of living
We live in the sun, casting a shadow
On all the others, the nameless, the toilers
And our sun-life, untouched by shadow
Is not a life, is a scorched blade.
There must be a way out for those in the shadow:
Can we join them, can it be found?

Moving over then, with the masses
Afraid to touch, and be friendly,   40
Afraid to be found out, and jeered at:
"You – you came from the sun!"
Fear dwindles, in the growing knowledge
The growing oneness of work to be done.
We look at the sun, and are not blinded
The sun our attainment, and its parasites
Blades of burnt grass to be trampled.
Was it so once for us? Were we once so,
Parasites burnt with a false possession?

Returning now to the trees felt then, not known,   50
To the leaves and the bulrush spikes
Returning with understanding, we have delight
Because there is no longer isolation in the valley
We come not to the marsh seeking self-effacement
We come now with others to share this joy.

Look, we have secrets comradely yielded:
Here is the earth, rounded and warm to be taken:
And the wind for all city lovers and children
Is a banner upshaken.

{1934}

Day and Night

i

Dawn, red and angry, whistles loud and sends
A geysered shaft of steam searching the air.
Scream after scream announces that the churn
Of life must move, the giant arm command.
Men in a stream, a moving human belt
Move into sockets, every one a bolt.
The fun begins, a humming, whirring drum —
Men do a dance in time to the machines.

ii

One step forward
Two steps back
Shove the lever,   10
Push it back

While Arnot whirls
A roundabout
And Geoghan shuffles
Bolts about.

One step forward
Hear it crack
Smashing rhythm —
Two steps back   20

Your heart-beat pounds
Against your throat
The roaring voices
Drown your shout

Across the way
A writhing whack
Sets you spinning
Two steps back —

One step forward
Two steps back.   30

    iii

Day and night are rising and falling
Night and day shift gears and slip rattling
Down the runway, shot into storerooms
Where only arms and a note-book remember
The record of evil, the sum of commitments.
We move as through sleep's revolving memories
Piling up hatred, stealing the remnants,
Doors forever folding before us —
And where is the recompense, on what agenda
Will you set love down? Who knows of peace?   40

Day and night
Night and day

Light rips into ribbons
What we say.

I called to love
Deep in dream:
Be with me in the daylight
As in gloom.

Be with me in the pounding
In the knives against my back   50
Set your voice resounding
Above the steel's whip crack.

High and sweet
Sweet and high
Hold, hold up the sunlight
In the sky!

Day and night
Night and day
Tear up all the silence
Find the words I could not say . . .   60

        iv

We were stoking coal in the furnaces; red hot
They gleamed, burning our skins away, his and mine.
We were working together, night and day, and knew
Each other's stroke; and without words, exchanged
An understanding about kids at home,
The landlord's jaw, wage-cuts and overtime.
We were like buddies, see? Until they said
That nigger is too smart the way he smiles

And sauces back the foreman; he might say
Too much one day, to others changing shifts.   70
Therefore they cut him down, who flowered at night
And raised me up, day hanging over night –
So furnaces could still consume our withered skin.

Shadrach, Meshach and Abednego
Turn in the furnace, whirling slow.
   Lord, I'm burnin' in the fire
   Lord, I'm steppin' on the coals
   Lord, I'm blacker than my brother
   Blow your breath down here.

   Boss, I'm smothered in the darkness   80
   Boss, I'm shrivellin' in the flames
   Boss, I'm blacker than my brother
   Blow your breath down here.
Shadrach, Meshach and Abednego
Burn in the furnace, whirling slow.

   v

Up in the roller room, men swing steel
Swing it, zoom; and cut it, crash.
Up in the dark the welder's torch
Makes sparks fly like lightning reel.

Now I remember storm on a field   90
The trees bow tense before the blow
Even the jittering sparrows' talk
Ripples into the still tree shield.

We are in storm that has no cease
No lull before, no after time

When green with rain the grasses grow
And air is sweet with fresh increase.

We bear the burden home to bed
The furnace glows within our hearts:
Our bodies hammered through the night   100
Are welded into bitter bread.

Bitter, yes:
But listen, friend:
We are mightier
In the end.

We have ears
Alert to seize
A weakness
In the foreman's ease

We have eyes   110
To look across
The bosses' profit
At our loss.

Are you waiting?
Wait with us
After evening
There's a hush —

Use it not
For love's slow count:
Add up hate   120
And let it mount

Until the lifeline
Of your hand
Is calloused with
A fiery brand!

Add up hunger,
Labour's ache
These are figures
That will make

The page grow crazy   130
Wheels go still,
Silence sprawling
On the till –

Add your hunger,
Brawn and bones,
Take your earnings:
Bread, not stones!

    vi

Into thy maw I commend my body
But the soul shines without
A child's hands as a leaf are tender   140
And draw the poison out.

Green of new leaf shall deck my spirit
Laughter's roots will spread:
Though I am overalled and silent
Boss, I'm far from dead!

One step forward
Two steps back

Will soon be over:
Hear it crack!

The wheels may whirr   150
A roundabout
And neighbour's shuffle
Drown your shout

The wheel must limp
Till it hangs still
And crumpled men
Pour down the hill

Day and night
Night and day
Till life is turned   160
The other way!

[1936] {1944}

SEA SEQUENCE

i

The sea is our season: neither dark nor day,
Autumn nor spring, but this inconstancy
That yet is continent: this self-contained
Organic motion, our mind's ocean
Limitless as thought's range, yet restrained
To narrow beaches, promontories
Accepting her in silence: the land's ear
Forming a concave shell along the sands
To hear sea's shuffle as she leaps in gear

Spuming her poems upon our ribbèd hands   10
Crying against our poor timidity:
O come to bed in bending water, be
Swept to these arms, this sleep, beloved and proud!
You'll need no linen; nor, thereafter, any shroud.

ii

Now that I walk alone along the stones
I am compelled to cry, like the white gull
Light as snow on the undulating wave
Riding, lamenting. Though he lie
Forever feasting on the sea's blue breast
And I am shorebound, sucked to the hot sand   20
Crunching the mussels underfoot, scuttling the crabs
And seared by sun — still we are, each one,
The bird, the human, striding a world alone
Calling for colleague who could share the song
Yet bow to the denial: laugh or be mute:
Calling, and yet reluctant to forego
For otherness, the earth's warm silences
Or the loquacious solace of the sea.

iii

I think of you as being continually near
As the sea is, sounding upon the ear   30
Through night's carousel into dazzling day
In sea's spectacular and changing way.
Sometimes at morning, open-minded, clear
As blue-washed water, never a scowl of foam
Easy to live with, a countenance of home —
Then sudden tempest, lashing out at fear
Moody at folly, clouding out the noon;

Yet through all moods your mind remains the same
Low-breathing or breath-taking, calling the name
Of constancy, whatever time and moon: 40
With such companion ever at my side
I go alone, not lonely, feeding upon the tide.

{1948}

SIGNATURE

Livesay the name god them gave
and now lives aye indeed they have.
                    – Lines on an English tombstone

Born by a whim
This time
On a blowing plain
I am as wind
Playing high sky
With a name –
Winnipeg!

So prairie gave breath:
Child head, anemone
Raised from winter grass   10
Pushing the mauve-veined cup
Upward to world all sky
Peopled with cloud.

Ages before
These violet veins
Fingered their mauve
Through England's green;

These crocus eyes
Glowed in stone
Or a poplar row   20
Sturdy with Normandy;
Or a sea-wall —
War's peep-hole.

And longer than summers
Of conquering blood
Were my feet running
In a Roman wood
And my hair bound
In a vestal hood.

Stretched on the solitary sand   30
Of Egypt, I lay asunder:
Till the lover came,
The flowering night
Shaped me a name
And the earth shook under.

Now when I waken here
Earthbound
Strapped to the sound
Of a Winnipeg wind;
I dream of the next step   40
On into time —
Casting off skin,
Bones, veins and eyes,
Flower without root,
Dancer without feet —
Gone in a cone of spiralled air,
And I only wind
Sucked to the sun's fire!

The prairie gave breath; I grew and died:
Alive on this air these lives abide.   50

[1951] {1957}

BARTOK AND THE GERANIUM

She lifts her green umbrellas
Towards the pane
Seeking her fill of sunlight
Or of rain;
Whatever falls
She has no commentary
Accepts, extends,
Blows out her furbelows,
Her bustling boughs;

And all the while he whirls   10
Explodes in space,
Never content with this small room:
Not even can he be
Confined to sky
But must speed high and higher still
From galaxy to galaxy,
Wrench from the stars their momentary notes
Steal music from the moon.

She's daylight
He is dark   20
She's heaven-held breath
He storms and crackles
Spits with hell's own spark.

Yet in this room, this moment now
These together breathe and be:
She, essence of serenity,
He in a mad intensity
Soars beyond sight
Then hurls, lost Lucifer
From heaven's height.   30

And when he's done, he's out:
She leans a lip against the glass
And preens herself in light.

{1952}

LAMENT

FOR J.F.B.L.

What moved me, was the way your hand
Lay in my hand, not withering,
But warm, like a hand cooled in a stream
And purling still; or a bird caught in a snare
Wings folded stiff, eyes in a stare,
But still alive with the fear,
Heart hoarse with hope –
So your hand, your dead hand, my dear.

And the veins, still mounting as blue rivers,
Mounting towards the tentative finger-tips,   10
The delta where four seas come in –
Your fingers promontories into colourless air
Were rosy still – not chalk (like cliffs
You knew in boyhood, Isle of Wight):

But blushed with colour from the sun you sought
And muscular from garden toil;
Stained with the purple of an iris bloom,
Violas grown for a certain room;
Hands seeking faïence, filagree,
Chinese lacquer and ivory —   20
Brussels lace; and a walnut piece
Carved by a hand now phosphorus.

What moved me, was the way your hand
Held life, although the pulse was gone.
The hand that carpentered a children's chair,
Carved out a stair
Held leash upon a dog in strain
Gripped wheel, swung sail,
Flickered horse's rein
And then again   30
Moved kings and queens meticulous on a board,
Slashed out the cards, cut bread, and poured
A purring cup of tea;

The hands so neat and nimble
Could make a tennis partner tremble,
Write a resounding round
Of sonorous verbs and nouns —
Hand that would not strike a child, and yet
Could ring a bell and send a man to doom.

And now unmoving in this Spartan room   40
The hand still speaks:
After the brain was fogged
And the tight lips tighter shut,
After the shy appraising eyes
Relinquished fire for the sea's green gaze —

The hand still breathes, fastens its hold on life;
Demands the whole, establishes the strife.

What moved me, was the way your hand
Lay cool in mine, not withering;
As bird still breathes, and stream runs clear —   50
So your hand; your dead hand, my dear.

[1953] {1957}

ON LOOKING INTO HENRY MOORE

i

Sun   stun me   sustain me
turn me to stone:
Stone   goad me   gall me
urge me to run.

When I have found
passivity in fire
and fire in stone
female and male
I'll rise alone
self-extending and self-known.   10

ii

The message of the tree is this:
aloneness is the only bliss
Self-adoration is not in it
(Narcissus tried, but could not win it)

Rather, to extend the root
tombwards, be at home with death

But in the upper branches know
a green eternity of fire and snow.

  iii

The fire in the farthest hills
is where I'd burn myself to bone: 20
clad in the armour of the sun
I'd stand anew alone

Take off this flesh this hasty dress
prepare my half-self for myself:
one unit as a tree or stone
woman in man and man in womb.

{1957}

THE TOUCHING

    i

Caress me
shelter me now
   from the shiver
of dawn
"the coldest hour"

pierce me again
   gently

so the penis completing
      me
rests in the opening
      throbs
and its steady pulse
      down there
is my second heart
      beating

ii

Light nips the darkness
      a white frost
breaking in ripples
      on a dark ground
like light your kisses hover
      touching my nipples
under the cover

iii

Each time you come
      to touch   caress
me
      I'm born again
            deaf   dumb
each time
      I whirl
            part of some mystery
I did not make or earn
that seizes me
      each time
I drown
      in your identity

I am not I

     but root

          shell

               fire

each time you come   40

I tear through the womb's room

     give birth

and yet   alone

     deep in the dark

     earth

I am the one   wrestling

the element re-born

{1967}

Leda Again

The hand that warms my belly

Is the sun's

He thrusts my legs apart and strokes the hair

Undoes me on a bed of moss and crushed sea pinks

And rolls me over sweet again

Pricks my flesh green again –

Writhing, the body breaks.

The body breaks. As bread is torn, devoured,

The body yields and shakes

The bones dissolve in moss and stone   10

And rock's rib shapes the spine.

I lie, accepted: by the earth,

By humming wind whose sound

Tree-sifted, shifts its tone
To underpass the silences;
I lie, accepted: by the clouds
That change their angles in the lake
Sever their shadows, re-unite;
And by the wild hawk hovering
Who veers, sun-blinded, from my body's light.   20

The hand that takes me knows me at day's end
Stone still, all glowing gone —
And yet, pulsing within
Fire's embryo at the bone.

{c. 1969}

LEO KENNEDY

1907–2000

Leo Kennedy was born in Liverpool, England, and came to Canada at the age of five. After six years of school he went to sea. In the mid-1920s he was writing covertly ironic advice columns in the Montreal *Star*. A.J.M. Smith and F.R. Scott invited him to contribute to the *McGill Fortnightly Review*, an affiliation that gave significant impetus to Kennedy's poetry and criticism. He and Scott subsequently founded the *Canadian Mercury* (1928–29); though short-lived, the periodical published important work by the editors (including Kennedy's manifesto "The Future of Canadian Literature") as well as by Smith and A.M. Klein. During the Depression he regularly contributed poems, short stories, and essays to the *Canadian Forum* and *Saturday Night*. In 1933, at the urging of E.J. Pratt, Macmillan published Kennedy's only collection, *The Shrouding;* it was dedicated to the recently deceased Raymond Knister. By the time he appeared with Smith, Scott, Klein, Pratt, and Robert Finch in *New Provinces* in 1936, Kennedy had repudiated his early work and was seeking a poetry that could contribute to social and political reform. He joined the editorial committee of *New Frontier* (1936-38), a journal of left-wing opinion and culture, and contributed essays and verse. Shortly after its cessation he left for the United States to pursue an advertising career and soon stopped writing poetry. He returned to Montreal in the 1970s, where he worked on literary memoirs he was not to finish. He died in Pasadena, California.

Epithalamium

This body of my mother, pierced by me,
In grim fulfilment of our destiny,
Now dry and quiet as her fallow womb
Is laid beside the shell of that bridegroom
My father, who with eyes towards the wall
Sleeps evenly; his dust stirs not at all,
No syllable of greeting curls his lips,
As to that shrunken side his leman slips.

Yet! these are two of unabated worth
Who in the shallow bridal bed of earth   10
Find youth's fecundity, and of their swift
Comminglement of bone and sinew, lift
— A lover's seasonable gift to blood
Made bitter by a parchèd widowhood —
This bloom of tansy from the fertile ground:
My sister, heralded by no moan, no sound.

{1933}

Rite of Spring (A Fragment)

INTERMENT OF THE LIVING

April is no month for burials.
Blood root and trillium break out of cover,
And crocuses stir blindly in their cells,
Hawthorns bloom whitely, laburnums shudder
Profusion from dim boughs — slight daffodils
Defy the pale predominance of colour.
April is rather a month for subtle spells

And incantations chanted from old poets
By tremulous girls who are sick with the April weather
And boys whose glances are craven and bold together.   10
April is no month for burials.

And yet we must take the old loves and bury them under,
Empty the heart of ghosts that grieve and stumble
Down corridors sealed up to air and light:
We must gather last year's laurels before they crumble
And bury them out of sight.

For we must hurry them into the earth, and spread
A coverlet to hide each sheeted head, .
And stamp the mound out flat without misgiving –
Then gather flowered offerings for the living!   20

Lay them austerely in grave cloths scented with lilac.

Do not weep for the dead, Remorseful Lovers.
Do not regret the hawthorn spray that mattered
And is now crumbled and piteously scattered
With heat and frost between you and its flowering.
Do not recall the fragrance overpowering!
Do not remember the folded hands nor the eyes
Under the violet lids, nor the April bosom
Caressed to a breathless tumult of delight –
Make no dolorous plaint for the spilled bright   30
Hair, or for the brow too dearly cherished –
All these have perished
With the bent throat, the lips that wooed and flattered –
The words best understood when left unspoken –

All these things endured their time and are broken.

New loves await you with every burst of lilac,
Do not remember the dead in their lilac shrouds;
Do not recall their lilac-scented dust!
Strange mouths await your mouth, and other fingers
Prepare to touch you with a touch that lingers . . .   40

Where sapling boys and girls are sweetly aching
For sudden April gusts, perfumed and heady —
For willow sprouts, and the smell of fresh earth breaking.

Set them into the earth to sprout and blossom.

{1933}

AUDREY ALEXANDRA BROWN
1904–1998

Discovered and championed by Pelham Edgar, E.J. Pratt's colleague at Victoria College of the University of Toronto, in 1928, Audrey Alexandra Brown produced five collections of brilliant Romantic poetry from 1931 to 1948 that satisfied the yearning for cultural continuity of conservative Canadian readers. She was born in Nanaimo, British Columbia; a voracious reader, she appears to have been largely self-taught after the age of twelve. An attack of rheumatic fever in 1927 left her unable to walk until a successful operation in 1934; she told the story of this experience in her *Log of a Lame Duck* (1938). Her first volume, *A Dryad in Nanaimo,* appeared with Macmillan in 1931, followed by an expanded second edition in 1934. Her final collection, *All Fools' Day,* was published by Ryerson in 1948. Thereafter she withdrew from literary life, although she continued to publish articles and columns as a freelance journalist in the *Nanaimo Free Press* and to exchange correspondence with Ryerson's director Lorne Pierce. In 1944 she was the first woman poet to receive the Lorne Pierce Medal for contributions to Canadian literature from the Royal Society of Canada. She was made an Officer of the Order of Canada in 1968.

DANTE'S BEATRICE

Beatrice di Portinari long ago
Went out to walk in Florence; fair as snow

Was she, with hair like rippled wheat, and eyes
Dark as brown wallflowers where the late dew lies:

Light though her foot, she had an art which knew
How to be gracious-lipped yet stately too –

A lady of great name and little gold
And April beauty – all at eight years old!

Many a rolling hundred-years has been,
But still, immortal, in her velvet-green   10

Of kirtle, with the garnet-coloured hood,
Her beauty is a flame to warm the blood.

Across the bridge she went; and half-way over,
He raised his eyes to hers, her silent lover –

Fixing her with a gaze so dreamy-dim
It drew her own bright look to dwell on him.

She knew – (although she never knew his love) –
The man: had heard him ill reported of,

Though of old blood: some tinct of dubious fame
Did half-dishonour to an ancient name.   20

But none the less, the mutely-hungering face
Moved her, she knew not why, and asked her grace;

So, while the dimples dipped about her mouth
Swift as a charm of swallows flying south,

She made her courtesy: and she passed from sight.
– His grey eyes followed far as any might,

Wondering that dark-veined petals did not stir
And flower betwixt the flags for love of her!

Beatrice di Portinari grew a bride,
Was wedded, had a gold-haired son, and died: 30

Nor ever knew her beauty stored apart,
Wine in the chalice of a poet's heart.

She never thought with quickened pulse astir
Of the pale face that once had gazed on her —

Nor in the fields immortal does she guess
The memory of her dear dead loveliness

Took angel-raiment (as his scribings tell)
And drew the soul of Dante up from hell.

{1934}

CANDLES IN THE GLASS

Here in this ivory room whose pale casket
Holds bright-gowned women like bright fruit heaped in a basket,
A man at the piano strikes out chords
Of a crashing march; silent we sit and listen
To the great notes that glisten, wheel and glisten
With the hard brilliance of the play of swords.

Silent we sit and listen, each in our places;
Yet I am aware behind the stilled faces
Of a restless hovering like the wings of birds —
Of small inconsequent currents of thought leaping   10

From mind to mind, never silenced or sleeping
Or able to appease themselves in words.

There is a mirror on the wall nearest:
I need not lift my eyes to see this clearest
Of clear lovely things, in which I have found
A lovelier, whose beauty makes me ache with yearning —
Three tall reflected candles quietly burning
Without flicker of flame in that bright round.

The currents of thought dart under — over — under —
The music mounts till it shakes the air with its thunder: 20
And all the while unmoved in that clear plane
Is the delicate fire of the three candles burning,
Like that serene far Light towards which our yearning
Beats up from the dark forever, sick to attain.

[1937] {1948}

To Chopin

Frederic Chopin, laid in Paris earth,
    Do you sleep sound, as if no battle were?
    Is there no movement in your dust, no stir
Like a new bloodless agony of birth?
    Clay that was flesh of the broken patriot once,
    Have you not heard, far off, the mutter of the guns?

The books say wrong; it was not love but life
    That killed you, melancholy bright-haired ghost;
    And life was many things, but Poland most —
Poland, beloved as a man loves his wife   10

And a son his mother: Poland, wept-for long,
Till she bloomed out of your heart in a red rose of song.

You did not live to know her free at last —
    The clarions of her great triumphant stand
    Against the arch-usurper of her land
Did not awake you with their silver blast:
    No vision of white city and crowned keep
Slid like a shining dream into your starless sleep.

Two decades as a nation: twenty years
    To lay foundations and to build thereon;   20
    And they built well, and all they built is gone:
Their bread is anguish and their drink is tears.
    "We have lost all but honour" — so he said,
Who spoke for living Poland and for Poland's dead.

Did you not see them, Chopin — girls and boys
    In Warsaw, heaped like wreckage of the tide?
    The starveling little ones and how they died?
Surely your voice was with Starzynski's voice
    Comforting — exhorting — crying "Stand fast!" —
And they stood firm, Chopin, to the very last.   30

Hourly the bombers came in wave on wave —
    The folk of Warsaw died in square and street;
    Their blood was dabbled on the passing feet,
A common bed they had, the common grave:
    Death took them at the wall and by the gate —
But not one cried for mercy, not one flinched from fate.

. . . What was he thinking, your compatriot
    And fellow-pianist at the keyboard set?

A year ago I saw, and see him yet:
The overcrowded room was close and hot,   40
    But with remote still face he sat, and breathed
Another air than ours. He was like a sword sheathed.

Under his hands your ecstasy, your pain
    Took our breath and tore our hearts; but he
    Was like a rock on which the harmony
Beat like a breaking wave and beat in vain.
    His soul was in some valley that lies fair
Far beyond hope and very far beyond despair.

It may be that the sound was in his head
    Of the day his country rang with marching men: 50
    He had a wife and child in Cracow then;
They may be alive and likelier they are dead –
    But living or dead, O never in sun or rain
Shall he kiss his wife's lips or stoop to his child again . . .

The tall cities lie a heap of stone,
    Eaten by famine, drugged with pestilence;
    But never had they such magnificence
As now, stripped, shattered, overthrown –
    Having fought long as flesh and sinew can,
Singlehanded for the free soul of man.   60

And these your people, Chopin, though they bleed
    Cannot be broken: fire is in their blood,
    Wings in their soul: they stand as they have stood.
Let their deliberate murderers take heed –
    A dark wave musters where the winds are met
To hurl them down in ruin. *Poland is not lost yet.*

{1943}

KENNETH LESLIE
1892–1974

Kenneth Leslie was born in Pictou, Nova Scotia, and grew up there and in Halifax. His early poetry was encouraged by his involvement in the mid-1920s with the Song Fishermen, a group of Maritime writers whose membership, including Confederation-period poets Charles G.D. Roberts and Bliss Carman and newcomer Charles Bruce, affirmed the lines of continuity between nineteenth- and twentieth-century Canadian poetics but welcomed Leslie's socialist convictions. He published three books of poetry before *By Stubborn Stars* won the Governor General's Award for poetry for 1938. Shortly after moving to the United States he established *Protestant Digest* (1938-1953; later simply *Protestant*), a popular monthly magazine of religious speculation and politics dedicated substantially to the battle against anti-Semitism and Fascism. In 1949, partly as the result of a damaging *Life* magazine photo-spread depicting him alongside supposed Communist fellow travellers Arthur Miller, Charlie Chaplin, and Thomas Mann, Leslie returned to Halifax, where he made a constrained living as a taxi driver and substitute teacher. He continued to publish minor periodicals along the lines of *Protestant* until the end of his life. Sean Haldane edited *The Poems of Kenneth Leslie* in 1971, but Leslie objected to the volume's exclusion of much of his political verse; he issued his own comprehensive volume, *O'Malley to the Reds and Other Poems,* the following year. Leslie died in Halifax in 1974.

EARLY SUMMER STORM

TO EILEEN CURRAN

Shaken, torn,
by my yearly getting born,
waiting while my Mother weaves
                      leaves,

clothing me
as she clothes each naked tree,
and giving me, instead of singing birds,
                        words,

fiercely warm
comes an early summer storm,   10
twists from all my wintry length
                      strength.

{1934}

THE SKI RUNNER

TO ROBERT LESLIE

Shod with impatient wood, on the crest I stand,
my sticks of easy balance in either hand.
The sun has closed a mountain in my face
chilling my thoughts to home fires and the homeward race.

Two ways for home: one undulating and slow,
the other sheer and swift; how shall I go?

My mind sets firmly, choosing the safer path,
while sullen blood cries kin to this steep wrath,
this slope, fir-bristled, spiked with flinty points,
a calculus to be reckoned in the joints   10
of knee and ankle on the precipice
where death would wet my dry lips with her kiss.

What is the news I wait for, treading the snow?
It is for the mind to learn what the veins know.

{1934}

MY LOVE IS SLEEPING . . .

My love is sleeping; but her body seems
awake within itself, secure from ills
of consciousness; her veins are buried streams,
her flanks are ghostly vales, her breasts are hills
of some far planet finding its sure way
beyond the orbit of this night of fears,
beyond the burnished darkness of this day;
my love is sleeping out of reach of tears.
How can her limbs dance motionless, what makes
her lips curve smiling to a crescent moon,   10
what does her hand reach out for, what dawn breaks
beneath her eyelids, to her ears what tune?
I shall not sleep, nor seek that yonder land
where her hand yearns, but not to touch my hand.

{1938}

THE SILVER HERRING . . .

The silver herring throbbed thick in my seine,
silver of life, life's silver sheen of glory;
my hands, cut with the cold, hurt with the pain
of hauling the net, pulled the heavy dory,
heavy with life, low in the water, deep
plunged to the gunwale's lips in the stress of rowing,
the pulse of rowing that puts the world to sleep,
world within world endlessly ebbing, flowing.
At length you stood on the landing and you cried,
with quick low cries you timed me stroke on stroke   10
as I steadily won my way with the fulling tide
and crossed the threshold where the last wave broke
and coasted over the step of water and threw
straight through the air my mooring line to you.

{1938}

ROBERT FINCH
1900–1995

Robert Finch was born on Long Island, New York, but his parents moved when he was six to the Albertan foothills of the Rocky Mountains, where he grew up. He attended the University of Toronto from 1919 to 1925 and then did post-graduate work at the Sorbonne in Paris. He returned to Toronto in 1928 to teach in the French department in University College. A noted scholar of French poetry, Finch was also a skilled harpsichordist and a respected painter with several solo exhibitions to his credit. A.J.M. Smith and F.R. Scott included his early poetry in *New Provinces: Poems of Several Authors* in 1936. Finch would win two Governor General's Awards: the first, for his first book *Poems* (1946), occasioned a now notorious controversy when John Sutherland ridiculed the choice and Finch's book in a sarcastic editorial in *Northern Review*. While vigorous protests were lodged against Sutherland's tone, it encouraged subsequent condescension to Finch's mannered, archly traditional poetics and played a part in the lack of critical attention to his uniquely realized visions of nature, time, and intimate life. His third book, *Acis in Oxford and Other Poems,* earned a second Governor General's Award in 1961. After his retirement from teaching in 1968 he became highly prolific and published eight books of poetry after the age of eighty.

WINDOW-PIECE

Trees: hands upthrust in tattered black lace mitts,
enormous brooms stuck handle down in snow,
the nervous roots of giant buried flowers;
old willows in spun copper periwigs,
and many-fingered firs smoothing white stoles
beside the drained rococo lily-pool
whose shuddering cherub wrings an icicle
from the bronze gullet of his frozen swan.

The hedge, the driveway, mock in counterpoint
the inverted canon of the winding creek   10
whose little fall boils in a bowl of ice
under the bent back of the patient bridge.
Lacks a blue buck bearing vermilion horns
led by a groom in tightest daffodil?
The silent steam shovel gathers its dark mass
to leap upon the pale red water-tower.

[1936] {1948}

SCROLL-SECTION

You who practise the four elegant occupations
tea music calligraphy and checkers
follow me over the snow in search of plum blossom.

Leave kingdom breakers
to juggle nations,
and care's broad
cloud
to the white hare that with mortar and pestle
sits in the moon by the cassia tree,

leave your lacquer trestle
of puppets, your aviary
of pets in petrified wood,
your malachite lion with its ball of brocade,
your clique to scribble the past
on dust,
and with no inlaid saddle,
no jewelled bridle,
follow me over the snow in search of plum blossom.

The leaping salmon rainbows the cataracts,
the dragon in chase of a pearl skips space
and the phoenix, alighting, first selects a place
to arrange its tail. Emulate in a degree these agreeable acts.

Silent though peach and plum
a path is trod to them.
Every rustic talent
till seen is silent.
Even the hollow bamboo
has leaves that droop.

Come back over the snow,
set up
wrist-rests, paint in ink
mountains trees creepers clouds
gorges rivers cascades
the brink
of wind, monasteries in mist,
beauties that have no best,
that through your purpose a longing be learned, earned,
the seal of your mind borrowed and not returned.

[1943] {1946}

Train Window

The dark green truck on the cement platform
is explicit as a paradigm.
Its wheels are four black cast-iron starfish.
Its body, a massive tray of planking,
ends in two close-set dark green uprights
crossed with three straight cross-pieces, one
looped with a white spiral of hose.

The truck holds eleven cakes of ice,
each cake a different size and shape.
Some look as though a weight had hit them.   10
One, solid glass, has a core of sugar.
They lean, a transitory Icehenge,
in a moor of imitation snow
from the hatchet's bright wet-sided steel.

Five galvanized pails, mottled, as if
of stiffened frosted caracul, three
with crescent lids and elbowed spouts,
loom in the ice, their half-hoop handles
linking that frozen elocution
to the running chalk-talk of powder-red   20
box-cars beyond, while our train waits here.

[1943] {1946}

The Smile

The lake has drawn a counterpane of glass
On her rock limbs up to her island pillows

And under netting woven by the swallows
Sleeps in a dream and is a dream that has

Strayed to sleep in the library of space
Whose ceiling beams are purple over yellows
And whose blue shelves behind a cloudy trellis
Wait for tomorrow's volumes of new grace;

Her restless hound at the western fireplace
Stretches a coaxing crimson claw to tell his   10
Mistress the hunt is on, not over, zealous
For a last smile before resuming chase:

See the lake wake! you would take it for the dawn
But for the flashlight of night's watchman moon.

{1946}

The Statue

A small boy has thrown a stone at a statue,
And a man who threatened has told a policeman so.
Down the pathway they rustle in a row,
The boy, the man, the policeman. If you watch you

Will see the alley of trees join in the chase
And the flower-beds stiffly make after the boy,
The fountains brandish their cudgels in his way
And the sky drop a blue netting in his face.

Only the statue unmoved in its moving stillness
Holds the park as before the deed was done   10
On a stone axis round which the trio whirls.

Stone that endured the chisel's cutting chillness
Is tolerant of the stone at its foot of stone
And the pigeon sitting awry on its carved curls.

{1946}

FLORIS CLARK MCLAREN
1904–1978

Floris Marion Clark was born in Skagway, Alaska. After completing normal school at Western Washington University in Bellingham, Washington, she taught in Skagway from 1923 to 1925. In 1925 she married John McLaren; the couple lived in Whitehorse, Yukon Territory, from 1925 to 1932, then moved to Victoria, British Columbia, where she lived until her death in 1978. She published her only volume of poems, *Frozen Fire,* in 1937. In Easter 1941 she met with Dorothy Livesay, Doris Ferne, and Anne Marriott to discuss the discouraging situation for younger poets in Canada. They agreed on the need for a new periodical and invited Alan Crawley, a Vancouver lawyer who had retired after losing his eyesight, to found and edit *Contemporary Verse.* It ran quarterly from late 1941 until 1953, thus both preceding and surviving *Preview* and *First Statement,* the better-known Montreal little magazines of the era. Livesay has stressed Crawley's accomplishment, revolutionary for the time, of gender balance among included poets. McLaren was *Contemporary Verse*'s business manager and worked indefatigably to establish its reputation across Canada. She published new poems in the journal throughout its run, but only a handful elsewhere after its suspension in 1953.

BITS OF THE PATTERN

There were things she remembered as she grew,
Small bright bits of the pattern of things she knew:

203

There was always the Valley,
Always a strong wind blowing,
And the bay, and the mountains,
So that she grew up knowing
Stars and their changes,
White windflowers in spring;
And that darkness could be
A safe and friendly thing.   10

Sometimes in winter, when the north wind tore
Down through the rocky funnel of the hills,
Her father met her at the schoolhouse door.
The tears froze on her face before they fell,
But seeing him there she was suddenly unafraid
Of the stinging snow and the bitter howling day;
And stepping carefully behind his steps
She found the only shelter on the way,
The small safe haven that his broad back made.

Through spring and summer she watched the brush piled high   20
In the south clearing, seasoned, tinder-dry;
Till one rain-threatened afternoon in fall,
Just at first dusk, she heard her father call,
And running close beside him where the trees
Had taken strangeness with the night, she reached
The clearing; watched him bend to light
A tiny flame that wavered, kindled, spread,
Till orange banners leaped above her head
And swarming sparks whirled bright against the sky.
So she learned the wonder of flame and spark,   30
Of sudden roaring beauty in the dark.

Sharper than other terrors was the ford:
The pitch and jolting as the horses stepped
Into the current, and the rising swirl
Of cold green water pulling at the wheels,
Foaming hub-deep to splash the wagon floor;
The sickening roll of glacier-polished stones
And that eternity in full mid-stream,
Always the same, that moment when it seemed
She moved and not the water; strangely swept   40
With sure and dreadful swiftness up the tide.
That was the worst. Too terrified to cry
She clutched the wagon edge until they came
To splashing shallows, and the horses strained
In a last plunging scramble up the bank
To sun-warmed willows on the other side.

All through her life the smell of dawn could bring
A sudden choking memory of the way
The great bulk of East Mountain rode the sky,
With sun behind it, and the morning haze   50
Thin-drifting; overshadowing her days
So that she never quite forgot how small
The town, the people, looked beneath that wall.

Clouds and their shadows; always the keen wind blowing;
The grey light of spring evenings, water flowing;
These were things she remembered as she grew,
Clear bright bits of the pattern of things she knew.

{1937}

FROZEN FIRE

I

The air is full of diamond dust tonight,
Cold glittering sparks between us and the snow:
The hills are ragged etchings, black and white, pointed with stars;
The crowding spruces go,
A still black army, down to the curving shore.
The frost lights glitter on every twig and brier
Till we set intruding feet on the jewelled floor
And shatter the cranberry bushes' frozen fire.

II

The still cold sharpens as the sun goes down;
The frost-fog thickens;   10
Plumes of white smoke stand
Straight up from every chimney.
Near at hand
A husky lifts a wailing quivering cry;
The low hills hold the sound
Answered, repeated, till from all around
The husky chorus swells to the winter sky.

III

Against the blue of spruces, and the grey
Of bare-boughed poplar, suddenly
As though a snowdrift burst in scattering fragments,   20
Ptarmigan rise with heavy whir of wings,
Show for a moment clear among the branches,
Then disappear,
White lost on white again.

The northern sky
Is pale transparent green
Where one lost star
Has climbed the snowy peak, to see
The world.

V

No whisper stirs the valley   30
Where blue dusk already lies;
But where that sunset-reddened tusk
Stabs the cold skies,
The air is lashed and torn,
As great winds blow
Across the peak, to lift the frozen snow
In gleaming haze,
Till streaming snow plumes fly
Above the valley in the sunset sky.

VI

The hills are changed today,   40
The white mist shows
Ravines unseen before.
The bare peaks stand
Separate; as though last night
They moved apart, and pausing now
Exchange slow stare for stare,
Like grey old men
With ragged shawls tight-drawn.

VII

The pines stand dark against the sky,
Northern lights are streaming high,   50
Far along the snowy trail
Sounds the prowling wolf-pack's wail;
Cold and swift the night comes down:
How bitter black that trail to town!

{1937}

L.A. MACKAY

1901–1982

Louis Alexander Mackay published his early work and first chapbook, *Viper's Bugloss* (1938), under the pseudonym of John Smalacombe. His major volume, *The Ill-Tempered Lover and Other Poems* (1948), appeared under his own name. He was born in Hensall, Ontario, and educated at the University of Toronto, where he had some success as a student playwright and saw at least two of his plays, one written in French, produced. He attended Balliol College, Oxford, as a Rhodes scholar. He was an associate editor of *Canadian Forum* in the early 1930s and remained a frequent contributor of poems, essays, and reviews throughout the Depression. He taught Classics at the University of Toronto, the University of British Columbia, and the University of California (Berkeley). His major critical volume, *The Wrath of Homer,* was published in the same year as *The Ill-Tempered Lover.* He was a specialist in the Roman poets and composed in Latin himself; he gave highly reputed writing workshops in Latin verse composition at Berkeley long after his retirement in 1968.

ADMONITION FOR SPRING

Look away now from the high lonesome hills
So hard on the hard sky since the swift shower;
See where among the restless daffodils
The hyacinth sets his melancholy tower.

Draw in your heart from vain adventurings;
Float slowly, swimmer, slowly drawing breath.
See, in this wild green foam of growing things
The heavy hyacinth remembering death.

{1938}

Now There Is Nothing Left

Now there is nothing left of all our sorrow,
Or only this: to know that sorrow dwindles,
And broken hearts may take their place tomorrow
With love, in the routine of minor swindles.

Doubtless we still shall find that we are able
To call a ghost up, with a little trying,
And learn, like many more, that life's a cable
Twisted of tedious, small, unfinished dyings.

{1938}

Rend Your Heart and Not Your Garments

Pity the innocent. There are none innocent, none.
Not all the quiet kindly men of good will.
We were weak who should have been strong, we were disunited,
We were smug, and lazy, and gullible, and short-sighted.
Whatever we did, there was more we should have done
Before there was nothing left to do but kill.

Now we squeal and squirm and shift and shuffle blame
On the paltry paladins that hold command

Because we let them. But God is not mocked.
Hell-gates are open; we could have kept them locked.   10
If it be shame to slay, on us the shame,
And if we die, we die by our own hand.

{1948}

ANNE MARRIOTT

1913–1997

Anne Marriott was born in Victoria and educated in private schools. In 1939 she published *The Wind Our Enemy*, a long poem voicing the experience of the Depression and drought on the Prairies; Dorothy Livesay's "Day and Night" (1936) had helped to inspire her method. Her 1941 volume *Calling Adventurers!*, originally written as a series of choruses for a CBC radio documentary, won the Governor General's Award. Marriott met with Floris Clark McLaren, Doris Ferne, and Livesay in Vancouver in 1941; they founded the new quarterly *Contemporary Verse* under the editorship of Alan Crawley. Marriott was on the journal's editorial board and published regularly in its pages. In the war years she published *Salt Marsh* (1942) and *Sandstone* (1945). In 1945 she moved to Ottawa as a script editor for the National Film Board; P.K. Page was a co-worker. In 1950 she moved to Prince George, British Columbia, where she briefly edited the "women's pages" of the Prince George *Citizen*. After the closure of *Contemporary Verse* in 1953 Marriott would publish little until *Countries* in 1971. *The Circular Coast: New and Selected Poems* appeared in 1980; later work was published in *Letters from Some Island* (1985) and *Aqua* (1991).

The Wind Our Enemy

I

Wind
flattening its gaunt furious self against
the naked siding, knifing in the wounds
of time, pausing to tear aside the last
old scab of paint.

Wind
surging down the cocoa-coloured seams
of summer-fallow, darting in about
white hoofs and brown, snatching the sweaty cap
shielding red eyes.   10

Wind
filling the dry mouth with bitter dust
whipping the shoulders worry-bowed too soon,
soiling the water pail, and in grim prophecy
greying the hair.

II

The wheat in spring was like a giant's bolt of silk
Unrolled over the earth.
When the wind sprang
It rippled as if a great broad snake
Moved under the green sheet
Seeking its outward way to light.   20
In autumn it was an ocean of flecked gold
Sweet as a biscuit, breaking in crisp waves
That never shattered, never blurred in foam.
That was the last good year . . .

The wheat was embroidering
All the spring morning
Frail threads needled by sunshine like thin gold
A man's heart could love his hand
Smoothly self-yielding,   30
Its broad spread promising all his granaries might hold.
A woman's eyes could kiss the soil
From her kitchen window,
Turning its black depths to unchipped cups – a silk crepe dress –
(Two-ninety-eight, Sale Catalogue)
Pray sun's touch be gentleness,
Not a hot hand scorching flesh it would caress.
But sky like a new tin pan
Hot from the oven
Seemed soldered to the earth by horizons of glare . . .   40

The third day he left the fields . . .

Heavy scraping footsteps
Spoke before his words, "Crops dried out – everywhere –"

IV

They said, "Sure, it'll rain next year!"
When that was dry, "Well, next year anyway."
Then, "Next –"
But still the metal hardness of the sky
Softened only in mockery.
When lightning slashed and twanged
And thunder made the hot head surge with pain   50
Never a drop fell;
Always hard yellow sun conquered the storm.

So the soon sickly-familiar saying grew,
(Watching the futile clouds sneak down the north)
"Just empties goin' back!"
(Cold laughter bending parched lips in a smile
Bleak eyes denied.)

v

Horses were strong so strong men might love them,
Sides groomed to copper burning the sun,
Wind tangling wild manes, dust circling wild hoofs,   60
Turn the colts loose! Watch the two-year-olds run!
Then heart thrilled fast and the veins filled with glory
The feel of hard leather a fortune more sweet
Than a girl's silky lips. He was one with the thunder,
The flying, the rhythm, of untamed, unshod feet!

But now —
It makes a man white-sick to see them now,
Dull — heads sagging — crowding to the trough —
No more spirit than a barren cow.
The well's pumped dry to wash poor fodder down,   70
Straw and salt — and endless salt and straw
(Thank God the winter's mild so far)
Dry Russian thistle crackling in the jaw —
The old mare found the thistle pile, ate till she bulged,
Then, crazily, she wandered in the yard,
Saw a water-drum, and staggering to its rim
Plodded around it — on and on in hard
Madly relentless circle. Weaker — stumbling —
She fell quite suddenly, heaved once and lay.
(Nellie the kid's pet's gone, boys.   80
Hitch up the strongest team. Haul her away.
Maybe we should have mortgaged all we had

Though it wasn't much, even in good years, and draw
Ploughs with a jolting tractor.
Still – you can't make gas of thistles or oat straw.)

VI

Relief.
   "God, we tried so hard to stand alone!"

Relief.
   "Well, we can't let the kids go cold."
They trudge away to school swinging half-empty lard-pails 90
to shiver in the schoolhouse (unpainted seven years),
learning from a blue-lipped girl
almost as starved as they.

Relief cars.
   "Apples, they say, and clothes!"
The folks in town get their pick first,
Then their friends –
"Eight miles for us to go so likely we
 won't get much –"
"Maybe we'll get the batteries charged up and have   100
the radio to kind of brighten things –"

Insurgents march in Spain

Japs bomb Chinese

Airliner lost

"Maybe we're not as badly off as some –"
"Maybe there'll be a war and we'll get paid to fight –"

"Maybe —"
"See if Eddie Cantor's on to-night!"

VII

People grew bored
Well-fed in the east and west
By stale, drought-area tales,
Bored by relief whinings,
Preferred their own troubles.
So those who still had stayed
On the scorched prairie,
Found even sympathy
Seeming to fail them
Like their own rainfall.

"Well — let's forget politics,
Forget the wind, our enemy!
Let's forget farming, boys,
Let's put on a dance tonight!
Mrs. Smith'll bring a cake.
Mrs. Olsen's coffee's swell!"

The small uneven schoolhouse floor
Scraped under big work-boots
Cleaned for the evening's fun,
Gasoline lamps whistled.
One Hungarian boy
Snapped at a shrill guitar,
A Swede from out north of town
Squeezed an accordion dry,
And a Scotchwoman from Ontario
Made the piano dance

110

120

130

In time to "The Mocking-Bird"
And "When I Grow Too Old to Dream,"
Only taking time off
To swing in a square-dance,
Between ten and half-past three.

Yet in the morning   140
Air peppered thick with dust,
All the night's happiness
Seemed far away, unreal
Like a lying mirage,
Or the icy-white glare
Of the alkali slough.

VIII

Presently the dark dust seemed to build a wall
That cut them off from east and west and north,
Kindness and honesty, things they used to know,
Seemed blown away and lost   150
In frantic soil.
At last they thought
Even God and Christ were hidden
By the false clouds
— Dust-blinded to the staring parable,
Each wind-splintered timber like a pain-bent Cross.
Calloused, groping fingers, trembling
With overwork and fear,
Ceased trying to clutch at some faith in the dark,
Thin, sick courage fainted, lacking hope.   160

But tightened, tangled nerves scream to the brain
If there is no hope, give them forgetfulness!

The cheap light of the beer-parlour grins out,
Promising shoddy security for an hour.
The Finn who makes bad liquor in his barn
Grows fat on groaning emptiness of souls.

IX

The sun goes down. Earth like a thick black coin
Leans its round rim against the yellowed sky.
The air cools. Kerosene lamps are filled and lit
In dusty windows. Tired bodies crave to lie   170
In bed forever. Chores are done at last.

A thin horse neighs drearily. The chickens drowse,
Replete with grasshoppers that have gnawed and scraped
Shrivelled garden leaves. No sound from the gaunt cows.
Poverty, hand in hand with fear, two great
Shrill-jointed skeletons stride loudly out
Across the pitiful fields, none to oppose.
Courage is roped with hunger, chained with doubt.
Only against the yellow sky, a part
Of the jetty silhouette of barn and house   180
Two figures stand, heads close, arms locked,
And suddenly some spirit seems to rouse
And gleam, like a thin sword, tarnished, bent,
But still shining in the spared beauty of moon,
As his strained voice says to her, "We're not licked yet!
It must rain again – it *will!* Maybe – soon –"

X

Wind
in a lonely laughterless shrill game

with broken wash-boiler, bucket without
a handle, Russian thistle, throwing up
sections of soil.

God, will it never rain again? What about
those clouds out west? No, that's just dust, as thick
and stifling now as winter underwear.
No rain, no crop, no feed, no faith, only wind.

{1939}

PRAIRIE GRAVEYARD

Wind mutters thinly on the sagging wire
binding the graveyard from the gouged dirt road,
bends thick-bristled Russian thistle,
sifts listless dust
into cracks in hard gray ground.
Empty prairie slides away
on all sides, rushes toward a wide
expressionless horizon, joined
to a vast blank sky.

    Lots near the road are the most expensive   10
    where heavy tombstones lurch a fraction
    tipped by splitting soil.
    Farther, a row of nameless heaps
    names weatherworn from tumbled sticks
    remember now the six thin children
    of a thin, shiftless home.

Hawk, wind-scouring, cuts
a pointed shadow in the drab scant grass.

Two graves apart by the far fence
are suicides, one with a grand   20
defiant tombstone, bruising at the heart
"Death is swallowed up in victory."
(And may be, God's kindness being more large
than man's, to this, who after seven years
of drought, burned down his barn,
himself hanged in it.)
The second, nameless, set around
with even care-sought stones
(no stones on this section)
topped with two plants, hard-dried,   30
in rust-thick jam-tins set in the caked pile.

A gopher jumps from a round cave,
sprints furtively, spurts under fence, is gone.
Wind raises dead curls of dust, and whines
under its harsh breath on the limp dragged wires,
then leaves the graveyard stiff with silence, lone
in the centre of the huge lone land and sky.

{1942}

STATION

This is a place of portentous movings,
Never the simple coming and going
Of people not caring of coming and going,
Minds on bargains or markets or bridge.
This impersonal gray-slabbed building
With impersonal men's faces striped behind wickets,
Thick and impervious holds summit emotions
Like radium in a lead tube.

Motion the fierce inexorable deity
Of this hard building, these blank-eyed forms   10
Stiff on brown benches, squared round
With cases, humped parcels, listlessly-turned magazines
Until he snaps them to speed, to a train;
Motion that brings hands against hands, the blessing relief
Of physical presence, lips babbling joy;
Motion that drags hands from hands, starts
The long ache of parting, makes heart
Run weeping to memory for comfort, find memory slipping,
And stare numbly at taut face dim in a window
Against jolting night.   20
This is a place of portentous movings —
Spring-river beginnings and ends like winter-cold stone.

{1942}

BERTRAM WARR

1917–1943

After completing high school in Toronto, Bertram Warr worked as office clerk and hotel porter before hitchhiking to Halifax and stowing away on an England-bound ocean liner. He worked at menial jobs to support informal studies at the University of London, where he became committed to socialism. In 1941 *Yet a Little Onward,* a chapbook of fourteen poems, was published in Favil Press's Resurgam Younger Poets Series. The work received favourable notice from Robert Graves and G.S. Fraser and was anthologized in *Poems of this War* (Cambridge, 1942). Despite pacifist convictions Warr did not resist conscription into the Royal Air Force in 1941. In an unfinished essay, included by Len Gasparini in *Acknowledgment to Life: The Collected Poems of Bertram Warr* (1970), Warr foresaw his death in action, an outcome he tries to forestall rhetorically in "The Heart to Carry On." He was shot down over Essen, Germany, on April 3, 1943. A.J.M. Smith included Warr's poems in the second and third editions of the *Book of Canadian Poetry*. A tribute issue of *Contemporary Verse* in October 1945 reproduced several of Warr's poems alongside a critical article by editor Alan Crawley. Since that time, apart from Gasparini's preface and Keith Garebian's entry in Gale's *Dictionary of Literary Biography,* Warr's writing has been forgotten by critics.

WORKING CLASS

We have heard no nightingales singing
in cool, dim lanes, where evening

comes like a procession through the aisles at passion-tide,
filling the church with quiet prayer dressed in white.
We have known no hills where sea-winds sweep up thyme perfume,
and crush it against our nostrils, as we stand by hump-backed trees.

We have felt no willow leaves pluck us timidly
as we pass on slack rivers;
a kiss, and a stealing away, like a lover who dares no more.
For we are the walkers on pavement,   10
who go grey-faced and given-up through the rain;
with our twice turned collars crinkled,
and the patches bunched coarsely in our crotches.
They have gashed the lands with cities,
and gone away afraid when the wounds turned blue.
Beauty has crept into the shelves of squat buildings,
to stare out strangely at us from the pages of Keats,
and the wan and wishful Georgian leaves.
These are our birthright, smoke and angry steel,
and long stern rows of stone, and wheels.   20
We are left with the churches, the red-necked men who eat oysters,
and stand up to talk at us in the approved manner.
We are left with the politicians who think poorly of us,
and who stand back with chaos in their pale old eyes
whimpering, "That is not what we wanted. No,
it was not to have gone that way."
They are very old, but we have been very ill,
and cannot yet send them away.

But there are things that still matter, something yet within us:
nights of love, bread and the kids,   30
and the cheek of the woman next door,
thoughts that glitter sometimes like a ruby on a mud-flat,
dreams that stir, and remind us of our blood.
Though the cities straddle the land like giants, holding us away,

we know they will topple some day,
and will lie over the land, dissolving and giving off gases.
But a wind will spring up to carry the smells away
and the earth will suck off the liquids and the crumbling flesh,
and on the bleached bones, when the sun shines,
we shall begin to build.   40

[1941] {1957}

THE DEVIATOR

I sat here this morning, detached, summoning up, I think
Something metaphysical;
And wishing peevishly for a thick fur to parcel up
The many distractions:
All that I felt, which was not to be released;
All that I saw, blue-blotched wallpaper, the wooden bear,
And the mirror, mirror on the wall;
All that I heard – all that I hear now, for today I hear sounds:
The hungry, unhopeful wail of a rag-and-bone man in the street;
His cart will be filled before nightfall, if God will.   10
The hover and drift of a voice through a sluggish
Gypsy lament;
She is from home, and the distance beats like a piston
Against her.
Plate and knife discord, fulfilling, and water
Rushing downward through pipes.
The satisfied slam of a door returning, adjusted again.
And the words of the woman across the court,
Muted through the vibrating films of phlegm in her throat.
In resignation, for the phlegm has long been with her,   20
Belonging, not to be cleared, and only strangers mind.
And as I sat here this morning, thinking my thoughts,

Amid the sounds,
Suddenly, all these, the definables,
Began telling their meanings to me,
Saying there is no aloneness, there can be no dark cocoon,
With room for one, and an empty place, if love should come.

[1941] {1957}

THE HEART TO CARRY ON

Every morning from this home
I go to the aerodrome.
And at evening I return
Save when work is to be done.
Then we share the separate night
Half a continent apart.

Many endure worse than we:
Division means by years and seas.
Home and lover are contained,
Even cursed within their breast.   10

Leaving you now, with this kiss
May your sleep tonight be blest,
Shielded from the heart's alarms
Until morning I return.
Pray tomorrow I may be
Close, my love, within these arms,
And not lie dead in Germany.

[*by 1943*] {1970}

PATRICK ANDERSON

1915–1979

Born in Ashstead, Surrey, England, in 1915, Patrick Anderson took B.A. and M.A. degrees at Oxford before coming to New York on a Commonwealth Scholarship in 1938. There he married Peggy Doernbach, a painter. They moved to Montreal in 1940; in 1942 he joined F.R. Scott, P.K. Page and others in founding *Preview*, a literary newsletter publishing the group's poetry, editorials, reportage, and essays. *Preview* appeared until 1945, when it amalgamated with *First Statement*, a rival Montreal little magazine, as *Northern Review*. Anderson had published two volumes privately as an adolescent; his first Canadian volumes were *A Tent for April* (1945,with First Statement Press) and *The White Centre* (1946). Suffering from a nervous condition during the mid-forties, Anderson was treated by Montreal's first Freudian psychoanalyst. By 1948, after a year in which he returned to England and divorced his wife, he had accepted his homosexuality (which remained a felony in Canada until 1969). From 1948 to 1950 he taught in the English department at McGill University. In 1950 he left Canada, but he retained literary ties: his *The Colour as Naked* was published by McClelland and Stewart in 1953. Anderson subsequently established a reputation as a popular travel writer. In 1961 he co-edited *Eros: An Anthology of Friendship*, a ground-breaking anthology of the literature of male-male desire. Critical interest in the *Preview* period in the 1960s encouraged return visits to Canada and the publication of his selected poems as *Return to Canada* in 1977. Anderson died of cancer in 1979.

Drinker

Loping and sloped with heat, face thatched and red,
hating his engine boots spraying mechanical pebbles
he slowly comes through the white blocked light to the fountain:
his shirt clinging about him wet and rose
hangs heavily in front with his chest's sour bracket.

He crouches then: he turns with a serious hand
the little wheel: hangs, trembles over the jet
rising in a crush of water towards his burning mouth:
his eyes are wide and grave, his act seems private
and as his hand spreads on the greenstained stone   10
his massive working throat is a column of pure love.

He tastes with the iron pipe the very roots of water
spreading under the ground, which in multitudinous dirt
and infinite threaded dark are purified:
he draws the long stalk of water up between his lips
and in his mouth there bursts its melting flower.

[1942] {1945}

Rink

Here I am drifting, darkness in my heels,
while out of little winds they crouch and prey,
handling their sticks across these frozen zones
where I am gliding, twilight in my skates

on tallow ice and murky shallowness –
and they are furious, candles in their heels,

braggart and target from the lovely circles
they build and kill across their misting zones

spurting a dirty powder from their skates –
how distant like a dying of the day
that saffron placard for Sweet Caporals
blurs in the rafters of this gloomy barn

where tarnished echoes break from schoolboys' yells –
I whistle like a bird to mark half time –
the kids stretch out and freeze their sweaty curls
but one goes skidding round the female goal.

Rubbery puck is whipped against the boards:
begin again, again. My whistle pares
the twilight with the muscle of a bird –
the afternoon, the game, the cold seem endless.

And I am master adult and alone,
inexpert, alien, and responsible,
make a mystique of motion like a swan
or lose myself in loving the description,

in which some meaning meets me on these zones
where they sweep by with murder in their heels,
echoes enormously surrounding them
from caves the darker for their happy yells.

{1945}

BOY IN A RUSSIAN BLOUSE

First, twelve year old with the mouse fringe, you wear that blouse
slippery with boyhood and a cold grace
which looser than your body and wrinkling with light
reminds me of the neutral texture of water
and is neither male nor female, neither a shirt nor a dress.

It ruffles, Timofyey, about you though stricter at your waist
with almost breasts maybe or a panic shiver
but for the rest you have how strangely the big boots
that leather you under with a heavy walk —
though even these have high heels and sharp toes for the
    dancer.   10

And when you stamp on the floor it is not only your eyes
under the fringe, or the green blouse so careless
simple subtle with light that I notice,
but how you shoot out and strut your legs,
how you stand and are strapping, like an acrobat.

Why does the icy silence that folds your torso
go with the making bold of the legs, the crude
hand snap? And why, Timofyey,
are you so manic like this and so much a bride,
so awkwardly human, O brutal and half a-girl?   20

{1946}

WINTER IN MONTREAL

Going home one night through the frozen fall
I kicked a kettle of ice on the lonely street,

scampered a black cat down the drifts of an alley
where shadow was shot a Picasso went cantering
while over the dusty parlours like crusts of wounds
the bandaging blinds drew down in a brown shadow.

One day I woke and took the milk like a flower
protruding its frozen neck on the outdoor steps
and a pole from my battered skis that were stacked in the hall
and began to jab furiously at the wonderful crystal   10
chandelier that had grown down from the roof in the night,
a theatrical piece of ice,

and the next day it had grown again to glisten
exactly as before, and a fungoid mirror
had sealed the garbage can to the balcony floor.
O, when shall we be free of the winter palace?
Armorial in air my breath was plantagenet
and my heels were spurred.

And, climbing the mountain, I saw in a bird's eye view
the city below with its way of a photograph,   20
its iron wood brick but never quite real tones –
I had not thought such silver in statistics
could play such a trick in the mist. Around me the skiers
rushed silently. The snow like chloroform
masked my face. And I turned to one

of the skiers whose nervous curve neatly missed me
and saw his heart spread out in a fluttering tartan
for the delicate pleasures which he was suffering,
and I said: Can you tell me? Is this Canadian
to ski – I mean, to dare so silently   30
with nothing in front and blue behind like a railway?
I waited for his answer but it was

wafted away in the sanitarium snow
where the skiers flushed like the hectic tubercular
schussed down the fever of their feathery pillow.

And afterwards on the rinks boys mashed their sticks
in the vivid colours of their awkward age
with D'Arcy McGee and Loyola over their breasts
knots on their knees bunches of lumps on their shoulders
and on their loins a strap and a codpiece –   40
in the extreme rabble of their being suspended
within the tarnished mirror of their game and their youth I glided,

I glided amongst them a whistle held in my hand
and watched them long and haltered, all shoulder and hip,
trip and go down by the boards, silvering their sides
slithering their thickset hair. Their faces fierce,
over the ice their cheeks and stockings slipped
and chewing gum they rose cursing indifferent.
In the climate of a mirror they moved and massed
and mashed their sticks in a season of frozen mist.   50

In this swan neck of the woods, these crystal sticks,
a hick town, icicle thick, such frozen bumpkins,
knockabout boys, knobbly with sex, flick their black
puck in the net. But I moralise
on the righteous quiet that makes the colony:
those who live in the capitalists' crystal
surge like a revolutionary future about me.

The double windows closed upon January
I hear the decrepit movement of this time
crepitate with ice and creep with shadow,   60
precipitate dust and frost in my room.
I hear the skinny wind in the chimney slightly

moaning all night. I wonder what will come –
what comes with a limping stride is February

and on my pane a prism burns in the fern
the frost has made, a wind begins to gnaw
at an ivory tower as if it had found a bone,
and in the suspension of the hour that is
not really so immobile at all, I hear
Ortona, Anzio and the bombing of Rome!   70

In the routine of snow and the dreaming season
I hear the avalanche fall from the villa roof
like the plush of a crash in sleep's debility
or Berlin dying, the gloved and female gash
of a great wound gliding into a soldier's body –
a crumpled thunder and faintness so far away
that the listener does not stir nor the skier wake
nor I, nor I. Drowsing upon this poem
which puns and purrs in the gap the armies make.

{1946}

THE BALL

I saw the child reach out for it. It was
suddenly his. The house became a tree
and grew it, and it dropped upon the grass
fresh, shining, round, a bit of world come free

able to mix with him. His fingers crept
around and felt its hardness like a knob;
and gripped it, and it was himself he gripped,
for it gave back to him his pulse's throb.

And then he threw it and himself away
quite wildly, and it drew his emptying stare   10
up through the azure branches of the sky.
It fell. The sun fell. So he caught them there.

Always it shines with luck. It never will
tamely obey. There's danger — when he throws
his strength against the dull suburban wall
outspring great vines, their shoots as sharp as arrows,

whiplash-stemmed, fierce flowering in the palm.
But now between the volley and recoil
he misses, it leaps off, then far from home
and time for bed he follows down the hill.   20

[*c. 1944*] {1953}

Spiv Song

Where are you going, my spiv, my wide boy,
down what grey streets will you shake your hair,
what gutters shall know the flap of your trousers
and your loud checked coat, O my young despair?

Have you been in a blind pig over whisky
where bedbugs spot the discoloured walls,
did you play *barbotte* and lose all your money
or backroom billiards with yellowed balls?

It's midnight now and the sky is dusty,
the police are going their rounds in the square,   10
the coffee is cold and the chromium greasy
and the last bus leaves, O my young despair.

Don't you just hate our personal questions
with your "Take me easy and leave me light,"
with your meeting your friends in every direction
– and sucking in private the thumb of guilt.

There are plenty of friends, my man, my monster,
for a Ganymede kid and a Housman lad
and plenty more you would hate to discover
what you do for a living, my spiv, my id.   20

And isn't it awkward, their smiles so friendly,
their voices so bright as they ask where you work:
a job in a store, or driving a taxi,
or baseball still in the sunlit park?

O why do you sit in the nightclub so sulky,
why so dramatic breaking the glass:
you've heard again that your mother is dying?
You think that you've caught a social disease?

Your looks are black, my spiv, my wide boy,
will you jump from the bridge to the end of the world   30
and break on the ice, my pleasure, my puppy,
your forehead so hot and your kisses so cold?

What desperate plan is this job that you talk of –
we'll read tomorrow what happens tonight . . . ?
and where are you off to, my son, my shadow,
with the bill unpaid, as the door swings shut?

{1953}

P.K. PAGE

1916–2010

Patricia Kathleen Page was born in Swanage, Dorset, England, while her father was serving with the Canadian army during the First World War. The family moved to Red Deer, Alberta in 1919; she was educated in a private school in Calgary. After brief residence in Saint John, New Brunswick, she moved to Montreal in 1941 and worked as a filing clerk. She soon met the members of the *Preview* group and was inspired by the example of British expatriate Patrick Anderson's dense, Freudian, politically suffused poetry. Her early work appeared regularly in *Preview*. She won *Poetry*'s Oscar Blumenthal Prize for a selection published in 1944, and she was well-represented in that year's Ryerson mini-anthology *Unit of Five*. As Judith Cape she published the novella *The Sun and the Moon* in 1944; the pseudonym reflected her skepticism of the early romance's merit. She published her first collection of poetry, *As Ten As Twenty*, in 1946. In the same year she left for Ottawa to work for the National Film Board as a researcher and script-writer. In 1950 she married William Arthur Irwin, and in 1953 Page left Canada for over eleven years as her husband took up ambassadorial postings in Australia, Brazil, and Mexico. Page recorded the social and creative challenges of the Brazilian experience in her later published *Brazilian Journal* (1987). Although *The Metal and the Flower* of 1954 won the Governor General's Award for poetry, Page's verse waned during her absence from Canada. Instead she established herself as a visual artist and, as P.K. Irwin, mounted solo exhibitions in Toronto in 1960 and Mexico City in 1962. She returned to Canada in 1964; new critical interest in the Montreal literary culture of the 1940s helped to spur her return to poetry. Two retrospective volumes of 1967 and 1974 contained new work, but she would not produce a collection of entirely new poems until *Evening Dance of the Grey Flies* (1981). Since then she has published more than a dozen volumes of new poetry, collected poems, verse and prose memoirs, children's literature, and short fiction. Of particular note is *Hologram: A Book of Glosas* (1994), in which she turned the courtly medieval Spanish verse form into a vehicle of modernist retrospect and exacting self-examination and inspired a generation of young poets to its use.

GENERATION

Schooled in the rubber bath,
promoted to scooter
early, to evade and dart;
learning our numbers
adequately, with a riveting tongue;
freed from the muddle of sex
by the never-mention method
and treading
the treacherous tightrope
of unbelieved religion,   10
we reached the dreadful
opacity of adolescence.

We were an ignored
and undeclared ultimatum
of solid children;
moving behind our flesh
like tumblers on the lawn
of an unknown future,
taking no definite shape —

shifting and merging
with an agenda
of unanswerable questions
growing like roots.

Tragically, Spain was our spade;
the flares went up in the garden.
We dug at night;
the relics within the house
sagged.
Walking down country lanes
we committed arson –
firing our parent-pasts;
on the wooded lands
our childhood games grew real:
the police and robbers
held unsmiling faces
against each other.

We strapped our hands in slings
fearing the dreaded
gesture of compromise:
became a war,
knew love roll from a bolt
long as the soil
and, loving, saw
eyes like our own
studding the map like cities.

Now we touch continents
with our little fingers,
swim distant seas
and walk on foreign streets

wearing crash helmets   50
of permanent beliefs.

[1942] {1946}

THE STENOGRAPHERS

After the brief bivouac of Sunday,
their eyes, in the forced march of Monday to Saturday,
hoist the white flag, flutter in the snowstorm of paper,
haul it down and crack in the midsun of temper.

In the pause between the first draft and the carbon
they glimpse the smooth hours when they were children –
the ride in the ice-cart, the ice-man's name,
the end of the route and the long walk home;

remember the sea where floats at high tide
were sea marrows growing on the scatter-green vine   10
or spools of grey toffee, or wasps' nests on water;
remember the sand and the leaves of the country.

Bell rings and they go and the voice draws their pencil
like a sled across snow; when its runners are frozen
rope snaps and the voice then is pulling no burden
but runs like a dog on the winter of paper.

Their climates are winter and summer – no wind
for the kites of their hearts – no wind for a flight;
a breeze at the most, to tumble them over
and leave them like rubbish – the boy-friends of blood.   20

In the inch of the noon as they move they are stagnant.
The terrible calm of the noon is their anguish;
the lip of the counter, the shapes of the straws
like icicles breaking their tongues are invaders.

Their beds are their oceans – salt water of weeping
the waves that they know – the tide before sleep;
and fighting to drown they assemble their sheep
in columns and watch them leap desks for their fences
and stare at them with their own mirror-worn faces.

In the felt of the morning the calico-minded,   30
sufficiently starched, insert papers, hit keys,
efficient and sure as their adding machines;
yet they weep in the vault, they are taut as net curtains
stretched upon frames. In their eyes I have seen
the pin men of madness in marathon trim
race round the track of the stadium pupil.

[1942] {1946}

IF IT WERE YOU

If it were you, say, you
who scanning the personal map one day knew
your sharp eyes water and grow colour-blind,
unable to distinguish green from blue
and everything terribly run together as if rain
had smudged the markings on the paper –
a child's painting after a storm –
and the broad avenue erased,
the landmarks gone;
and you, bewildered – not me this time and not   10

the cold unfriendly neighbour or the face in the news —
who walked a blind circle in a personal place;

and if you became lost, say, on the lawn,
unable to distinguish left from right
and that strange longitude that divides the body
sharply in half —that line that separates
so that one hand could never be the other —
dissolved and both your hands were one,
then in the garden though birds went on with their singing
and on the ground   20
flowers wrote their signatures in coloured ink —
would you call help like a woman assaulted,
cry to be found?

No ears would understand. Your friends and you
would be practically strangers, there would be no face
more familiar than this unfamiliar place
and there would be walls of air, invisible, holding
you single and directionless in space.

First you would be busy as a woodsman marking
the route out, making false starts and then   30
remembering yesterday when it was easy
you would grow lazy.

Summer would sit upon you then as on a stone
and you would be
tense for a time beneath the morning sun
but always lonely
and birds perhaps would brush your coat and become
angels of deliverance
for a moment only;
clutching their promising wings you would discover   40

they were elusive and gone
as the lost lover.
Would you call Ariel, Ariel, in the garden,
in a dream within a dream be Orpheus
and for a certain minute take a step
delicately across the grass?

If so, there would be no answer or reply
and not one coming forward from the leaves.
No bird nor beast with a challenging look
or friendly.   50
Simply nothing but you and the green garden,
you and the garden.

Then there would be the things your head
had prepared for your fingers:
rooting the dandelion from the lawn and training
the runner up the pole
or clipping the privet hedge
and always explaining
your actions by the phrase:
There's work to be done.   60
And when the garden was complete, the stones
stacked in the rockery
and the trees pruned,
the slugs and the cutworms dead,
your fingers then would signal to your head
wanting a meaning for their continuing movements.
And there would be shoots again to be clipped on the hedge
and weeds entangling the flower beds.

There you might stay forever, mechanically
occupied, but if you raised your head   70
madness would rush at you from the shrubbery

or the great sun, stampeding through the sky,
would stop and drop –
a football in your hands –
and shrink as you watched it
to a small dark dot
forever escaping focus
like the injury to the cornea which darts
hard as a cinder across the sight but dims
fading into the air like a hocus-pocus   80
the minute that you are aware
and stare at it.

Might you not, if it were you,
bewildered, broken,
slash your own wrists, commit
an untidy murder in the leafy lane
and scar the delicate air with your cries or sit
weeping, weeping in the public square
your flimsy butterfly fingers in your hair
your face destroyed by rain?   90

If it were you, the person you call "I,"
the one you loved and worked for,
the most high
now become Ishmael,
might you not
grow phobias about calendars and clocks,
stare at your face in the mirror, not knowing it
and feel an identity with idiots and dogs
as all the exquisite unborns of your dreams
deserted you to snigger behind their hands?   100

{1946}

STORIES OF SNOW

Those in the vegetable rain retain
an area behind their sprouting eyes
held soft and rounded with the dream of snow
precious and reminiscent as those globes –
souvenir of some never nether land –
which hold their snowstorms circular, complete,
high in a tall and teakwood cabinet.

In countries where the leaves are large as hands
where flowers protrude their fleshy chins
and call their colours   10
an imaginary snowstorm sometimes falls
among the lilies.
And in the early morning one will waken
to think the glowing linen of his pillow
a northern drift, will find himself mistaken
and lie back weeping.
And there the story shifts from head to head,
of how, in Holland, from their feather beds
hunters arise and part the flakes and go
forth to the frozen lakes in search of swans –   20
the snow light falling white along their guns,
their breath in plumes.
While tethered in the wind like sleeping gulls
ice boats await the raising of their wings
to skim the electric ice at such a speed
they leap jet strips of naked water,
and how these flying, sailing hunters feel
air in their mouths as terrible as ether.
And on the story runs that even drinks
in that white landscape dare to be no colour;   30

how, flasked and water clear, the liquor slips
silver against the hunters' moving hips.
And of the swan in death these dreamers tell
of its last flight and how it falls, a plummet,
pierced by the freezing bullet
and how three feathers, loosened by the shot,
descend like snow upon it.
While hunters plunge their fingers in its down
deep as a drift, and dive their hands
up to the neck of the wrist   40
in that warm metamorphosis of snow
as gentle as the sort that woodsmen know
who, lost in the white circle, fall at last
and dream their way to death.

And stories of this kind are often told
in countries where great flowers bar the roads
with reds and blues which seal the route to snow –
as if, in telling, raconteurs unlock
the colour with its complement and go
through to the area behind the eyes   50
where silent, unrefractive whiteness lies.

{1946}

THE PERMANENT TOURISTS

Somnolent through landscapes and by trees
nondescript, almost anonymous,
they alter as they enter foreign cities –
the terrible tourists with their empty eyes
longing to be filled with monuments.

Verge upon statues in the public squares
remembering the promise of memorials
yet never enter the entire event
as dogs, abroad in any kind of weather,
move perfectly within their rainy climate.   10

Lock themselves into snapshots on the steps
of monolithic bronze as if suspecting
the subtle mourning of the photograph
might, later, conjure in the memory
all they are now incapable of feeling.

And track all heroes down: the boy who gave
his life to save a town: the stolid queen;
forgotten politicians minus names;
the plunging war dead, permanently brave,
forever and ever going down to death.   20

Look, you can see them nude in any café
reading their histories from the bill of fare,
creating futures from a foreign teacup.
Philosophies like ferns bloom from the fable
that travel is broadening at the café table.

Yet, somehow beautiful, they stamp the plaza.
Classic in their anxiety they call
all the memorials of naked stone
into their passive eyes, as placid rivers
are always calling to the ruined columns.   30

[1948] {1954}

PHOTOS OF A SALT MINE

How innocent their lives look,
how like a child's
dream of caves and winter, both combined:
the steep descent to whiteness
and the stope
with its striated walls
their folds all leaning as if pointing to
the greater whiteness still,
that great white bank
with its decisive front,   10
that seam upon a slope,
salt's lovely ice.

And wonderful underfoot the snow of salt,
the fine
particles a broom could sweep,
one thinks
muckers might make angels in its drifts,
as children do in snow,
lovers in sheets,
lie down and leave imprinted where they lay   20
a feathered creature holier than they.

And in the outworked stopes
with lamps and ropes
up miniature Matterhorns
the miners climb,
probe with their lights
the ancient folds of rock –
syncline, anticline –
and scoop from darkness an Aladdin's cave:
rubies and opals glitter from its walls.   30

But hoses douse the brilliance of these jewels,
melt fire to brine.
Salt's bitter water trickles thin and forms
slow fathoms down
a lake within a cave
lacquered with jet –
white's opposite.
There grey on black the boating miners float
to mend the stays and struts of that old stope
and deeply underground   40
their words resound,
are multiplied by echo, swell and grow
and make a climate of a miner's voice.

So all the photographs like children's wishes
are filled with caves or winter,
innocence
has acted as a filter,
selected only beauty from the mine.
Except in the last picture, shot
from an acute high angle. In a pit   50
figures the size of pins are strangely lit
and might be dancing but you know they're not.
Like Dante's vision of the nether hell
men struggle with the bright cold fires of salt
locked in the black inferno of the rock:
the filter here, not innocence but guilt.

[1951] {1954}

PORTRAIT OF MARINA

Far out the sea has never moved. It is
Prussian forever, rough as teaselled wool
some antique skipper worked into a frame
to bear his lost four-master.
                          Where it hangs
now in a sunny parlour, none recalls
how all his stitches, interspersed with oaths
had made his one pale spinster daughter grow
transparent with migraines – and how his call
fretted her more than waves.
                          Her name
Marina, for his youthful wish –   10
boomed at the font of that small salty church
where sailors lurched like drunkards, would, he felt
make her a water woman, rich with bells.
To her, the name Marina simply meant
he held his furious needle for her thin
fingers to thread again with more blue wool
to sew the ocean of his memory.
Now, where the picture hangs, a dimity
young inland housewife with inherited
clocks under bells and ostrich eggs on shelves   20
pours amber tea in small rice china cups
and reconstructs
how great-great-grandpappa at ninety-three
his fingers knotted with arthritis, his
old eyes grown agaty with cataracts
became as docile as a child again –
that fearful salty man –
and sat, wrapped round in faded paisley shawls
gently embroidering.
While Aunt Marina in grey worsted, warped   30

without a smack of salt, came to his call
the sole survivor of his last shipwreck.

                    *

Slightly offshore, it glints. Each wave is capped
with broken mirrors. Like Marina's head
the glinting of these waves.
She walked forever antlered with migraines
her pain forever putting forth new shoots
until her strange unlovely head became
a kind of candelabra – delicate –
where all her tears were perilously hung   40
and caught the light as waves that catch the sun.
The salt upon the panes, the grains of sand
that crunched beneath her heel
her father's voice, "Marina!" – all these broke
her trembling edifice. The needle shook
like ice between her fingers.
In her head
too many mirrors dizzied her and broke.

                    *

But where the wave breaks, where it rises green
turns into gelatine, becomes a glass   50
simply for seeing stones through, runs across
the coloured shells and pebbles of the shore
and makes an aspic of them
then sucks back
in foam and undertow –
this aspect of the sea
Marina never knew.

For her the sea was Father's Fearful Sea
harsh with sea serpents
winds and drowning men.   60
For her it held no spiral of a shell
for her descent to dreams,
it held no bells.
And where it moved in shallows it was more
imminently a danger, more alive
than where it lay offshore full fathom five.

[1951] {1954}

AFTER RAIN

The snails have made a garden of green lace:
broderie anglaise from the cabbages,
Chantilly from the choux-fleurs, tiny veils –
I see already that I lift the blind
upon a woman's wardrobe of the mind.

Such female whimsy floats about me like
a kind of tulle, a flimsy mesh,
while feet in gumboots pace the rectangles –
garden abstracted, geometry awash –
an unknown theorem argued in green ink,   10
dropped in the bath.
Euclid in glorious chlorophyll, half drunk.

I none too sober slipping in the mud
where rigged with guys of rain
the clothes-reel gauche
as the rangy skeleton of some
gaunt delicate spidery mute
is pitched as if

listening;
while hung from one thin rib   20
a silver web —
its infant, skeletal, diminutive,
now sagged with sequins, pulled ellipsoid,
glistening.

I suffer shame in all these images.
The garden is primeval, Giovanni
in soggy denim squelches by my hub,
over his ruin
shakes a doleful head.
But he so beautiful and diademed,   30
his long Italian hands so wrung with rain
I find his ache exists beyond my rim
and almost weep to see a broken man
made subject to my whim.

O choir him, birds, and let him come to rest
within this beauty as one rests in love,
till pears upon the bough
encrusted with
small snails as pale as pearls
hang golden in   40
a heart that knows tears are a part of love.

And choir me too to keep my heart a size
larger than seeing, unseduced by each
bright glimpse of beauty striking like a bell,
so that the whole may toll,
its meaning shine
clear of the myriad images that still —
do what I will — encumber its pure line.

[1954] {1967}

ARRAS

Consider a new habit – classical,
and trees espaliered on the wall like candelabra.
How still upon that lawn our sandalled feet.

But a peacock rattling its rattan tail and screaming
has found a point of entry. Through whose eye
did it insinuate in furled disguise
to shake its jewels and silk upon that grass?

The peaches hang like lanterns. No one joins
those figures on the arras.
                            Who am I
or who am I become that walking here   10
I am observer, other, Gemini,
starred for a green garden of cinema?

I ask, what did they deal me in this pack?
The cards, all suits, are royal when I look.
My fingers slipping on a monarch's face
twitch and go slack.
I want a hand to clutch, a heart to crack.

No one is moving now, the stillness is
infinite. If I should make a break . . .
take to my springy heels . . . ? But nothing moves.   20
The spinning world is stuck upon its poles,
the stillness points a bone at me. I fear
the future on this arras.
                            I confess:

It was my eye.
Voluptuous it came.

Its head the ferrule and its lovely tail
folded so sweetly; it was strangely slim
to fit the retina. And then it shook
and was a peacock – living patina,
eye-bright – maculate!   30
Does no one care?

I thought their hands might hold me if I spoke.
I dreamed the bite of fingers in my flesh,
their poke smashed by an image, but they stand
as if within a treacle, motionless,
folding slow eyes on nothing. While they stare
another line has trolled the encircling air,
another bird assumes its furled disguise.

{1954}

THE METAL AND THE FLOWER

Intractable between them grows
a garden of barbed wire and roses.
Burning briars like flames devour
their too innocent attire.
Dare they meet, the blackened wire
tears the intervening air.

Trespassers have wandered through
texture of flesh and petals.
Dogs like arrows moved along
pathways that their noses knew.   10
While the two who laid it out
find the metal and the flower
fatal underfoot.

Black and white at midnight glows
this garden of barbed wire and roses.
Doused with darkness roses burn
coolly as a rainy moon;
beneath a rainy moon or none
silver the sheath on barb and thorn.

Change the garden, scale and plan;   20
wall it, make it annual.
There the briary flower grew.
There the brambled wire ran.
While they sleep the garden grows,
deepest wish annuls the will:
perfect still the wire and rose.

{1954}

REFLECTIONS IN A TRAIN WINDOW

There is a woman floating in a window –
transparent –
Christmas wreaths in passing houses
shine now in eye and now in hair, in heart.
How like a saint with visions, the stigmata
marking her like a martyr.

Merged with a background of mosaic
she drifts
through tenement transoms, independent stars,
while in between her and herself the sharp   10
frost crystals prick the pane with thorns.

She without substance, ectoplasmic, still,
is haloed with the reading lamps of strangers
while brass and brick pass through her.

                              Yet she stirs
to some soft soundless grieving and tears well
in her unseeing eyes and from the sill
her trembling image falls, rises and falls.

{1954}

GIOVANNI AND THE INDIANS

They call to pass the time with Giovanni
and speak an English none can understand
as Giovanni trims the weeping willow,
his ladder teetering in the yellow leaves.

They make him teeter even when he's steady;
their tatters blow and catch him through the trees;
those scraps of colour flutter against stucco
and flash like foreign birds;

and eyes look out at eyes till Giovanni's
are lowered swiftly – one among them is   10
perhaps the Evil Eye. The weather veers.
Pale leaves flap wetly on the metal trees.

                        *

Bare winter is pure glass. Past panes of air
he peers but sees no colour flicking raw
behind the little twigs; no movement shakes
the sunlight on the berries, no branch cracks

till quakes of spring unsettle them. Their flocks
emerge, they sprinkle paths with petals.
Now Giovanni pauses, stares and shrugs
hiding behind a golden blind of wattle.   20

                              *

One on a cycle, like a ragged sail
that luffs and sags, comes tacking up the hill.
Does Giovanni smile as he darts off, low
over the handlebars of his spinning wheel?

And one, his turban folded like a jug,
and frocked, walks brittle on his blanco'd legs —
a bantam cockerel. Giovanni looks
and laughs and laughs and lurches in great loops

and stoops to bend above a bed and gather
hyacinths, tulips, waterblue and yellow;   30
passes his offering through the rainy willow
nodding, "Good fellow," smiling, "much good fellow."

[1956] {1967}

CRY ARARAT!

I

In the dream the mountain near
but without sound.
A dream through binoculars
seen sharp and clear:
the leaves moving, turning

in a far wind
no ear can hear.

First soft in the distance,
blue in blue air
then sharpening, quickening   10
taking on green.
Swiftly the fingers
seek accurate focus
(the bird
has vanished so often
before the sharp lens
could deliver it)
then as if from the sea
the mountain appears
emerging new-washed   20
growing maples and firs.
The faraway, here.

Do not reach to touch it
or labour to hear.
Return to your hand
the sense of the hand;
return to your ear
the sense of the ear.
Remember the statue,
that space in the air   30
which with nothing to hold
what the minute is giving
is through each point
where its marble touches air.

Then will each leaf and flower
each bird and animal

become as perfect as
the thing its name evoked
when busy as a child
the world stopped at the Word   40
and Flowers more real than flowers
grew vivid and immense;
and Birds more beautiful
and Leaves more intricate
flew, blew and quilted all
the quick landscape.

So flies and blows the dream
embracing like a sea
all that in it swims
when dreaming, you desire   50
and ask for nothing more
than stillness to receive
the I-am animal,
the We-are leaf and flower,
the distant mountain near.

II

So flies and blows the dream that haunts us when we wake
to the unreality of bright day:
the far thing almost sensed by the still skin
and then the focus lost, the mountain gone.
This is the loss that haunts our daylight hours   60
leaving us parched at nightfall
blowing like last year's leaves
sibilant on blossoming trees
and thirsty for the dream of the mountain
more real than any event:
more real than strangers passing on the street

in a city's architecture white as bone
or the immediate companion.

But sometimes there is one
raw with the dream of flying: 70
"I, a bird,
landed that very instant
and complete —
as if I had drawn a circle in my flight
and filled its shape —
find air a perfect fit.
But this my grief,
that with the next tentative lift
of my indescribable wings
the ceiling looms   80
heavy as a tomb.

"Must my most exquisite and private dream
remain unleavened?
Must this flipped and spinning coin that sun
could gild and make miraculous become
so swiftly pitiful?
The vision of the flight it imitates
burns brightly in my head as if a star
rushed down to touch me where I stub against
what must forever be my underground."   90

III

These are the dreams that haunt us,
these the fears.
Will the grey weather wake us,
toss us twice in the terrible night to tell us
the flight is cancelled
and the mountain lost?

O, then cry Ararat!

The dove believed
in her sweet wings and in the rising peak
with such a washed and easy innocence   100
that she found rest on land for the sole of her foot
and, silver, circled back,
a green twig in her beak.

The leaves that make the tree by day,
the green twig the dove saw fit
to lift across a world of water
break in a wave about our feet.
The bird in the thicket with his whistle
the crystal lizard in the grass
the star and shell   110
tassel and bell
of wild flowers blowing where we pass,
this flora-fauna flotsam, pick and touch,
requires the focus of the total I.

A single leaf can block a mountainside;
all Ararat be conjured by a leaf.

{1967}

ANOTHER SPACE

Those people in a circle on the sand
are dark against its gold
turn like a wheel
revolving in a horizontal plane
whose axis – do I dream it? –

vertical
invisible
immeasurably tall
rotates a starry spool.

Yet *if* I dream   10
why in the name of heaven are fixed parts
within me set in motion
like a poem?

Those people in a circle reel me in.
Down the whole length of golden beach I come
willingly pulled by their rotation
slow
as a moon pulls waters
on a string
their turning circle winds around its rim.   20

I see them there in three dimensions yet
their height implies another space
their clothes'
surprising chiaroscuro postulates
a different spectrum.
What kaleidoscope
does air construct
that all their movements make a compass rose
surging and altering?
I speculate   30
on some dimension I can barely guess.

Nearer I see them dark-skinned.
They are dark. And beautiful.
Great human sunflowers spinning in a ring
cosmic as any bumble-top

the vast
procession of the planets in their dance.
And nearer still I see them – "a Chagall" –
each fiddling on an instrument – its strings
of some black woollen fibre   40
and its bow – feathered –
an arrow almost.

                       Arrow *is*.

For now the headman – one step forward shoots
(or does he bow or does he lift a kite
up and over the bright pale dunes of air?)
to strike the absolute centre of my skull
my absolute centre somehow
with such skill
such staggering lightness   50
that the blow is love.

And something in me melts.
It is as if a glass partition melts –
or something I had always thought was glass –
some pane that halved my heart
is proved, in its melting, ice.

And to-fro all the atoms pass
in bright osmosis
hitherto
in stasis locked   60
where now a new
direction opens like an eye.

[1969] {1974}

KAY SMITH

1911–2004

Kay Smith was born in Saint John, New Brunswick and educated at Mount Allison University in Sackville and at Columbia University. She taught English and drama at the Saint John Vocational School and later organized creative writing workshops at the University of New Brunswick and in local schools. Her first significant publication was in Montreal's little magazine *First Statement*. Its editor John Sutherland included a generous sampling of her poetry, alongside that of Louis Dudek and Irving Layton, in the twelfth issue and gave her a central place in the forties canon by including her in *Other Canadians: An Anthology of the New Poetry in Canada, 1940–1946*. Her first book, *Footnote to the Lord's Prayer*, appeared with First Statement Press in 1951. Although she continued to publish in periodicals, her next volume, *At the Bottom of the Dark*, would not appear for twenty years. In 1987 *The Bright Particulars: Poems Selected and New* gathered the work she considered her finest, though it excludes some of the strong early poems Sutherland so valued.

You in the Feathery Grass

You in the feathery grass, dropping the nubbled berry
into the thick bowl, you who linger in country roads
with naked feet, knowing the heat and texture of the steaming dust,
you, woman, standing in the doorway filling with twilight,
feeling a soft head on your breast, a harder pushing against your thigh,

you hired boy, sitting on a snake fence in the summer moonlight,
thinking of the crazy fiddle under the hanging lamps,
the city guys with laughter in their eyes like dry sticks burning,
thinking of the musty sweetness of hay in barns,
with knotted breath thinking of the bodies of women;   10

and you, moving on the wild March sky
as on cloud-driven mornings since time began to form
in your boy's mind, moving on the plunging sky
with the long sweeping rhythm of a scythe through tall grasses,
hoping behind the closed face for warm days soon and sowing,
feeling against the blunt hand familiar hardness of seed
like hail falling on the ready ground;

you, all of you who know affinity with the dust, speak it soon,
scatter the seed of your knowing quickly,
reckon it up in debits and credits,   20
have it written in the yellowing account book on the kitchen mantel,
before dust chokes the single outline,
blurs the individual mouth.

[1942] {1978}

WHEN A GIRL LOOKS DOWN

When a girl looks down out of her cloud of hair
And gives her breast to the child she has borne,
All the suns and the stars that the heavens have worn
Since the first magical morning
Rain through her milk in each fibre and cell of her darling.

Hand baring the gift touches the hidden spring,
Source of all gifts, the womb of creation;

From the wide-open door streams the elation
Shaping all things, itself shapeless as air,

That models the nipple of girl, of bud, the angel 10
Forms unscrolling their voices over fields of winter,
That whittles the ray of a star to a heart's splinter
For one lost in his palace of breath on the frozen hill,
Flying the big-bellied moon for a sail.

And releases the flood of girl, of bud, of the horn
Whose music starts on a morning journey.
In mother, child and all, the One-in-the-many
Gathers me nearer to be born.

{1951}

WORDS FOR A BALLET

Wilderness is not desert, wilderness is mirrors.
When the sun burns the glass the image performs,
Sun-worshipper makes an arch of hands, flows a river,
And conjures in columns of bone white birds in storms.

He coaxes, cajoles, dances the sun yet light
But gilds the dance, his heart is no gold trumpet.
Guess the time and season when wings collect from flight
In a group of static birds lodged in a sweetheart locket.

Wilderness is not desert, no devil leaps boulders,
Wilderness reflects a morning of April, 10
In matching sash of blue the artist changes gender,
Under rocketing bush of hair the dancer virginal

Spends her wandlike beauty in the lake of your eyes,
Fetches a cowl of cloud with her twigfine fingers,
And when the curving limbs publish their delicate lies
Covers them with the candour clinging of the air.

All seems but nothing is in that country of mirrors,
Costumes change the contours but not the heart
No simulated sunlight of stages discovers.
When will the lovely honest darkness start,   20

And wilderness become itself the map of a journey
Where the shoes of false selves travel the road,
But the discoverer never moves from the centre of that city
That a sudden dawn will light in the darkness of God?

{1951}

The One Stem

In the green and silver chorus of the grass
they lose themselves, the bright particulars.

Discovery begins
in the single that is singular,
the one stem your eyes are suddenly unsealed to see,
jointed with the latest, fragile, golden light.

Go hand in hand with generalities,
you will never be surprised,
you will never cross over

to the child dancing to herself   10
in a swirl of sunlight in the blind street,

to the travelling star in the running stream,
or the lucky clover.

You will never reach that tall one
talking with clouds as he mends a roof,
or the naiad rising from birth of waters in the stone fountain,
or under birds crossing the air, your voice will never carry
to the old saint sweeping leaves and frost jewels in the autumn
    morning.

[1958] {1978}

MIRIAM WADDINGTON

1917–2004

Miriam Dworkin was born in Winnipeg to recent Russian immigrants and educated in a Yiddish school. She received a B.A. from the University of Toronto in 1939 and in the same year married journalist Patrick Waddington. She completed a Master's degree in social work at the University of Pennsylvania in 1945 and then moved to Montreal, where she practised and taught in McGill's School of Social Work. John Sutherland's *First Statement* published her early poems and her first volume, *Green World* (1945), a title that spoke to Waddington's orientation towards the organic to counter what she perceived as the entropic bleakness of modernist poetry. In 1955 *The Second Silence* appeared, followed by *The Season's Lovers* in 1958. In 1960 she separated from her husband and moved to Toronto. In 1964 she began to teach in the English department at York University, where she remained until her retirement in 1983. *The Glass Trumpet* appeared in 1966; she would go on to publish nine more volumes of poetry. She also edited *John Sutherland: Essays, Controversies, and Poems* (1972), *The Collected Poems of A.M. Klein* (1974), and *Canadian Jewish Short Stories* (1990). Her own fiction was collected in *Summer at Lonely Beach and Other Stories* (1982). She published a collection of essays, *Apartment Seven: Essays New and Selected*, in 1989.

THE BOND

On Jarvis street the Jewish whore
Smiles and stirs upon the bed.

Sleep is the luxury of the poor
But sweeter sleep awaits the dead.

Sweeter sleep awaits the dead
Than all the living who must rise
To join the march of hunger fed
Under the dawn of city skies.

Under the dawn of city skies
Moves the sun in presaged course   10
Smoothing out the cunning lies
That hide the evil at the source.

I sense the evil at the source
Now at this golden point of noon,
The misdirected social force
Will grind me also, and too soon.

On Jarvis street the Jewish whore
The Jewish me on Adelaide –
Both of the nameless million poor
Who wear no medals and no braid.   20

Oh woman you are kin to me,
Your heart beats something like my own
When idiot female ecstasy
Transforms in love the flesh and bone;

And woman, you are kin to me
Those tense moments first or last,
When men deride your ancestry
Whore, Jewess, you are twice outcast.

Whore, Jewess, I acknowledge you
Joint heirs to varied low estate,   30
No heroes will arise anew
Avenging us twice isolate.

  . . . .

I who start from noonday sleep
To cry of triumph, "aeroplane!"
Hear nothing but the slippered creep
Of famine through the surplus grain.

Exultant females shriek, "parade!"
And crowd a hundred windows high,
From offices on Adelaide
They wave the khaki boys goodbye.   40

  . . . .

The heavy night is closing in,
Signal omens everywhere,
You woman who have lived by sin,
And I who dwelt in office air,

Shall share a common rendezvous
Arranged by madness, crime, and race.
Sister, my salute to you!
I will recognize your face.

[1942] {1955}

GREEN WORLD

When I step out and feel the green world
its concave walls must cup my summer coming
and curving hold me

beyond all geography in a transparent place
where water images cling to the inside sphere
move and distend as rainbows in a mirror
cast out of focus.

This crystal chrysalis
shapes to green rhythms to long ocean flowings
rolls toward the sun with sure and spinning speed   10
and under the intensely golden point
it warms expands
until walls crack suddenly
uncup me into large and windy space.

{1945}

THOU DIDST SAY ME

Late as last summer
thou didst say me, love
I choose you, you, only you.
oh the delicate del-
icate serpent of your lips,
the golden lie bedazzled
me with wish and flash
of joy and I was fool.

I was fool, bemused
bedazed by summer, still   10
bewitched and wandering
in murmur hush in green-
ly sketched-in fields
I was, I was, so sweet

I was, so honied with
your gold of love and love
and still again more love.

Late as last autumn
thou didst say me, dear
my doxy, I choose you and   20
always you, thou didst pledge
me love and through the red-
plumed weeks and soberly
I danced upon your words
and garlanded these
tender dangers.

Year curves to ending now
and thou dost say me, wife
I choose another love, and oh
the delicate del-   30
icate serpent of your mouth
stings deep, and bitter
iron cuts and shapes
my death, I was so fool.

[1945] {1955}

CHILDLESS

October promised me a son
and April hid a daughter,
But father they had none;
My children swam the spidery path
Of their mortality, were lost like stars

Between the distant worlds
And now their faces melt in the catalpa tree.

Wind gossïps in the leaves
And down below their voices
Blur the lilacs trailing sweet,   10
Translucent, hushed, their sadness
Follows me through time,
Space encompasses their loss
But neither space nor time
Give form to mine which featureless,
Remains vast, crying out.

Their unforgiving nymphid faces plead
My guilt, in my despair I feel
Their smiles snarl the night and pull
The ropes of darkness down until   20
At last the sky collapses on my solitude.
And still the children's faces follow me;
Everywhere waylaid
I feel their lacy bubblings flay
The hardened grave inside and hear
Their bitter cries upbraid
My barren womb.

{1955}

THE JOURNEYING

Trapped in such a paradise
(old Adam in a stuffy lair) —
pity the guilty self again;

my own last soul at mercy's end
begins once more the journeying.
Cell has starved from cell
and fallen from the bone,
body becomes a part again
and sloughs the dying whole.

Alive I burn: and burn beyond   10
archaic wastes of total snow,
no winter bird can sing the mean
of distance between yes and no,
or beast asleep can wake to know
if part can live apart from whole:
no man, no talking fish can tell
whose death will fire the heaven-slow-
time-blackened chimneys of the soul.

{1958}

THE SEASON'S LOVERS

In the daisied lap of summer
The lovers lay, they dozed
And lay in sun unending,
They lay in light, they slept
And only stirred
Each one to find the other's lips.
At times they sighed
Or spoke a word
That wavered on uneven breath,
He had no name and she forgot   10
The ransomed kingdom of her death.

When at last the sun went down
And chilly evening stained the fields,
The lovers rose and rubbed their eyes:
They saw the pale wash of grass
Heighten to metallic green
And spindly tongues of granite mauve
Lick up the milk of afternoon,
They gathered all the scattered light
Of daisies to one place of white,
And ghostly poets lent their speech
To the stillness of the air,
The lovers listened, each to each.

Into the solid wall of night,
The lovers looked, their clearer sight
Went through that dark intensity
To the other side of light.
The lovers stood, it seemed to them
They hung upon the world's rim –
He clung to self, and she to him;
He rocked her with his body's hymn
And murmured to her shuddering cry,
You are all states, all princes I,
And sang against her trembling limbs,
Nothing else is, he sang, *but I.*

They lifted the transparent lid
From world false and world true
And in the space of both they flew.
He found a name, she lost her death,
And summer lulled them in its lap
With a leafy lullaby.
There they sleep unending sleep,

20

30

40

The lovers lie
He with a name, she free of death,
In a country hard to find
Unless you read love's double mind
Or invent its polar map.

{1958}

MARGARET AVISON

1918–2007

Margaret Avison was born the daughter of a Methodist minister in Galt, Ontario, and grew up in Regina, Calgary, and Toronto. In her profound empathy with Depression-era starvation on the prairies she required three years of treatment for an anorexia-like condition. Her first poem appeared in the *Canadian Poetry Magazine,* then under the editorship of E.J. Pratt, in 1939. A.J.M. Smith's inclusion of several of her poems in the *Book of Canadian Poetry* in 1943 gave a major impetus to her poetry and to its recognition; she appeared in *Poetry* in 1947, but thereafter she published little until the late 1950s. She worked as a librarian, secretary, archivist, editor, and professional writer; she also toured France in 1950 as governess to an affluent family. While attending a creative writing program at the University of Chicago on a Guggenheim fellowship, she began to write the poems of her first volume, *Winter Sun,* which won the Governor General's Award for 1960. In 1963 she experienced a religious conversion that made her Christianity devout and exigent; the poetry of that new vision, written in two months following her conversion, was published in her second volume, *The Dumbfounding* (1966). After completing an M.A. on Byron at the University of Toronto in 1964, she began a lifelong commitment to community and Christian service as a social worker for Toronto's Presbyterian Church Mission and later for the Mustard Seed Mission. Three volumes of her collected poems were published as *Always Now* from 2003 to 2005.

THE BUTTERFLY

An uproar,
a spruce-green sky, bound in iron,
the murky sea running a sulphur scum,
I saw a butterfly, suddenly.
It clung between the ribs of the storm, wavering,
and flung against the battering bone-wind.
I remember it, glued to the grit of that rain-strewn beach
that glowered around it, swallowed its startled design
in the larger iridescence of unstrung dark.

That wild, sour air, those miles of crouching forest, that moth   10
when all enveloping space
is a thin glass globe, swirling with storm
tempt us to stare, and seize analogies.
The Voice that stilled the sea of Galilee
overtoned by the new peace, the fierce subhuman peace
of such an east sky, blanched like Eternity.

The meaning of the moth, even the smashed moth, the
meaning of the moth —
can't we stab that one angle into the curve of space
that sweeps so unrelenting, far above,   20
towards the subhuman swamp of under-dark?

{1943}

NEW YEAR'S POEM

The Christmas twigs crispen and needles rattle
Along the window-ledge.
A solitary pearl

Shed from the necklace spilled at last week's party
Lies in the suety, snow-luminous plainness
Of morning, on the window-ledge beside them.
And all the furniture that circled stately
And hospitable when these rooms were brimmed
With perfumes, furs, and black-and-silver
Crisscross of seasonal conversation, lapses   10
Into its previous largeness.
            I remember
Anne's rose-sweet gravity, and the stiff grave
Where cold so little can contain;
I mark the queer delightful skull and crossbones
Starlings and sparrows left, taking the crust,
And the long loop of winter wind
Smoothing its arc from dark Arcturus down
To the bricked corner of the drifted courtyard,
And the still window-ledge.   20
            Gentle and just pleasure
It is, being human, to have won from space
This unchill, habitable interior
Which mirrors quietly the light
Of the snow, and the new year.

[1956] {1959}

BIRTH DAY

Saturday I ran to Mytilene.

Bushes and grass along the glass-still way
Were all dabbled with rain
And the road reeled with shattered skies.

Towards noon an inky, petulant wind
Ravelled the pools, and rinsed the black grass round them.

Gulls were up in the late afternoon
And the air gleamed and billowed
And broadcast flung astringent spray
                    All swordy-silver.   10
I saw the hills lie brown and vast and passive.

The men of Mytilene waited restive
Until the yellow melt of sun.
I shouted out my news as I sped toward them
That all, rejoicing, could go down to dark.

All nests, with all moist downy young
Blinking and gulping daylight; and all lambs
Four-braced in straw, shivering and mild;
And the first blood-root up from the ravaged beaches
Of the old equinox; and frangible robins' blue   20
Teethed right around to sun:
These first we loudly hymned;
And then
The hour of genesis
When first the moody firmament
Swam out of Arctic chaos,
Orbed solidly as the huge frame for this
Cramped little swaddled creature's coming forth
To slowly, foolishly, marvellously
Discover a unique estate, held wrapt   30
Away from all men else, which to embrace
Our world would have to stretch and swell with strangeness.

This made us smile, and laugh at last. There was
Rejoicing all night long in Mytilene.

{1959}

Snow

Nobody stuffs the world in at your eyes.
The optic heart must venture: a jail-break
And re-creation. Sedges and wild rice
Chase rivery pewter. The astonished cinders quake
With rhizomes. All ways through the electric air
Trundle candy-bright discs; they are desolate
Toys if the soul's gates seal, and cannot bear,
Must shudder under, creation's unseen freight.
But soft, there is snow's legend: colour of mourning
Along the yellow Yangtze where the wheel   10
Spins an indifferent stasis that's death's warning.
Asters of tumbled quietness reveal
Their petals. Suffering this starry blur
The rest may ring your change, sad listener.

{1959}

The Dumbfounding

When you walked here,
took skin, muscle, hair,
eyes, larynx, we
withheld all honour: "His house is clay,
how can he tell us of his far country?"

Your not familiar pace
in flesh, across the waves,
woke only our distrust.
Twice-torn we cried "A ghost"
and only on our planks counted you fast.   10

Dust wet with your spittle
cleared mortal trouble.
We called you a blasphemer,
a devil-tamer.

The evening you spoke of going away
we could not stay.
All legions massed. You had to wash, and rise,
alone, and face
out of the light, for us.

You died.   20
We said,
"The worst is true, our bliss
has come to this."

When you were seen by men
in holy flesh again
we hoped so despairingly for such report
we closed their windpipes for it.

Now you have sought
and seek, in all our ways, all thoughts,
streets, musics – and we make of these a din   30
trying to lock you out, or in,
to be intent. And dying.

Yet you are
constant and sure,
the all-lovely, all-men's-way
to that far country.

Lead through the garden to
trash, rubble, hill,
where, the outcast's outcast, you
sound dark's uttermost, strangely light-brimming, until   40
time be full.

{1966}

A.G. BAILEY

1905–1997

Alfred Goldsworthy Bailey was born in Quebec City to a family descended from Loyalists. He was educated at the University of New Brunswick and completed M.A. and Ph.D. degrees at the University of Toronto. From 1935 to 1937 he was Curator of the New Brunswick Museum in Saint John. He then accepted an offer from the University of New Brunswick to head their new Department of History; he remained until his retirement in 1970. Before he had any significant exposure to contemporary poetry he had published *Songs of the Saguenay* (1927) and *Tao* (1930). Partly as a result of friendships with Earle Birney and Robert Finch, and of hearing Roy Daniells read T.S. Eliot's *The Waste Land* aloud in 1931, Bailey began to modernize his poetry. His third volume, *Border River*, would not appear until 1952. Many of its poems reflect the interests of his ground-breaking doctoral dissertation, *The Conflict of European and Eastern Algonkian Cultures, 1504-1700* (published in 1937 and 1969). With a group of student writers he founded *The Fiddlehead* literary journal in 1945 and edited it until 1953. A fourth volume, *Thanks for a Drowned Island*, appeared in 1973. His poems have been collected in *Miramichi Lightning: The Collected Poems of Alfred Goldsworthy Bailey* (1981).

Plague Burial

The bright matrix of the brain
contains a box to put one's values in:

the work well done, a bargain fairly made,
virtue rewarded with fat satisfactions.

An oblong box, say five feet and a bit,
to hold the bones on this side of the scales.
Who weights the values on the other side
may weight to no end, it may be
there's nothing adequate to bones gone dry.

Although the box is made specifically   10
these bones are no less fond
(and bones no more for garments gaily donned).
An empire's lamentation for all these ducal bones;
for all these duchesses who fondled them, no less,
with fond caress.

The drawn blind, the silent house.
The fat mouse nibbles a cheese
equal in kind to coronets worn well,
equal to the tolling bell
that travels over refuse heaps and restaurants.   20
And *café noir* is comforting no less,
no less a value hailing from Brazil
for pounds and pence
and ledgers fat as cheese.

Weevil in a green-rot,
green-rot weevil,
know he is a green-rot
for good or for evil.

The drawn blind, the day that does not break.
Tread silently lest someone wake   30
to sense the peace that passeth here.

Handle the creaking hinge with fear
and into the yard tread softly
over by the chicken coop
dig us a hole, say five feet and a bit.
A close fit, 'twill closer bye and bye.
There is no need for too much sky
for bones.
Spade and gravel grate.
A hen squawks like a throat torn open.   40
Hurry! It grows late.

[1943] {1952}

Thanks for a Drowned Island

Into the flooding tide
to seek the consolation of the waters,
to find the depths a life of blessed peace
after the sable ride:

I would lie in the sea
and light not cease,
nor water gather stagnant in the grave,
nor rampant furies of the land and air
gibber about the tomb;
where tides hold concourse with the fragile weed   10
while broad shapes loom,
gather in groups to feed,
shining and indistinct against the green sea grass,
and with a casual flick of the tail dart home
moving cold currents to a body's need,
sending the deep sea echo of a wave
washing about the entrance to a cave:

there to grow strength of body, faith of mind,
accustomed to the water's way
and understanding of its kind 20
there
in the green sea day.

{1952}

LOUIS DUDEK

1918–2001

Louis Dudek's conviction that poets must control the means of their own production fundamentally altered Canadian publishing. He was a major contributor of poems, essays, and editorial direction to *First Statement* (1942–45); he was a mentor-editor of *Civ/n* (1953–55), a co-editor of *Contact* (1952–54), and a co-director of Contact Press (1952–67); he edited his own little magazine *Delta* (1957–66) and its affiliated press as Delta Canada (1966–70), then as DC Books. He was by turns social realist, Imagist, aphorist, didacticist, prose poet, and pioneer of the Canadian modernist long poem, which he took to its extreme form in the deliberate unfinishing of *Continuation,* his last major project. Dudek was born to recent Polish immigrants in Montreal. He completed a B.A. degree at McGill University and worked briefly in advertising. He left for New York in 1943 for post-graduate work at Columbia University, where his eminent teachers included Jacques Barzun and Lionel Trilling. While in New York he met Ezra Pound, then incarcerated in Saint Elizabeth's Hospital, and became his informal literary assistant; Dudek published Pound's letters to him as *Dk / Some Letters of Ezra Pound* in 1974. In 1951 he joined the English department at McGill University, where he would remain until retirement in 1984. Dudek's first solo volume was *East of the City* (1946). Two more of his own books appeared before he joined with Layton and Raymond Souster in the trio publication *Cerberus* (1952), the first volume from their new Contact Press. Contact subsequently published *Europe* (1954) and *En Mexico* (1958), experimental long poems arising partly from Dudek's travels. In *Atlantis* (1967) travel and temporal organization itself are secondary to the spontaneous flow of the persona's mind. Dudek published his *Collected Poetry*, including the first fragment of *Continuation*, in 1971 and thereafter produced ten more books of new poetry, as well as epigrams and prose poems, anthologies, collected essays and lectures, diaries and notebooks. Near the end of his life he prepared a volume of what he felt to be his finest work, *The Poetry of Louis Dudek: Definitive Edition* (1998).

A WHITE PAPER

Butterfly wing,
silver diver of the air
held in my pocket,
who danced of your own free will
with the dancing wind,
was lost in a cloud
and then came down
to a lawn,
to a rooftop,
missing the rooftop,   10
to a street, to the edge of the sidewalk —

you, destined to return
to rest in my hand,
belong in a book to keep for a keepsake!
Shall I place you in a museum?
You are a record of me, as I of you.

Once, I traced with my finger
the delicate ribs
and bones of a dancer
who died in the sea   20

and buried his body in stone;
Dalmanites . . . today's museum piece, I saw
playing among corals
in a green sea,
dancing among sunbeams,
running from a shadow.

So you be a record of me,
a print I traced with my eye
one afternoon
that someone time hence   30
may lift like a layer, and see
me, white in the sunlight.

[1943] {1946}

ON POETRY

The flame of a man's imagination should be organic with his body,
coincident with an act, like an igniting spark.
But mostly, he fails in the act
and expels his bad humour in visions. A man curses,
seeing the thing he hates in pain, cursed by his vision:
this is poetry, action unrealized:
what we want most we imagine most, like self-abusing boys.

Lately, of woman man has been deprived
– the smaller man and the greater too –
and in all the language of his verse   10
love, love, love
he cries, never having enough.

Formerly, it was different.
Hairy and sensible, he needed food
when he painted steak chops (bison meat)
in a gaping cave; a bird, or juicy calves of mammoth,
his midday meals.
He carved these also on his spears
and on the handles of knives,
handing the art down the generations.   20

But with the coming of civilization
his body desired other food at times, less personal,
but unattainable. So the poet, who had vision,
wanted to be capable of commanding God, like Jeremiah;
but denied, he ranted poetry.

The poet should have been a king,
Shakespeare should have been all his monarchs, ruling England,
Homer should have been Achilles
frowning for Briseis, or fighting for his friend.
These great ones imagined grandly,   30
the life of their body having defaulted.

So in our time, the poet,
in need of quiet, order in chaos,
complete community, wants something he does not have
in all nakedness. And so he wrestles
with the maiden, his wild dream, in his sleep.

{1946}

A Street in April

Look now, at this February street in April
where not a flower blossoms, or if one broke
would be like water from a blister, a yellow poke,
new bird lime on a rail, or jet from a yolk.

Neither the fire-escapes making musical patterns
nor the filigree of stone flowery and decorating
can now accompany young April; the iron grating
jars, someone dropped a kettle in the orchestrating.

There a pale head rising from an eyeless cavern
swivels twice above the street, and swiftly dips   10
back into the gloom of the skull, whose only lips
are the swinging tin plate and the canvas strips.

And here are infants too, in cribs, with wondrous eyes
at windows, the curtains raised upon a gasping room,
angelic in white diapers and bibs, to whom
the possibilities in wheels and weather – bloom.

But I have seen a dove gleaming and vocal with peace
fly over them, when his sudden wings stirred
and cast the trembling shadow of a metal bird;
so April's without flower, and no song heard.   20

{1946}

19

The commotion of these waves, however strong, cannot disturb
                    the compass-line of the horizon
nor the plumb-line of gravity, because this cross coordinates
                    the tragic pulls of necessity
that chart the ideal endings, for waves, and storms
                    and sunset winds:
the dead scattered on the stage in the fifth act
– Cordelia in Lear's arms, Ophelia, Juliet, all silent –
show nature restored to order and just measure.
                    The horizon is perfect,   10
and nothing can be stricter
than gravity; in relation to these
                    the stage is rocked and tossed,
kings fall with their crowns, poets sink with their laurels.

48

Paris, more stinking royal than any city:
            city of republicans, of the Conciergerie, Bastille!
(Some 10,000 visit Versailles on a Sunday?
            Nothing but sentiment. O the great age
                    of the Roi Soleil!)
The city is filled with palaces and baroque horrors
and such filthy flamboyant statues
            as deface the corners of the best cathedrals,
                    even Chartres –
eighteenth-century additions, twentieth-century   10
                    legs et dons.

And buried under Paris, under the Palais de Justice,
         under St. Germain & the Louvre,
you will find the stained glass
            of the Sainte Chapelle,
and a small Greek church of very early date,
and St. Séverin, perfect and harmonious, and quiet
and the staring face of Notre Dame.

95

The sea retains such images
      in her ever-unchanging waves;
for all her infinite variety, and the forms,
inexhaustible, of her loves,
she is constant always in beauty,
        which to us need be nothing more
      than a harmony with the wave on which we move.
All ugliness is a distortion
of the lovely lines and curves
        which sincerity makes out of hands   10
          and bodies moving in air.
Beauty is ordered in nature
      as the wind and sea
shape each other for pleasure; as the just
know, who learn of happiness
        from the report of their own actions.

{1954}

FROM *En Mexico*

It is most quiet
where it is most violent.
That's why we appear so good.

In a tropical cemetery
hardly a grave is to be seen,
so much is overgrown.

And where Cortés with his men
      (their pockets full of booty)
waded in blood, they've drained the lake
and streetcars glide   10
where he shook the Indian by the arm and cried:
"You have destroyed the most beautiful city in the world —
                  Tenochtitlan!"

He opened the continent
      like a cornucopia.

Now the jungle has an oceanic luxury:
boys by a heap of papaya
(above them, the cornfields,
            maguey rows, cactus)
and thatched native huts   20
with little children in the puddles.
Rain, out of a solitary cloud,
then sun, more sun —
building pyramids of green
and *las flores*
in the Huastecan jungle,
the pre-Aztec world.

***

That it should come into being out of nothing.
(Grass . . . bird . . . machine and metal,
    that they should come into being.)
Man, come to shape out of smoking matter,
    out of male secretion in the womb, take form.
All things, all bodies:
    that they should come out of nothing,
rise, as projectiles out of rock,
with spicules, with eyes, limbs,
with objects, accoutrements, skills,   10
amid an abundance of flora and fauna,
each to itself all —
in a jungle devouring graves.

We have passed through the earth's middle
and emerged as we are.
Climbing mountains, living in valleys,
can we miss the end of living?
(Since we have looked death in the face.)
To be is the palm of creation,
and all that we are is seed from a pod.   20

You may hate the jungle,
its inimical insects, flies,
and the chaos of growing
everything at once;
but we return for fertility
to its moist limbs and vaginal leaves.

{1958}

FROM *ATLANTIS*

How seagulls know what they are!

So to be, whatever you are —
        a white bird,
                        a man with a blue guitar.
But there is room for more, more.

It is the part of us
not yet finished as seagull or man
that worries us at the pit of creation,

hanging over cliffs, drowning,
                        or lifted in flight   10

to new states of being, asking always what we are.

Like this ship leaving, gently, to silent tears
                falling all around,
the infinite poem begins, with its power
    of a great ocean-liner greeting the waves,
bound for the sea, its home.

So the waves of the sea (it all comes back to me
                as when I first heard it),
the white snowcaps breaking,
the power of repetition, multitudes,   20
like the universe of atoms —

ephemeral, too, the making and breaking of crested forms.

It comes back to me
          (like a wave in these waters)
in the repetition of these lines.

          * * *

Marble is the cross-section of a cloud.
What, then, if the forms we know
                    are sections of a full body
whose dimensions are timeless
                         and bodiless, like poems,
whose unseen dimension is mind?

I want to learn how we can take life seriously,
   without afflatus, without rhetoric;
to see something like a natural ritual,
          maybe an epic mode unrevealed,   10
in the everyday round of affairs.

          {1967}

JOHN GLASSCO
1909–1981

John Glassco is best known for his *Memoirs of Montparnasse* (1970), the exuberantly fictionalized record of his years as a young dilettante in Paris in the late 1920s. His first collection of poetry, *The Deficit Made Flesh,* would not be published until 1958, yet his cultural sensibility is profoundly that of the 1920s, with its self-conscious Decadent postures and its mood of harsh regret for a lost Jazz-Age energy and freedom. He was born in Montreal and studied at McGill University, without graduating, from 1925 to 1927. He published fugitive pieces in A.J.M. Smith and F.R. Scott's *McGill Fortnightly Review* but was not of its inner circle. He left Montreal for the bohemian literary life in Paris in 1928, where he lived until 1931, when tuberculosis forced him to return to Montreal. After the removal of a lung stabilized his health, he moved to Quebec's Eastern Townships, where he delivered the rural mail and began to make a pseudonymous reputation as a pornographer. His best-known work in this line, *Harriet Marwood, Governess,* was eventually re-published under his own name (1976). His poems appeared regularly in periodicals by 1947. In the 1950s he also began to translate Canada's francophone poets, particularly Hector de Saint-Denys Garneau, whose *Journal* and *Complete Poems* he published in 1962 and 1975. He edited the anthology *The Poetry of French Canada in Translation,* including many of his own adaptations, in 1970. In 1963 he organized a conference in Foster, Quebec, on English poetry in Quebec and published its proceedings in 1965. Glassco's second collection, *A Point of Sky,* appeared in 1964. His *Selected*

Poems (1971) won the Governor General's Award for that year. The long satiric poem *Montreal* (1973), a pastiche of many of Glassco's creative impulses, with its dominant elegiac mood and brief passages of verse pornography, showed little of his usual craftsmanship. He died in Montreal in 1981.

THE RURAL MAIL

These are the green paths trodden by patience.
I hang on the valley's lip, a bird's eye viewing
All that opposes to makers and masters of nations
Only its fierce mistrust of the word —
To the smashed records for gobbling and spewing,
Cows that exist in a slow-motion world.

For here is man on man's estate of nature,
Farmer on farm, the savage civilized
Into the image of his God the weather —
Only another anarchist, foiled highflyer   10
Whose years have grown as a minute in his eyes,
Whose grin reveals a vision of barbed wire:

Here birth evokes pleasure and a reflective pity,
Marriage or mating, much of the voyeur,
Sickness, an interest and some hope of booty,
And death strikes like an oddly barked command,
Confounding with its *Easy,* its *As you were,*
His stiff-kneed generation unused to bend.

I sense his hours marked by my two-wheeled cart
Descending the stony hill: as I stop by his box   20
The ring of tin as the *Knowlton News* goes in

Is a day's knell — and the countryside contracts
For an instant to the head of a pin;
Or he comes with a money-order, or to chat.

Getting good money, and money is always good,
We keep the high standards in the front parlour
Like a wedding-cake or a motto carved in wood,
The falling-out of enemies makes no friends.
"Far as I'm concerned, the war can go on forever!"
A man can *make* a dollar, with hens.   30

Scraping the crumbling roadbed of this strife
With rotten fenceposts and old mortgages
(No way of living, but a mode of life),
How sift from death and waste three grains of duty,
O thoughts that start from scratch and end in a dream
Of graveyards minding their own business?

But the heart accepts it all, this honest air
Lapped in green valleys where accidents will happen!
Where the bull, the buzz-saw and the balky mare
Are the chosen fingers of God for a farmer's sins,   40
Like the axe for his woods, and his calves and chicks and children
Destined for slaughter in the course of things.

[1943] {1958}

BRUMMELL AT CALAIS

A foolish useless man who had done nothing
All his life long but keep himself clean,
Locked in the glittering armour of a pose
Made up of impudence, chastity and reserve —
How does his memory still survive his world?

The portraits show us only a tilted nose,
Lips full blown, a cravat and curly wig,
And a pair of posturing eyes,
Infinitely vulnerable, deeply innocent,
Their malice harmless as a child's: 10

And he has returned to childhood now, his stature
That of the Butterfly whose *Funeral*
He sang (his only song) for one of his
Dear duchesses, Frances or Georgiana,
In the intolerable metre of Tom Moore –

To a childhood of sweet biscuits and curaçao;
Hair-oil and tweezers make him forget his debts,
The angle of his hat remains the same,
His little boots pick their way over the cobblestones,
But where is he going as well as going mad?   20

Nowhere: his glory is already upon him,
The fading Regency man who will leave behind
More than the ankle-buttoning pantaloon!
For see, even now in the long implacable twilight,
The triumph of his veritable art,

An art of being, nothing but being, the grace
Of perfect self-assertion based on nothing,
As in our vanity's cause against the void
He strikes his elegant blow, the solemn report of those
Who have done nothing and will never die.   30

[1947] {1964}

DESERTED BUILDINGS UNDER SHEFFORD MOUNTAIN

These native angles of decay
    In shed and barn whose broken wings
Lie here half fallen in the way
Of headstones amid uncut hay —
    Why do I love you, ragged things?

What grace unknown to any art,
    What beauty frailer than a mood
Awake in me their counterpart?
What correspondence of a heart
    That loves the failing attitude?   10

Here where I grasp the certain fate
    Of all man's work in wood and stone,
And con the lesson of the straight
That shall be crooked soon or late
    And crumble into forms alone,

Some troubled joy that's half despair
    Ascends within me like a breath:
I see these silent ruins wear
The speaking look, the sleeping air
    Of features newly cast in death,   20

Dead faces where we strive to see
    The signature of something tossed
Between design and destiny,
Between God and absurdity,
    Till, harrowing up a new-made ghost,

We half embrace the wavering form,
    And half conceive the wandering sense

Of some imagined part kept warm
And salvaged from the passing storm
  Of time's insulting accidents.   30

So I, assailed by the blind love
  That meets me in this silent place,
Lift open arms: Is it enough
That restless things can cease to move
  And leave a ruin wreathed in grace,

Or is this wreck of strut and span
  No more than solace for the creed
Of progress and its emmet plan,
Dark houses that are void of man,
  Dull meadows that have gone to seed?   40

{1958}

A Devotion: To Cteis

Well, I shall kneel, that the whole world can say
Here is desire too that has come to pray.
The poles of pleasure in our divided dust
Meet often in their own tropics, lust and lust,
Devotion and devotion, but to join
Either to other is this way of mine;
Here to confound the order that's been planned
In man's imagined globe, the seas and land
Huddle together, make fire from beneath
Burst on his Arctic, and in the rotten teeth   10
Of all his moralist-geographers
Hurl nature in his embrace, and mine in hers!
Now when my mouth, that holds my heart, has become

An infinite reverence's ciborium,
Now, when the surcharged spiritual part
Exhales its burden – marvel, O marvel at
This joining, this economy of love
That turns the pious breath, the gesture of
My extreme adoration to a kiss,
As if it were all that could be made of this!   20
– Soon, soon begins the long intense journey
My lips shall lead you and my care delay,
But ere we embark, and ere thou shalt – O stay ! –
Translate thy vision, seeing through closed eyes
The ideal form of carnal ecstasies;
Ere thou'rt become all sensible, and I
Am grown a very incubus thereby,
Oh let us hang, as the waves of ocean do,
An instant in the arrest of what we travel to.
See, I'd not slip from worshipper into man   30
A space yet, but remain as I began,
Give my lips holiday from the work of words,
Sabbath of silence, drifting pleasurewards,
And let my spirit, as my knees do, bow
Before this cloven idol – an altar now
As the old speechless misremembered year
Returns in noonlight, hunger and rage and fear
Cancelled forever, and as there bloom in me,
On the bare branches of my cynic tree,
Like mistletoe run wild, the devotee,   40
The lover and the child.

{1958}

UTRILLO'S WORLD

I

He sat above it, watching it recede,
A world of love resolved to empty spaces,
Streets without figures, figures without faces,
Desolate by choice and negative from need.
But the hoardings weep, the shutters burn and bleed;
Colours of crucifixion, dying graces,
Spatter and cling upon these sorrowful places.
— Where is the loved one? Where do the streets lead?

There is no loved one. Perfect fear
Has cast out love. And the streets go on forever   10
To blest annihilation, silently ascend
To their own assumption of bright points in air.
It is the world that counts, the endless fever,
And suffering that is its own and only end.

II

Anguished these sombre houses, still, resigned.
Suffering has found no better face than wood
For its own portrait, nor are tears so good
As the last reticence of being blind.
Grief without voice, mourning without mind,
I find your silence in this neighbourhood   20
Whose hideous buildings ransom with their blood
The shame and the self-loathing of mankind.

They are also masks that misery has put on
Over the faces and the festivals:
Madness and fear must have a place to hide,

And murder a secret room to call his own.
I know they are prisons also, these thin walls
Between us and what cowers and shakes inside.

{1958}

THE DEATH OF DON QUIXOTE

I

So this is what it is,
The world of things, arrested.
The music in my brain has stopped.
The armies are simply sheep, the giants windmills,
Dulcinea a cow-girl,
Mambrinus' helmet a barber's basin —
And the priest is delighted,
Fussing over me as I lie here
After my marvellous interminable journeys,
Shorn of my armour, extenuated,   10
Now in my five wits, restored,
Ready to make a good death.
— Rosinante and Dapple are dead too
Where are their bones?

Are we all as dead as my Amadis
Who slew so many giants, indomitable?
I who modelled my endeavour, who tried . . .

Yes, this is what it is to be alive,
To die, to cease
To force a folly on the world.   20

II

The trees beyond the window are blowing green
The long road white in the distance, the sunshine,
There are flowers at my window
What do I know?

Well, that nothing partakes of reality,
And I too am simply Alonso Quixano the Good,
The wise gentleman, the restored,
Lying in my bed, tended
By my loving people, ready
To make a good death . . .   30

I appear to have killed myself
By believing in some other God:
Or perhaps it was the drubbings did for me,
The horseplay, the jokes
Wore out my silly casing of flesh.
In any event, as I lie here,
The withdrawal of the vision,
The removal of the madness,
The supplanting of a world of beauty
By God's sticks and stones and smells   40
Are afflictions, I find, of something more absurd
Than any book of chivalry.

III

O my God
I have lost everything
In the calm of my sanity
Like a tree which regards itself
In still water

Seeing only another tree,
Not as when the crazy winds of heaven blew
Turning it to a perpetual fountain   50
Of shaken leaves,
The image of an endless waltz of being
So close to my heart I was always asking
Why should we not dance so for ever, be always
Trees tossed against the sky?
Why are we men at all if not to defy
This painted quietude of God's world?

Well, everything must have an end.
I have had my day
I have come home   60
I see things as they are.
My ingenious creator has abandoned me
With the insouciance of a nobleman
The fickleness of an author
The phlegm of an alguazil —

Only Sancho is faithful unto death
But in his eyes I discern the terrible dismay
For he sees that mine are at last a mirror of his own.

{1964}

BELLY DANCE

The corpsewhite column spiralling on slow feet
Tracing the seashell curve, the figure eight,
Coldly unwinds its flowing ribbon
With public motions of the private psalm
Of supposed woman to the thought of man;

And like that man of Bierce's wrestling
In the embrace of an invisible Thing,
Flaps in snakehead-strike doublejointed death –
An evocation of circumfluent air,
The adversary in a breath of air.   10

And the air is icy. Love, that is violence
Made easy, is here the end of all, a dance,
And man the viewless form, the animal
No longer animal but seeing-eye,
But super-member of impossible man.

So the man of air supplants the man of bone,
And it is he who writhes before a glass,
Before the figure of his only love,
The viewless member in his nerveless hand
Working within the adverse air.   20

{1971}

RALPH GUSTAFSON
1909–1995

A prominent anthologist of Canadian poetry and writer of short
fiction as well as a prolific poet, Ralph Gustafson was born in Lime
Ridge, Quebec, and grew up in Sherbrooke. At Bishop's College,
where he took B.A. and M.A. degrees (1929, 1930), his taste was
first shaped by the literary conservatism of two of his teachers,
poets Frank Oliver Call and F.G. Scott, the father of F.R. Scott.
His first collection, *The Golden Chalice*, won Quebec's Prix David
for 1935. Gustafson took a second B.A. at Oxford in 1933 and then
made a living as a freelance journalist and tutor in London until
1938. In New York by 1939, he began work on the landmark
Anthology of Canadian Poetry (English) (Penguin 1942). Intended
for distribution to Canadian soldiers at the front, the anthology
also sold over 50,000 copies. In the war years Gustafson printed
three volumes of poetry reflecting his steady turn away from
Romantic sources towards a modernity of tone and subject: *Poems*
(1940), *Epithalamium in Time of War* (1941), and *Lyrics Unromantic*
(1942). *Flight into Darkness*, arguably his first mature volume,
appeared in 1944. He worked for British Information Services in
New York (1942–46) and then, alongside freelance journalism and
editorial work, wrote short fiction through the 1950s. Marriage in
1958 and European travel renewed his poetry, and *Rocky Mountain
Poems* and *River among Rocks* (both 1960) established the lyric
travel poem as the major genre of his mid-career. He joined the
CBC as a music critic in the sixties and taught at Bishop's College
from 1963 (as poet-in-residence from 1966) to 1977. His 1974
volume, *Fire on Stone*, won the Governor General's Award. He

was at his most prolific in later life: he published twenty-five books from 1980 until his death.

FLIGHT INTO DARKNESS

We have fulfilled our apprehension, hope,
Matched our hands' delay against the sun,
Against a guttering candle written dreams.
Was it today we fumbled spiral of spring,
Clutched at the throat the knot of accurate winds,
Noose and thong by beauty slung?

Yesterday yesterday! the hills were bare of snow,
The hackneyed maple broke with leaf, the bough
Sprang colour along the sweetened air — whose action
Pledged our anger. O we have sworn our lives   10
Between the hyphened prologue of the crow,
The crimson coming of the rose!

Who now, regretting June with adult smiles,
Set nodding with a finger Buddha's porcelain head:
Hearing of marvels in the township, turned
Expensive keys against the empty street,
From possible cars saw moon eclipse the sun,
Cautious glass before our eyes.

And all that year the tamarack was green
And we who saw the tolerant seed and snow,   20
By leaning questions ambushed. Grace was then
The grateful turning-out of lamps at night,
Within the book the treacherous flower's clue,
The short escape of perjured love.

For we remembering our defense refused
The mirror's prosecution, praised the speaker
On the chairman's right: within the files,
Found brief anger for the anonymous clock,
Looking up, the calendar on startled walls –
Withdrawing truth from blundering sleep.   30

We have waited important letters from the west,
In evening cities heard the newspaper tossed
Against the door, under the prosperous valley
Guessed at oil, proved the legend false.
We dream wisely who once had loved too well.
And yet, coming on sun across

An alien street, stand suddenly surprised –
As Galileo, before his midnight window,
Cloak about his shoulders, coldly chose
A fatal planet – first, listened while   40
The solitary wagon passed along the road –
Then aimed his contradictory lens.

{1944}

ALL THAT IS IN THE WORLD

I John 2:16

Sick, sick with it! Scarp and scaffold wrenched
    Counter, opposite to God.
        Addled John abased it,
            Impotent Paul
            And all
    The self-appointed since

Who given flesh, ungraced it.
    Celestial fraud

Of churchmen's hairs and coddled crypts compounded —
    Who, snarled in Friday's crape, to make   10
        The Genesitic bother
          Sense, begin
            With sin —
    This hungered architecture —
On their own logic, no other —
    A damned mistake

Of God. Blackmail wholly, this sacerdotal
    Trade in bones and haloes — hoax.
        Beware of martyrs who
          The tangible rose   20
            Oppose
    As devious, sun, stars
Perverted cinders prove,
    Virgins coax.

Such joy and jostling nudge the elbow, anger's
    Love, damning those who roar
        Delight and sin, equation;
          A foot i' the grave
            To have
    Half goodness. Than Zion is,   30
This autumn's more persuasion,
    This maple, more.

In coitu inluminatio.
        On the path's a crimson leaf:
        Such present praise and glory
          Throughly thrust

This dust,
I blaspheme mightily.
The very spikes are sorry,
Tree, a thief.   40

{1960}

ARMORIAL

I lay down with my love and there was song
Breaking, like the lilies I once saw
Lovely around King Richard, murdered
Most foully and all his grace at Pomfret,
The roses of England stolen; our love
Was like gules emblazoned at Canterbury
Most kingly in windows and leo-pards
Passant on bars of gold. This
Was our heraldry.

Our love was larks and sprang from meadows   10
Far from kingdoms, which regal grew
With rod and bloodred weed and rush
Where water ran; this was our love,
The place where she chose, I could not but come,
A field without myth or rhetoric.
She lay down with love and my hand
Was gold with dust of lily. This
Was our province.

There was song in that kingly country
But I saw there, stuck like a porcupine   20
On Bosworth Field the arrows through him,
That regal and most royal other

Richard, runt and twitch in a ditch,
His hand wristdeep in lily where
Henry Tudor rolled him, the gules
Of England draining on his shirt.
My love wept.

{1960}

RAYMOND SOUSTER

B.1921

Raymond Souster was born in Toronto; the cityscape and his experience of it are so consistent in his imagination that he might be thought of as an urban regional poet. After completing high school in 1939 he entered the Imperial Bank of Commerce. In 1941 he enlisted in the Royal Canadian Air Force; for medical reasons he was stationed in Maritime airbases until the last days of the war. There he contributed poems to Montreal's *First Statement* and established his own little magazine, *Direction,* in which he published excerpts from the banned *Tropic of Cancer* by Henry Miller. At war's end he returned to banking. He was among the poets of *Unit of Five* (1944) and thereafter published *When We Are Young* (1946), *Go to Sleep, World* (1947), and *City Hall Street* (1951). In 1952, Louis Dudek showed Souster the poetry of William Carlos Williams; the experience profoundly changed Souster's voice, and a new minimalism of presentation and conception was fixed in his style thereafter. He established the little magazine *Contact* in 1952 and with Dudek and Irving Layton founded Contact Press later in the year. Until its closure in 1967 Contact Press was the premier publisher of Canadian poetry, producing crucial early volumes from most of the major poets of the 1960s and 1970s. Souster published seven more volumes of his own poetry before 1964's *The Colour of the Times,* which won a Governor General's Award. In 1966 he edited the controversial anthology *New Wave Canada: The New Explosion in Canadian Poetry.* His *Collected Poems* began to appear with Ottawa's Oberon Press in 1980 and now runs to ten volumes.

Night of Rain

Rain on the streets: go ahead, make up your little poem
about wet boughs and the silver sandals
of the rain: it's still one hell of a night,

and the old men on the Queen Street pavements
won't bum any cigarettes, the boys and girls on these other streets
    won't bloom
like any spring flowers tangled in dark rotted weeds,
while that tortuous stream of life that never ends, never ends,
along the pus-lines of this, my city,

will cage itself in the four trapped walls
of furnished and unfurnished rooms,   10
waiting for this night to go,

this night to go, this darkness of their lives.

{1944}

Young Girls

With night full of spring and stars we stand
here in this dark doorway and watch the young
girls pass, two, three together, hand in hand.
They are like flowers whose fragrance hasn't sprung
or awakened, whose bodies now dimly feel
the flooding, upward welling of the trees;
whose senses, caressed by the wind's soft fingers, reel
with a mild delirium that makes them ill at ease.

They lie awake at night, unable to sleep,
then walk the streets, kindled by strange desires;   10
they steal lightning glances at us, unable to keep
control upon those subterranean fires.
We whistle after them, then laugh, for they
stiffen, not knowing what to do or say.

{1946}

These Words, This Music

Although we've been singing now for more than an hour
it's only as the darkness builds, as stars pierce through,
that the music of the two accordions, the words of our mouths,
raised in these thousand-throated songs, take on beauty,

a pathos never intended, something we never dreamed
could or would ever happen. So we sing on and on,
not wanting to end this warmth, this comradeship
flowing suddenly like good wine, a feeling electric
flashing invisible sparks along the whole crowded deck length:
while this good ship speeding us home from Europe's madness,
        pulses, shivers,   10
as its funnels lay plumes on the wake of seething water.

These words we sing, this music playing,
our heartfelt thanks rising up to the heavenly angels.

{1947}

Study: The Bath

In the dim light
of the bathroom
a woman steps from white tub,
towel around her shoulders.

Drops of water glisten
on her body
from slight buttocks,
neck, tight belly,
fall at intervals
from the slightly plumed   10
oval of crotch.

The neck bent forward,
eyes collected,
her attention gathered
at the end of fingers,

lovingly removing
dead, flaked skin
from the twin nipples.

{1954}

FLIGHT OF THE ROLLER-COASTER

(Old Sunnyside Beach, Toronto)

Once more around should do it, the man confided . . .

and sure enough, when the roller-coaster reached the peak
of the giant curve above me, shrill screech of its wheels
almost drowned out by the shriller cries of its riders –

instead of the dip, then the plunge with its landslide of screams,
it rose in the air like a movieland magic carpet, some wonderful bird,

and without fuss or fanfare swooped slowly above the amusement-
    park,
over Spook's Castle, ice-cream booths, shooting-gallery;
then losing no height made the last yards across the beach,
where its brakeman cucumber-cool in the last seat solemnly
    saluted   10
a lady about to change to her bathing-suit:

ending up, as many witnesses reported later,
heading leisurely out above the blue lake water,
to disappear all too soon behind a low-flying flight of clouds.

{1955}

IRVING LAYTON

1912–2006

Irving Layton was born Israel Lazarovitch in Neamtz, Romania. His parents immigrated to Montreal, Quebec, in 1913. In his 1985 memoir *Waiting for the Messiah*, he recorded his childhood experience of poverty and anti-Semitism and his early adulthood as a dilatory student of economics and budding political orator. Layton enlisted in the army in 1942 but was granted a remarkable honourable discharge in 1943 for incompatibility with military discipline. In 1943 he began to contribute to *First Statement*, a little magazine edited by John Sutherland. He took a Master's degree at McGill in economics and political science, taught English to recent immigrants, and was employed by the Jewish parochial high school Herzliah. His first books appeared with First Statement Press (*Here and Now*, 1945; *Now Is the Place*, 1948). He would publish twelve more books of poetry at his own or friends' expense before McClelland and Stewart issued his collected poems, *A Red Carpet for the Sun*, in 1959; the book won the Governor General's Award. By 1954 the philosophy of Friedrich Nietzsche had inspired Layton to an image of the poet as a visionary madman, struggling against mortality and the bland hypocrisy and repression of the middle classes. In 1949 he began to teach in the English department at Sir George Williams University; after 1965 he was poet in residence. He then moved to Toronto for a similar position at York University (1969-78). By the late 1950s he enjoyed a high degree of celebrity and appeared regularly on radio and television. His poetry shifted its concern profoundly over the course of the sixties, in part because of his collaboration and friendship with Leonard Cohen; in the preface to *Balls for a One-Armed Juggler* (1963) Layton demanded a "poet who can make clear for us Belsen." In *Periods of the Moon* (1967) and *The Shattered Plinths* (1968) he expressed an outraged geo-political consciousness in denunciations of the Holocaust and celebrations of Israel's military victories of the period. *For My Brother Jesus* of 1976 offended many with its reclamation of the Jewish radical from those Layton saw as his Christian diluters. Collections of new poetry appeared regularly, though with decreasing notice and praise, until the late 1980s. A definitive volume of selected poems, *A Wild Peculiar Joy,* was re-issued by McClelland and Stewart in 2004.

THE SWIMMER

The afternoon foreclosing, see
The swimmer plunges from his raft,
Opening the spray corollas by his act of war —
The snake heads strike
Quickly and are silent.

Emerging see how for a moment,
A brown weed with marvellous bulbs,
He lies imminent upon the water
While light and sound come with a sharp passion
From the gonad sea around the poles
And break in bright cockle-shells about his ears.

He dives, floats, goes under like a thief
Where his blood sings to the tiger shadows
In the scentless greenery that leads him home,
A male salmon down fretted stairways
Through underwater slums. . . .

10

Stunned by the memory of lost gills
He frames gestures of self-absorption
Upon the skull-like beach;
Observes with instigated eyes   20
The sun that empties itself upon the water,
And the last wave romping in
To throw its boyhood on the marble sand.

{1945}

The Birth of Tragedy

And me happiest when I compose poems.
        Love, power, the huzza of battle
        are something, are much;
yet a poem includes them like a pool
        water and reflection.
In me, nature's divided things —
        tree, mould on tree —
        have their fruition;
I am their core. Let them swap,
bandy, like a flame swerve.   10
I am their mouth; as a mouth I serve.

And I observe how the sensual moths
        big with odour and sunshine
        dart into the perilous shrubbery;
or drop their visiting shadows
        upon the garden I one year made
of flowering stone to be a footstool
        for the perfect gods,
        who, friends to the ascending orders,
sustain all passionate meditations   20

and call down pardons
for the insurgent blood.

A quiet madman, never far from tears,
    I like a slain thing
    under the green air the trees
inhabit, or rest upon a chair
    towards which the inflammable air
tumbles on many robins' wings;
    noting how seasonably
    leaf and blossom uncurl   30
and living things arrange their death,
while someone from afar off
blows birthday candles for the world.

{1954}

THE COLD GREEN ELEMENT

At the end of the garden walk
the wind and its satellite wait for me;
their meaning I will not know
    until I go there,
but the black-hatted undertaker

who, passing, saw my heart beating in the grass,
is also going there. Hi, I tell him,
a great squall in the Pacific blew a dead poet
    out of the water,
who now hangs from the city's gates.   10

Crowds depart daily to see it, and return
with grimaces and incomprehension;

if its limbs twitched in the air
     they would sit at its feet
peeling their oranges.

And turning over I embrace like a lover
the trunk of a tree, one of those
for whom the lightning was too much
     and grew a brilliant
hunchback with a crown of leaves.   20

The ailments escaped from the labels
of medicine bottles are all fled to the wind;
I've seen myself lately in the eyes
     of old women,
spent streams mourning my manhood,

in whose old pupils the sun became
a bloodsmear on broad catalpa leaves
and, hanging from ancient twigs,
     my murdered selves
sparked the air like the muted collisions   30

of fruit. A black dog howls down my blood,
a black dog with yellow eyes;
he too by someone's inadvertence
     saw the bloodsmear
on the broad catalpa leaves.

But the Furies clear a path for me to the worm
who sang for an hour in the throat of a robin,
and misled by the cries of young boys
     I am again
a breathless swimmer in that cold green element.   40

{1955}

THE IMPROVED BINOCULARS

Below me the city was in flames:
the firemen were the first to save
themselves. I saw steeples fall on their knees.

I saw an agent kick the charred bodies
from an orphanage to one side, marking
the site carefully for a future speculation.

Lovers stopped short of the final spasm
and went off angrily in opposite directions,
their elbows held by giant escorts of fire.

Then the dignitaries rode across the bridges   10
under an auricle of light which delighted them,
noting for later punishment those that went before.

And the rest of the populace, their mouths
distorted by an unusual gladness, bawled thanks
to this comely and ravaging ally, asking

Only for more light with which to see
their neighbour's destruction.

All this I saw through my improved binoculars.

{1955}

THE BULL CALF

The thing could barely stand. Yet taken
from his mother and the barn smells

he still impressed with his pride,
with the promise of sovereignty in the way
his head moved to take us in.
The fierce sunlight tugging the maize from the ground
licked at his shapely flanks.
He was too young for all that pride.
I thought of the deposed Richard II.

"No money in bull calves," Freeman had said. 10
The visiting clergyman rubbed the nostrils
now snuffing pathetically at the windless day.
"A pity," he sighed.
My gaze slipped off his hat toward the empty sky
that circled over the black knot of men,
over us and the calf waiting for the first blow.

Struck,
the bull calf drew in his thin forelegs
as if gathering strength for a mad rush . . .
tottered . . . raised his darkening eyes to us, 20
and I saw we were at the far end
of his frightened look, growing smaller and smaller
till we were only the ponderous mallet
that flicked his bleeding ear
and pushed him over on his side, stiffly,
like a block of wood.

Below the hill's crest
the river snuffled on the improvised beach.
We dug a deep pit and threw the dead calf into it.
It made a wet sound, a sepulchral gurgle, 30
as the warm sides bulged and flattened.
Settled, the bull calf lay as if asleep,
one foreleg over the other,

bereft of pride and so beautiful now,
without movement, perfectly still in the cool pit.
I turned away and wept.

{1956}

BERRY PICKING

Silently my wife walks on the still wet furze
Now darkgreen the leaves are full of metaphors
Now lit up is each tiny lamp of blueberry.
The white nails of rain have dropped and the sun is free.

And whether she bends or straightens to each bush
To find the children's laughter among the leaves
Her quiet hands seem to make the quiet summer hush –
Berries or children, patient she is with these.

I only vex and perplex her; madness, rage
Are endearing perhaps put down upon the page;   10
Even silence daylong and sullen can then
Enamour as restraint or classic discipline.

So I envy the berries she puts in her mouth,
The red and spurting juice that stains her lips;
I shall never taste that good to her, nor will they
Displease her with a thousand barbarous jests.

How they lie easily for her hand to take,
Part of the unoffending world that is hers;
Here beyond complexity she stands and stares
And leans her marvellous head as if for answers.   20

No more the easy soul my childish craft deceives
Nor the simpler one for whom yes is always yes;
No, now her voice comes to me from a far way off
Though her lips are redder than the raspberries.

{1958}

CAIN

Taking the air rifle from my son's hand,
I measured back five paces, the Hebrew
In me, narcissist, father of children,
Laid to rest. From there I took aim and fired.
The silent ball hit the frog's back an inch
Below the head. He jumped at the surprise
Of it, suddenly tickled or startled
(He must have thought) and leaped from the wet sand
Into the surrounding brown water. But
The ball had done its mischief. His next spring   10
Was a miserable flop, the thrust all gone
Out of his legs. He tried – like Bruce – again,
Throwing out his sensitive pianist's
Hands as a dwarf might or a helpless child.
His splash disturbed the quiet pondwater
And one old frog behind his weedy moat
Blinking, looking self-complacently on.
The lin's surface at once became closing
Eyelids and bubbles like notes of music
Liquid, luminous, dropping from the page   20
White, white-bearded, a rapid crescendo
Of inaudible sounds and a crone's whispering
Backstage among the reeds and bulrushes
As for an expiring Lear or Oedipus.

But Death makes us all look ridiculous.
Consider this frog (dog, hog, what you will)
Sprawling, his absurd corpse rocked by the tides
That his last vain spring had set in movement.
Like a retired oldster, I couldn't help sneer,
Living off the last of his insurance: 30
Billows – now crumbling – the premiums paid.
Absurd, how absurd. I wanted to kill
At the mockery of it, kill and kill
Again – the self-infatuate frog, dog, hog,
Anything with the stir of life in it,
Seeing the dead leaper, Chaplin-footed,
Rocked and cradled in this afternoon
Of tranquil water, reeds, and blazing sun,
The hole in his back clearly visible
And the torn skin a blob of shadow   40
Moving when the quiet poolwater moved.
O Egypt, marbled Greece, resplendent Rome,
Did you also finally perish from a small bore
In your back you could not scratch? And would
Your mouths open ghostily, gasping out
Among the murky reeds, the hidden frogs,
We climb with crushed spines toward the heavens?

When the next morning I came the same way
The frog was on his back, one delicate
Hand on his belly, and his white shirt front   50
Spotless. He looked as if he might have been
A comic, tapdancer apologizing
For a fall, or an emcee, his wide grin
Coaxing a laugh from us for an aside
Or perhaps a joke we didn't quite hear.

{1958}

FOR MAO TSE-TUNG: A MEDITATION ON FLIES AND KINGS

So, circling about my head, a fly.
Haloes of frantic monotone.
Then a smudge of blood smoking
On my fingers, let Jesus and Buddha cry.

Is theirs the way? Forgiveness of hurt?
Leprosariums? Perhaps. But I
Am burning flesh and bone,
An indifferent creature between
Cloud and a stone;
Smash insects with my boot,   10
Feast on torn flowers, deride
The nonillion bushes by the road
(Their patience is very great).
Jivatma, they endure,
Endure and proliferate.

And the meek-browed and poor
In their solid tenements
(Etiolated, they do not dance).
Worry of priest and of commissar:
None may re-create them who are   20
Lowly and universal as the moss
Or like vegetation the winds toss
Sweeping to the open lake and sky.
I put down these words in blood
And would not be misunderstood:
They have their Christs and their legends
And out of their pocks and ailments
Weave dear enchantments –
Poet and dictator, you are as alien as I.

On this remote and classic lake   30
Only the lapsing of the water can I hear
And the cold wind through the sumac.
The moneyed and their sunburnt children
Swarm other shores. Here is ecstasy,
The sun's outline made lucid
By each lacustral cloud
And man naked with mystery.

They dance best who dance with desire,
Who lifting feet of fire from fire
Weave before they lie down   40
A red carpet for the sun.

I pity the meek in their religious cages
And flee them; and flee
The universal sodality
Of joy-haters, joy-destroyers
(O Schiller, wine-drunk and silly!),
The sufferers and their thick rages;
Enter this tragic forest where the trees
Uprear as if for the graves of men,
All function and desire to offend   50
With themselves finally done;
And mark the dark pines farther on,
The sun's fires touching them at will,
Motionless like silent khans
Mourning serene and terrible
Their Lord entombed in the blazing hill.

{1958}

WHATEVER ELSE POETRY IS FREEDOM

Whatever else poetry is freedom.
Forget the rhetoric, the trick of lying
All poets pick up sooner or later. From the river,
Rising like the thin voice of grey castratos – the mist;
Poplars and pines grow straight but oaks are gnarled;
Old codgers must speak of death, boys break windows,
Women lie honestly by their men at last.

And I who gave my Kate a blackened eye
Did to its vivid changing colours
Make up an incredible musical scale;   10
And now I balance on wooden stilts and dance
And thereby sing to the loftiest casements.
See how with polish I bow from the waist.
Space for these stilts! More space or I fail!

And a crown I say for my buffoon's head.
Yet no more fool am I than King Canute,
Lord of our tribe, who scanned and scorned;
Who half-deceived, believed; and, poet, missed
The first white waves come nuzzling at his feet;
Then damned the courtiers and the foolish trial   20
With a most bewildering and unkingly jest.

It was the mist. It lies inside one like a destiny.
A real Jonah it lies rotting like a lung.
And I know myself undone who am a clown
And wear a wreath of mist for a crown;
Mist with the scent of dead apples,
Mist swirling from black oily waters at evening,
Mist from the fraternal graves of cemeteries.

It shall drive me to beg my food and at last
Hurl me broken I know and prostrate on the road;   30
Like a huge toad I saw, entire but dead,
That Time mordantly had blacked; O pressed
To the moist earth it pled for entry.
I shall be I say that stiff toad for sick with mist
And crazed I smell the odour of mortality.

And Time flames like a paraffin stove
And what it burns are the minutes I live.
At certain middays I have watched the cars
Bring me from afar their windshield suns;
What lay to my hand were blue fenders,   40
The suns extinguished, the drivers wearing sunglasses.
And it made me think I had touched a hearse.

So whatever else poetry is freedom. Let
Far off the impatient cadences reveal
A padding for my breathless stilts. Swivel,
O hero, in the fleshy groves, skin and glycerine,
And sing of lust, the sun's accompanying shadow
Like a vampire's wing, the stillness in dead feet –
Your stave brings resurrection, O aggrievèd king.

{1958}

KEINE LAZAROVITCH: 1870–1959

When I saw my mother's head on the cold pillow,
Her white waterfalling hair in the cheeks' hollows,
I thought, quietly circling my grief, of how
She had loved God but cursed extravagantly his creatures.

For her final mouth was not water but a curse,
A small black hole, a black rent in the universe,
Which damned the green earth, stars and trees in its stillness
And the inescapable lousiness of growing old.

And I record she was comfortless, vituperative,
Ignorant, glad, and much else besides; I believe   10
She endlessly praised her black eyebrows, their thick weave,
Till plagiarizing Death leaned down and took them for his mould.

And spoiled a dignity I shall not again find,
And the fury of her stubborn limited mind:
Now none will shake her amber beads and call God blind,
Or wear them upon a breast so radiantly.

O fierce she was, mean and unaccommodating;
But I think now of the toss of her gold earrings,
Their proud carnal assertion, and her youngest sings
While all the rivers of her red veins move into the sea.   20

[1960] {1965}

BUTTERFLY ON ROCK

The large yellow wings, black-fringed,
were motionless

They say the soul of a dead person
will settle like that on the still face

But I thought: The rock has borne this;
this butterfly is the rock's grace,

its most obstinate and secret desire
to be a thing alive made manifest

Forgot were the two shattered porcupines
I had seen die in the bleak forest.   10
Pain is unreal; death, an illusion:
There is no death in all the land,
I heard my voice cry;
And brought my hand down on the butterfly
And felt the rock move beneath my hand.

{1963}

A TALL MAN EXECUTES A JIG

I

So the man spread his blanket on the field
And watched the shafts of light between the tufts
And felt the sun push the grass towards him;
The noise he heard was that of whizzing flies,
The whistlings of some small imprudent birds,
And the ambiguous rumbles of cars
That made him look up at the sky, aware
Of the gnats that tilted against the wind
And in the sunlight turned to jigging motes.
Fruitflies he'd call them except there was no fruit   10
About, spoiling to hatch these glitterings,
These nervous dots for which the mind supplied
The closing sentences from Thucydides,
Or from Euclid having a savage nightmare.

II

Jig jig, jig, jig. Like minuscule black links
Of a chain played with by some playful
Unapparent hand or the palpitant
Summer haze bored with the hour's stillness.
He felt the sting and tingle afterwards
Of those leaving their orthodox unrest,   20
Leaving the undulant excitation
To drop upon his sleeveless arm. The grass,
Even the wildflowers became black hairs
And himself a maddened speck among them.
Still the assaults of the small flies made him
Glad at last, until he saw purest joy
In their frantic jiggings under a hair,
So changed from those in the unrestraining air.

III

He stood up and felt himself enormous.
Felt as might Donatello over stone,   30
Or Plato, or as a man who has held
A loved and lovely woman in his arms
And feels his forehead touch the emptied sky
Where all antinomies flood into light.
Yet jig jig jig, the haloing black jots
Meshed with the wheeling fire of the sun:
Motion without meaning, disquietude
Without sense or purpose, ephemerides
That mottled the resting summer air till
Gusts swept them from his sight like wisps of smoke.   40
Yet they returned, bringing a bee, who, seeing
But a tall man, left him for a marigold.

IV

He doffed his aureole of gnats and moved
Out of the field as the sun sank down,
A dying god upon the blood-red hills.
Ambition, pride, the ecstasy of sex,
And all circumstance of delight and grief,
That blood upon the mountain's side, that flood
Washed into a clear incredible pool
Below the ruddied peaks that pierced the sun.   50
He stood still and waited. If ever
The hour of revelation was come
It was now, here on the transfigured steep.
The sky darkened. Some birds chirped. Nothing else.
He thought the dying god had gone to sleep:
An Indian fakir on his mat of nails.

V

And on the summit of the asphalt road
Which stretched towards the fiery town, the man
Saw one hill raised like a hairy arm, dark
With pines and cedars against the stricken sun   60
– The arm of Moses or of Joshua.
He dropped his head and let fall the halo
Of mountains, purpling and silent as time,
To see temptation coiled before his feet:
A violated grass-snake that lugged
Its intestine like a small red valise.
A cold-eyed skinflint it now was, and not
The manifest of that joyful wisdom,
The mirth and arrogant green flame of life;
Or earth's vivid tongue that flicked in praise of earth.   70

VI

And the man wept because pity was useless.
"Your jig's up; the flies come like kites," he said
And watched the grass-snake crawl towards the hedge,
Convulsing and dragging into the dark
The satchel filled with curses for the earth,
For the odours of warm sedge, and the sun,
A blood-red organ in the dying sky.
Backwards it fell into a grassy ditch
Exposing its underside, white as milk,
And mocked by wisps of hay between its jaws;   80
And then it stiffened to its final length.
But though it opened its thin mouth to scream
A last silent scream that shook the black sky,
Adamant and fierce, the tall man did not curse.

VII

Beside the rigid snake the man stretched out
In fellowship of death; he lay silent
And stiff in the heavy grass with eyes shut,
Inhaling the moist odours of the night
Through which his mind tunnelled with flicking tongue
Backwards to caves, mounds, and sunken ledges   90
And desolate cliffs where come only kites,
And where of perished badgers and raccoons
The claws alone remain, gripping the earth.
Meanwhile the green snake crept upon the sky,
Huge, his mailed coat glittering with stars that made
The night bright, and blowing thin wreaths of cloud
Athwart the moon; and as the weary man
Stood up, coiled above his head, transforming all.

{1963}

There Were No Signs

By walking I found out
Where I was going.

By intensely hating, how to love.
By loving, whom and what to love.

By grieving, how to laugh from the belly.

Out of infirmity, I have built strength.
Out of untruth, truth.
From hypocrisy, I wove directness.

Almost now I know who I am.
Almost I have the boldness to be that man.   10

Another step
And I shall be where I started from.

{1963}

Rhine Boat Trip

The castles on the Rhine
are all haunted
by the ghosts of Jewish mothers
looking for their ghostly children

And the clusters of grapes
in the sloping vineyards
are myriads of blinded eyes
staring at the blind sun

The tireless Lorelei
can never comb from their hair   10
the crimson beards
of murdered rabbis

However sweetly they sing
one hears only
the low wailing of cattle-cars
moving invisibly across the land

{1967}

FOR MY SONS, MAX AND DAVID

The wandering Jew: the suffering Jew
The despoiled Jew: the beaten Jew
The Jew to burn: the Jew to gas
The Jew to humiliate
The cultured Jew: the sensitized exile
     gentiles with literary ambitions aspire to be
The alienated Jew cultivating his alienation
     like a rare flower: no gentile garden is complete
     without one of these bleeding hibisci
The Jew who sends Christian and Moslem theologians   10
     back to their seminaries and mosques for new arguments
     on the nature of the Divine Mercy
The Jew, old and sagacious, whom all speak well of:
     when not lusting for his passionate, dark-eyed daughters
The Jew whose helplessness stirs the heart and conscience
     of the Christian like the beggars outside his churches
The Jew who can be justifiably murdered because he is rich
The Jew who can be justifiably murdered because he is poor
The Jew whose plight engenders profound self-searchings

in certain philosophical gentlemen who cherish him   20
to the degree he inspires their shattering aperçus
into the quality of modern civilization, their noble
and eloquent thoughts on scapegoatism and unmerited agony
The Jew who agitates the educated gentile, making him pace
    back and forth in his spacious well-aired library
The Jew who fills the authentic Christian with loathing for himself
    and his fellow Christians
The Jew no one can live with: he has seen too many conquerors
    come and vanish, the destruction of too many empires
The Jew in whose eyes can be read the doom of nations   30
    even when he averts them in compassion and disgust
The Jew every Christian hates, having shattered his self-esteem
    and planted the seeds of doubt in his soul
The Jew everyone seeks to destroy, having instilled self-division
    in the heathen

Be none of these, my sons
My sons, be none of these
Be gunners in the Israeli Air Force

{1968}

ROY DANIELLS

1902–1979

Born in London, England, Roy Daniells was raised in Victoria, B.C. He received a B.A. from the University of British Columbia in 1930 and took M.A. and Ph.D. degrees at the University of Toronto. He was Head of the English department at the University of Manitoba from 1937–46; in 1948 he returned to the University of British Columbia as Head of its English department. In that post he was instrumental in establishing now world-renowned creative writing courses and programmes, though he was often at odds with Earle Birney, who received much of the credit, on the shared dossier. He promoted research and teaching in Canadian literature at U.B.C. and elsewhere and helped to found the discipline's flagship journal, *Canadian Literature,* under the editorship of George Woodcock. Although his respected scholarship focussed on English poets John Milton and Thomas Traherne, he was among the editors of the *Literary History of Canada* and contributed notable entries on the Confederation poets. His first volume of poems, *Deeper into the Forest,* appeared in 1948; his second collection would not appear until 1963. Thereafter he published little poetry, though he continued to write it privately for the rest of his life. He was awarded the Lorne Pierce Medal for contributions to Canadian literature by the Royal Society of Canada in 1970.

Epithalamion in Time of Peace

Like pus, the dead corpuscular defenders,
They flow from wounds in cities and committees
Pallid and spent (O these defeats embitter);
Or like an auger seized upon and centered

They sink in earth, grating on startled stone;
Or like a bit thrust against muscular steel
Their cutting spiral, through the sinews squealing,
Twists in pain with the distempering strain;

Or they are oil, crowded by bullying rings:
In the smoking cylinder their bodies thin   10
Decomposing; blackened, drained out then
They have played their part; they have accomplished things.

II

The radio leaned far out the window-sill
Vomiting over the pavement; but the trees
Kept their majestic message, holding their leaves
High and still. I waited quiet until

At the meridian hour the green tree spoke;
There, in viridian shade of the cedar's cape,
The plumed helm showing on the dark sky's cope,
I heard the cedars through the darkness speak.   20

I heard the cedars speak as friend to friend,
Bending easily one to hear another,
Brother with brother, who have long lived together;
Only to life have the cedars learned to attend.

III

Now must the quick brown fox jump high as a typewriter;
Now must Reynard run pell-mell for cover;
New speeds his heart and lungs must now deliver
Faster than cry of sound or speed of light.

His mask adorns the doors of courtly stables
Or it is hammered to the beams of barns   30
In remote farms; now must he double and turn
Fast as Cain and twice as fast as Abel.

They are shooting foxes and the fox must fly
Higher than Plato's dream or Paul's epistle,
Swifter than a rocket or a guided missile
On the great circle of the cruel sky.

IV

While fearful Jove holds up the thunderbolt
Under this lowering curtain, this leaning wall
Silent with the portent of appalling fall
Suspended – now, now let us hold   40

Our nuptials; Hymen with flame of gold
And saffron robe waits; radio augurs tell
Of woes; below on sands there moves the swell
Of restless Neptune and his waters cold.

Hearken! you may hear the approaching roar
Oncoming up edges drear and naked stones;
Soon shall the blast leap, lifting long-buried bones;
Soon the vast tidal wave dismiss the shore.

O come with us into the farthest woods,
Unpretending and all unoffending,   50
For we have neither defenders nor defence
Nor are endowed with any wordly goods.

All pale, all blackened, O my wearied friends,
Only the trees can speak you back to peace,
Only the flying fox whose speeds increase
Can make life viable, can make amends.

Rest on this rock, then over the vast knife-
Edge of the cliff climb; down the utmost slope;
Escape into our refuge of green hope,
The forest wild, the fortress heart of life.   60

{1948}

Unsearchable Dispose

We who have been betrayed shall come again
Returning to our place of birth
(As the unhurrying, slow-recurving star
Of our nativity): long since forgotten,
With brows contracted, faces plowed with pain,
And inextinguishable eyes.

We who have been betrayed, sold to the galleys,
Shipped to plantations, pressed into the fleet,
Sent to the salt mines, shall yet return,
Shapes at evening walking in the lane,   10
Midnight shadows by the corner standing,
Morning figures on the sunbright hillside,

Leaping hedges, vaulting over gates,
And silently appearing in the doorway,
At the window showing, head behind steady head,
Necks grown firmer with toil and strong-set shoulders.

We who have been betrayed shall come to the trial
Trooping through market, gathering in the square,
Standing apart on steps like an ancient chorus,
Holding aloof, not bearing evidence,   20
Eddying beside this current of conflagration,
This wrath of God.

We shall return, climbing upon the gateway,
To watch the gallows, guillotine, four horses
Ready for drawing, rack, wheel, maskèd face.
With complacence shall we sit regarding
There being no pain with which we are unacquainted,
Having died the first death and the second death
And bearing death our portion.

Not of our own will do we thus return   30
But drawn like driftwood through the flooding straits,
Tossed by the waves with apparent aimlessness,
Pressing ever onward to the whirlpool
And circling slowly its devouring centre.

We who have been betrayed shall come again
Like bread on waters, bastards, younger brothers,
Like good intentions flung in the unconscious,
Like sailors beaten, sold by a great admiral,
After lost battle with fresh flags at masthead,
Soft and terrible, not to be resisted,   40
Into the roadstead moving quietly.

{1948}

DOUGLAS LEPAN
1914–1998

Douglas LePan was a distinguished poet, professor and university administrator, civil servant and diplomat, and double winner of the Governor General's Award. He was born in Toronto and educated at the University of Toronto and at Oxford. He taught at Harvard University from 1938 to 1941. From 1941 to 1943 he worked in London, England, on army education, and from 1943 to the war's end he was an artillery gunner in Italy. After the war he took an M.A. from Oxford (1948) and entered the diplomatic service in London. During this time LePan met novelist Elizabeth Bowen, who gave his poetry manuscript to Cecil Day Lewis; with their support it was published as *The Wounded Prince* in 1948. He left the Department of External Affairs as Under-Secretary of State in 1959. *The Net and the Sword* won the Governor General's Award for 1953; a novel, *The Deserter,* won in 1964. From 1959 to 1964 he was Professor of English at Queen's University, Kingston; in 1964 he was made Principal of University College, University of Toronto. He retired as Senior Fellow of Massey College and University Professor in 1980. He published a memoir, *Bright Glass of Memory,* in 1979. His collected poems, *Weathering It: Complete Poems, 1948-1987,* were published in 1987.

ANGELS AND ARTIFICERS

When the skies close,
When light has the eerie colour of a bruise,

When the heavy light tastes leaden on the tongue;
And the brave, deserted by all heavenly healers,
Are dying slowly into desperation;
When the shrunk light stiffens, mortifies —
Eclipse, crows call, quacks swarm along the streets —
In the yawning hour of funeral,
In plague

Still to remember the patience of the fiery artificers,   10
Who morning after morning from their own lips blew the reluctant
    flames;
Who, asking nothing of the bright seraphim,
Through the murkiest days shaped their gold images,
Fashioned them trophies, tripods, cups, libation bowls,
And trusted they would reappear; who failed often
But, always imagining some perfect icon, calm, reserved,
To resurrect the light, achieved it sometimes;
Who, believing in luck, were not embittered.
They looked up. But the nihilist heavens did not appal them.
They went about their work, making the metal ductile,   20
Hammering it into curious shapes, annealing, burnishing,
Intent about the smithy, blowing it to the pitch
Of their quick zeal. Their breath was ardent, flickering,
A Pentecost that played about the senseless mass
And conquered it. But like a lover. And would not rest.

Until one lucky morning, casually looking up.
No longer the hiatus;
The heavenly company!
Wing-tip to wing-tip, again in kind surveillance
To come at the call of the beaten, the oppressed,   30
Healers, to breathe into the sick an irrational hope.
The death-cloth plucked from the face of the dead day,
A miracle!

Flowers springing up in place of spotted leprosy,
Warmth glancing, pouring on the ulcered earth,
Joy coming out in every leaf and bough.
And there
Where mists unravelling reveal the mountain,
The sacred mountain where the vision flows,
The source, the head, the dayspring manifest,   40
Intelligence-and-Power, the lost archangel.

{1948}

A Country Without a Mythology

No monuments or landmarks guide the stranger
Going among this savage people, masks
Taciturn or babbling out an alien jargon
And moody as barbaric skies are moody.

Berries must be his food. Hurriedly
He shakes the bushes, plucks pickerel from the river,
Forgetting every grace and ceremony,
Feeds like an Indian, and is on his way.

And yet, for all his haste, time is worth nothing.
The abbey clock, the dial in the garden,   10
Fade like saint's days and festivals.
Months, years, are here unbroken virgin forests.

There is no law — even no atmosphere
To smooth the anger of the flagrant sun.
November skies sting, sting like icicles.
The land is open to all violent weathers.

Passion is not more quick. Lightnings in August
Stagger, rocks split, tongues in the forest hiss,
As fire drinks up the lovely sea-dream coolness.
This is the land the passionate man must travel.   20

Sometimes – perhaps at the tentative fall of twilight –
A belief will settle that waiting around the bend
Are sanctities of childhood, that melting birds
Will sing him into a limpid gracious Presence.

The hills will fall in folds, the wilderness
Will be a garment innocent and lustrous
To wear upon a birthday, under a light
That curls and smiles, a golden-haired Archangel.

And now the channel opens. But nothing alters.
Mile after mile of tangled struggling roots,   30
Wild-rice, stumps, weeds, that clutch at the canoe,
Wild birds hysterical in tangled trees.

And not a sign, no emblem in the sky
Or boughs to friend him as he goes; for who
Will stop where, clumsily constructed, daubed
With war-paint, teeters some lust-red manitou?

{1948}

THE WOUNDED PRINCE

In the eye is the wound.

Lancings of pity, blades of sensual disappointment
Have pierced the delicate pupil.

Transfixed, the bird of heavenly airs
Is struck at sundown,
Entering the leafy wood, under the heavy lintel.

Gathered in that point all sharp humiliations;
The strokes converge.
The feathered dreams fly home from fruitless voyages.
Light needles.   10
Still to and fro they hawk their costliest plumage.

In your dear eye . . .

The dark scar sings from the wanton thicket
Its princely grief;
Sets up in perilous leaves the crest of bravery;
Impaled, sings on;
Will not disown its fettering crest and crown;

So that what never could be dreamt of has been made.
From target's puny eye
Such liquid compass of this wide, aerial gaze;   20
From wounds, from wounds
By love inflicted, this strict and healing blade.

{1948}

MEDITATION AFTER AN ENGAGEMENT

Lack-lustre now the landscape, too long acquainted
With death and wounds. Only the orchard where
Persimmons smoulder in the darkening air,
Like cressets guttering to an orange glow,
Preserves the landscape the old masters painted;

A glimmer in green leaves and glossy bark,
A radiance rescued from the pouring dark,
A fragment of the glister of Uccello.

Through that green secrecy my limbs would drown
Drifting enfranchised down a still bay, preened   10
By art, a peacock lustre damascened
With meandering dreams and pleasures, where unconstrued
Would waters hide me with their amaranth crown.
Even the fishermen who fish night-long
With flares would never net my rapturous song,
Leafy with marvels like a romantic wood.

Pleasure? A romantic wood? The other trees
Have felt the venom of a senseless flail
And on the threshing-floor are dying, pale
As wounded men on whom the darkness hardens.   20
The farm is pock-marked with a strange disease.
The craters suppurate an acid sea
That, spreading, blots out old calligraphy.
A peasant points and says, "These all were gardens."

No. I cannot from a few leaves twist
A sheltering chaplet even of despair,
When trees and fields for miles around are bare.
If there is any comfort, then I must find
It in the open where the dead insist
How cold the earth has turned. This lingering swoon   30
Of colour is ambushed fatally, and soon
The fruit will fall like kings in a rebel wind.

O entropy that has involved our hearts!
A mother kindles withered twigs beneath
A pot and lets them die for lack of breath.

The farmer risks the dull, gun-metalled sky
And, slouching barefoot through the shell holes, starts
To shave more fodder from the dripping straw-stack,
Forgets his purpose and comes empty-handed back.
The age is guttering to senility.   40

But she (the woman who is my wisdom) writes
That every age has been faint-hearted, redeemed
By daring horsemen, whose gold stirrups gleamed
On the flanks of the lathered time, past the dark croup
Spattering brightness; and their extreme delights –
Turmoil, difficulty and a distant quarry –
Were frescoed as the background of their glory.
And I believe her – but hear no huntsmen up.

The soldiers, huddled in the night's neglect,
Know only that the weather here has broken,   50
Deep in their bones the coming snow has spoken
Death. With lonely men in the moon's eye
I stare at ruts and puddles that reflect
Clay-tarnished splendour and, in the doom of words,
Nail to my shuttered heart with pitted swords
The weather, exile and man's agony.

{1953}

GEORGE WHALLEY

1915–1983

Best known as critic and editor of the writings of Samuel Taylor Coleridge, popular biographer of Arctic adventurer John Hornby, and head of the Department of English at Queen's University, George Whalley left a rare body of wartime poetry from his service in the Royal Canadian Navy and in the intelligence service of the Royal Navy (1940–45). He rose to the rank of lieutenant-commander and was decorated for saving lives during naval action. He was born in Kingston, Ontario. He took B.A. and M.A. degrees from both Bishop's College in Sherbrooke, Quebec, and from Oxford University, which he attended as a Rhodes Scholar. After the war he taught briefly at Bishop's before taking up a professorship at Queen's in 1948, where he would serve twice as Head of the department. He was awarded the Ph.D. degree from King's College, London, in 1950. His two post-war volumes, *Poems: 1939-44* (1946) and *No Man an Island* (1948), contain almost all of his work; he wrote little new poetry after their appearance. In 1955 he organized the paradigm-shifting Canadian Writers Conference at Queen's and later edited the conference's proceedings as *Writing in Canada* (1956). His *Collected Poems* were edited by George Johnston in 1986.

DIEPPE

Ebbed now the cold fear
that turns the will to water,

fear of waiting ebbed,
and fierce joy of assault,
and killing; the fine defiance,
the shout on the lips, the zip-
whine of bullets and shells;
the leading, the delight
of high endeavour certain
of quick victory.   10
Nothing was clear then
but sharp feelings of fear
and joy; and they are seared
so deeply into the soul
that any could see them, even
now that they have ebbed.

The dull smack, dull
thud, dull dark
dropping down under wounds.
And now he sits in a cobbled   20
square above the seawall;
head in hands, alone,
shaken, cold, utterly
desolate: the ships
gone, the friends ebbed
homeward. Was it ever
fun to be young, to attack
(face blackened), to lead,
to kill? All ebbed out
to the cold trembling dread   30
of a small boy climbing
a dark stair.

        The tide,
turned from ebb, is flooding,

washing about the tracks
and turrets of the tanks
that never cleared the shingle:
burned out, broken, awry;
startled, questioning yet,
as somehow the living no longer   40
have power or desire to question.

{1948}

NORMANDY 1944

Forget about what's on the beaches. Tide,
wind and the blind muffling drift of sand
will care for that. Deeper inland, here
where the apples taste only the rumours of gales,
the wounds are subtler. One obliterating
sweep of a bulldozer crushes for all time
a sunken lane which never knew harsher uses
than murmur of lovers in mothlight. What do we care
for the splintered stillness of a Norman tower,
soiled (had it not been destroyed) by iron-shod   10
boots and spotter's glasses and the predatory
snap of a sniper's rifle? What to us
is the gnarled and immemorial apple orchard
under whose trees we heap up ammunition,
dig fox-holes and write V-letters home?
The tanks have made destructive harvesting
of fields patiently waiting for the scythe.
The bearded pale gold wheat and the poppies know
the sudden limp impersonality
of violent death. In Bayeux, while the guns   20
thunder round Caen preparing the final assault,

the houses, as though bemused, stare with blind
eyes at the tanks clattering over the cobbles
and the crowning impertinent insult of the jeeps.
And there's no wandering with a market basket,
no passing the time with gossip at a corner.
The silent villagers' eyes are dull, bewildered
with wondering how the refugees are faring.

Whether we do it or the enemy,
this second death in no wise rights the first.   30
Perhaps we need this blindness, need this hangman's
smiling complacency, because we know
the Army of Liberation strips the country girl
and, laughing, sets her to walk her native streets
naked and humbled in the lewd eye of the world.

{1948}

FROM *BATTLE PATTERN*

Finale

There is not elegy enough in all
the winds and waves of the world to sing the ships,
to sing the seamen to their rest, down
through the slow shimmering drift of crepuscule,
sinking through emerald green, through opal dimness
to darkness. Not all laving of all the world's
oceans, loving moonwash of warm
tropic seas can ever heal the hearts
smashed to fragments of desolated darkness.
Sink now, life ended, down through the haunts   10
of trumpetfish and shark and spermwhale, down

to the still siltless floor of the ocean where
no light sifts or spills through the liquid driftings
of darkness, where no eye sees the delicate
dark-wrought flowers that open to no moon.

With you is scattered what treasure to puzzle the eager
submarine historian when the sea
gives up her dead: the hammered, turned, polished,
riveted sleekness and sweet beauty of gun,
plate, turbine, screw, shell, torpedo,   20
anchor-fluke and studded cable (symbol of
what hope, what faith?), instruments
of electronic daintiness blind
inert unfunctional in ignorance;
perplexing fragments of ingenious skill
that bear no trace of their powerlessness to shield
the germ of life against the sudden steel,
the slow drowsy agony of drowning.

No pity or memory ever ruffled the iron
implacable will of ocean. Yet in its throat   30
is merciful secrecy, when hope is gone.
When life is a wafer dissolved on the lips of the sea
the desolation of waiting hearts may heal
in ignorance of the haunting dread of fear,
the numb hunger, and terror — dull tensions
that never uncoiled in the cool crystals of words.
In the vast silence of the tideless sea-floor,
fathoms deep, in the birthless womb of ocean,
let the jagged steel, and broken pitiful
beauty born of the smooth loins of women   40
sleep where the diatom and the coral sleep.

{1948}

JAMES REANEY
1926–2008

Poet and dramatist James Reaney was born on a farm near Stratford, Ontario. He took B.A. and M.A. degrees at the University of Toronto. At the age of twenty-three he won the Governor General's Award for his first collection of poetry, *The Red Heart* (1949). In the same year he left Toronto to teach English at the University of Manitoba. After doctoral studies at the University of Toronto he took up a permanent position at the University of Western Ontario in 1960. In 1958 he published *A Suit of Nettles,* which adapts the eclogues of Edmund Spenser's *The Shepherd's Calendar* to the voices and rivalries of a flock of emblematic geese on a Canadian farm; it won his second Governor General's Award. In 1960 he began the little magazine *Alphabet.* In its nineteen issues Reaney welcomed some of the most experimental poets of the 1960s and helped to push Canadian writing to the interface with visual art. Reaney had begun to write plays in the late 1950s; the first produced was *The Killdeer* (1960). In 1962 *The Killdeer and Other Plays* won Reaney his third Governor General's Award, which was simultaneously awarded to his volume of poems *Twelve Letters to a Small Town.* In the course of the 1960s Reaney concentrated increasingly on play-writing and pioneered new forms of theatre workshopping and communal theatre. His best-known plays are those of the trilogy *The Donnellys,* which enjoyed a hugely successful production in Toronto from 1973 to 1975. They were published in one volume in 2000 and again in 2008. Reaney's *Poems* were collected in 1972.

Antichrist as a Child

When Antichrist was a child
He caught himself tracing
The capital letter A
On a window sill
And wondered why
Because his name contained no A.
And as he crookedly stood
In his mother's flower-garden
He wondered why she looked so sadly
Out of an upstairs window at him.   10
He wondered why his father stared so
Whenever he saw his little son
Walking in his soot-coloured suit.
He wondered why the flowers
And even the ugliest weeds
Avoided his fingers and his touch.
And when his shoes began to hurt
Because his feet were becoming hooves
He did not let on to anyone
For fear they would shoot him for a monster.   20
He wondered why he more and more
Dreamed of eclipses of the sun,
Of sunsets, ruined towns and zeppelins,
And especially inverted, upside down churches.

{1949}

The Plum Tree

The plums are like blue pendulums
That thrum the gold-wired winds of summer.

In the opium-still noon they hang or fall,
The plump, ripe plums.
I suppose my little sister died
Dreaming of looking up at them,
Of lying beneath that crooked plum tree,
That green heaven with blue stars pied.
In this lonely haunted farmhouse
All things are voiceless save the sound   10
Of some plums falling through the summer air
Straight to the ground.
And there is no listener, no hearer
For the small thunders of their falling
(Falling as dead stars rush to a winter sea)
Save a child who, lolling
Among the trunks and old featherticks
That fill the room where he was born,
Hears them in his silent dreaming
On a dark engraving to a fairy-tale forlorn.   20
Only he hears their intermittent soft tattoo
Upon the dry, brown summer ground
At the edge of the old orchard.
Only he hears, and farther away,
Some happy animal's slow, listless moo.

{1949}

THE WINDYARD

I built a windyard for the wind;
  The wind like a wild vast dog came up
To play with weathervanes and corners
  My keyholes and my chinks.

And for the sea I built a well;
   The brookish tomcat gurgled in,
Waterfell and sprung about
   Hunting throats and boots.

I stood a house up for the earth;
   The mappy girl came in   10
With rut and footstep path
   That wind the traveller up.

A stove I hammered for the sun;
   In flew the golden oriole
To crackle sticks of time
   And sing the loaves of space.

Come girl well yard and stove,
   Come Flesh Heart Mind and Lyre,
Come Earth Water Wind and Fire.
      Well, when they came   20
Barking, meowing, talking and caroling,
I stepped above both house and yard
      Into myself.

[1956] {1972}

APRIL

ARGUMENT
With Duncan as judge the geese hold a bardic contest in honour of Spring.

Duncan   Raymond   Valancy

Here is a kernel of the hardest winter wheat
Found in the yard delicious for to eat.

It I will give to that most poetic gander
Who this season sings as well as swam Leander.
The white geese with their orange feet on the green
Grass that grew round the pond's glassy sheen
Chose then Valancy and Raymond to sing
And to hear them gathered about in a ring.

Raymond
I speak I speak of the arable earth,
Black sow goddess huge with birth;   10
Cry cry killdeers in her fields.

Black ogress ate her glacier lover
When the sun killed him for her;
The white owl to the dark crow yields.

Caw caw whir whir bark bark
We're fresh out of Noah's Ark;
Wild geese come in arrowheads

Shot from birds dead long ago
Buried in your negro snow;
Long water down the river sleds.   20

Black begum of a thousand dugs,
A nation at each fountain tugs;
The forests plug their gaps with leaves.

Whet whet scrape and sharpen
Hoes and rakes and plows of iron;
The farmer sows his sheaves.

Mr. Sword or Mr Plow
Can settle in your haymow,
All is the same to Mother Ground.

Great goddess I from you have come,
Killdeer crow geese ditch leaf plowman
From you have come, to you return
In endless laughing weeping round.

Valancy
Your limbs are the rivers of Eden.
From the dead we see you return and arise,
Fair girl, lost daughter:
The swallows stream through the skies,
Down dipping water,
Skimming ground, and from chimney's foul dusk
Their cousins the swifts tumble up as the tusk
Of roar day
In bright May
Scatters them gliding from darkness to sun-cusp.

Your face unlocks the bear from his den.
The world has come into the arms of the sun.
What now sulky earth?
All winter you lay with your face like a nun,
But now bring forth
From river up boxdrain underground
Fish crawling up that dark street without sound
To spawn
In our pond
Young suckers and sunfish within its deep round.

Your body is a bethlehem.
Come near the sun that ripened you from earth
Pushing south winds
Through lands without belief till this pretty birth
The faithful finds:
Fanatic doves, believing wrens and orioles

Devoted redwinged blackbirds with their calls,   60
Archilochus alexandri,
Melospiza georgiana,
All surround you with arched cries of Love's triumphals.

Your mind is a nest of all young things, all children
Come to this meadow forest edge;
Put her together
From this squirrel corn dogtooth young sedge
And all this weather
Of the white bloodroots to be her skin
The wake robin to be her shin   70
Her thighs pockets
Of white violets
Her breasts the gleaming soft pearly everlasting.

For her limbs are the rivers of Eden;
Her face unlocks
The brown merry bear from his den,
From his box
The butterfly and her body is a bethlehem
Humming
With cherubim   80
And her mind is a cloud of all young things, all children.

The prize to this one goes cried eagerly some
And others cried that to Raymond it must come,
So that Duncan Goose turned to the plantain leaf
And chopped the prize in half with beak-thrust brief.

{1958}

GIFTS

Existence gives to me
What does he give to thee?

He gives to me :   a pebble
He gives to me :   a dewdrop
He gives to me :   a piece of string
He gives to me :   a straw

Pebble   dewdrop   piece of string   straw

The pebble is a huge dark hill I must climb
The dewdrop's a great storm lake you must cross
The string was a road he could not find   10
The straw will be a sign whose meaning they forget

Hill   lake   road   sign

What was it that quite changed the scene
So desert fades into meadows green?

The answer is that they met a Tiger
The answer is that he met a Balloon,
A Prostitute of Snow, a Gorgeous Salesman
As well as a company of others such as
Sly Tod, Reverend Jones, Kitty Cradle and so on

Who was the Tiger?   Christ   20
Who was the Balloon?   Buddha
Emily Brontë and the Emperor Solomon
Who sang of his foot in the doorway.
All these met him. They were hopeful and faithful.

Now the mountain becomes   a pebble in my hand
The lake calms down   to a dewdrop in a flower
The weary road   is a string around your wrist
The mysterious sign   is a straw that whistles "Home"

Pebble   dewdrop   piece of string   straw

[1965] {1972}

ELIZABETH BREWSTER

B.1922

Elizabeth Brewster was born in Chipman, New Brunswick. During B.A. studies at the University of New Brunswick, she was influenced by A.G. Bailey and helped to found *The Fiddlehead* in 1945. After a Master's degree at Radcliffe College and brief studies in London she received a degree in library science from the University of Toronto (1953); in 1962 she completed her doctoral dissertation on the poetry of George Crabbe at the University of Indiana. She worked in many different parts of the country, as a librarian, university instructor, and teacher of creative writing. From 1972 until her retirement in 1990 she was a member of the English department at the University of Saskatchewan. She began to publish in the 1940s; her first volume was *East Coast* (1951). *Lillooett*, a collection of vignettes and portraits from the small British Columbia town, appeared in 1954, and *Roads and Other Poems* in 1957. She has published fifteen books of poetry. Her *Selected Poems* appeared in 1985, in two volumes. *The Collected Poems of Elizabeth Brewster* was published in 2003 by Oberon Press. She has also published short stories and two novels. Her most recent collection, *Jacob's Dream*, appeared in 2002. She lives in Victoria, British Columbia.

IN THE LIBRARY

Believe me, I say to the gentleman with the pince-nez,
Framed forever with one hand in his pocket,
With passion, with intensity I say it —

Believe me, oh believe me, you are not I.
Making my chair squeak on the chilly floor,
Catching up my pencil, I say —
But of course I am myself.

And all the while time flows, time flows, time flows;
The minutes ripple over the varnished tables.
This is June, I say, not yesterday or tomorrow.   10
This is I, not Byron or Vanessa. I am not in the moon.
I must differentiate my body from all other bodies,
Realizing the mole on my neck, the scar on my hand.
I must wind my watch, say it is ten o'clock.
But I know I am not convinced, feel uneasily the lie.
Because actually I am Byron, I am Vanessa,
I am the pictured man with the frigid smile.

I am the girl at the next table, raising vague eyes,
Flicking the ash from her cigarette, the thoughts from her mind.
The elastic moment stretches to infinity,   20
The elastic moment, the elastic point of space.
The blessed sun becomes the blessed moon.

{1951}

IF I COULD WALK OUT INTO THE COLD COUNTRY

If I could walk out into the cold country
And see the white and innocent dawn arise:
The mist stealing away, leaving the low hills
Bathed in pale light; the pink, unreal sun;
The jagged trees stabbing the cold, bright sky;
If I could walk over stubble fields white with frost
And see each separate small beaded blade

Loaded and edged with white; or climb the fence
Of grey and twisted wood, to find and eat
The crab-apples in the pasture, sharp with frost;   10
If I could shelter, shivering in a clump of woods
To watch the chill and beautiful day go past;
Perhaps I might find again my lost childhood,
A ghost blowing with the November wind,
Or buried in the wood, like those dead pioneers
Whose tumbled tombstones I found overgrown with brambles,
Their names erased, in an unfrequented way.

[1957] {1962}

RETURN OF THE NATIVE

This is the true land of fairy-tales,
this countryside of sullen beauty
heavy beneath dark trees. The brown smell of wood
lingers about it. Sawdust penetrates
every corner. You smell it, mixed with manure,
in the restaurant with its moosehead, or, like dim must,
in the little movie house.

The short street swims in dust and sunshine, slides
into a country road, and crosses the bridge
across the log-filled river where men walk,   10
balancing on the logs, and a single rowboat
holds a group of boys, their dark, round heads
bent close together. Sunshine, wind and water
carry together the floating smell of boards.

Across the bridge is pasture; later, woods.
This is a land

not settled yet by its generations of settlers.
Wildness still lingers, and the unfriendly trees
suffer, but do not shelter, man, their neighbour.
No Eden this, with parks and friendly beasts,   20
though hopeful settlers, not far distant, called
their country Canaan, New Jerusalem,
or even Beulah. Yet beauty here is solemn,
with the freshness of some strange and morning world.

At the last house on the edge of the woods, two children
sit on their swings, reading aloud to each other
a fairy tale of children in a wood.
Their mother, hanging up her Monday wash,
stops for a minute and watches flying over
the shining crows flapping their heavy wings.   30

[*of the Fifties* – *E.B.*] {1985}

GEORGE JOHNSTON

1913–2004

Gearge Johnston was born in Hamilton, Ontario, and grew up in Toronto. In 1932 he entered Victoria College at the University of Toronto, where he studied under E.J. Pratt and Pelham Edgar. He spent much of the late 1930s as a freelance writer in London, England, and travelling in Europe. From 1939 to 1944 he served as a reconnaissance pilot in the Royal Canadian Air Force. After the war he returned to the University of Toronto; his Master's thesis was supervised by Northrop Frye. After beginning a doctoral degree he took up an assistant professorship at Mount Allison University in Sackville, New Brunswick, in 1947 and began to publish poems in Canadian literary periodicals. In 1950 he moved to Ottawa to take up a position at Carleton College. His best-known book of poems, *The Cruising Auk,* was published in 1959. He was an eminent translator of Norse saga; of these the best-known is *The Saga of Gisli* (1963). Later collections of his own poetry include *Home Free* (1966) and *Ask Again* (1984). Robyn Sarah edited *The Essential George Johnston* for Porcupine's Quill in 2007.

WAR ON THE PERIPHERY

Around the battlements go by
Soldier men against the sky,
Violent lovers, husbands, sons,
Guarding my peaceful life with guns.

My pleasures, how discreet they are!
A little booze, a little car,
Two little children and a wife
Living a small suburban life.

My little children eat my heart;
At seven o'clock we kiss and part,
At seven o'clock we meet again;
They eat my heart and grow to men.

I watch their tenderness with fear
While on the battlements I hear
The violent, obedient ones
Guarding my family with guns.

[1951] {1959}

POOR EDWARD

Whose hat is moving on the water's face
Making towards the sea a doubtful pace?
Poor Edward's, I'm disconsolate to say,
He owed me twenty dollars, by the way.
I look along the darkening bank and wonder
How Edward and his wisdom came asunder.

The air grows cool, the crowd has partly gone;
The lights begin to fidget off and on;
The boats kechunk and creak as to and fro
And up and down and through the bridge they go
Fishing, fishing where the water's deep
For Edward and his trouble, sound asleep.

{1959}

Queens and Duchesses

Miss Belaney's pleasure is vast,
    Indeed it fills the night;
She doesn't remember who kissed her last
    But he did it good, all right.

She doesn't remember who broke her flowers
    When her fastenings came undone;
Her lipstick hasn't been straight for hours,
    She's had a night of fun.

Around her head is a haze of gold,
    Pleasure shines in her dress   10
Illuminating its every fold,
    Blessing each drunken tress.

Queens, queens, a little bit lighter
    They go, than we of the town;
And jewelled duchesses, grander and brighter
    When they step down, step down.

Queens, queens, they smile and go,
    Their loves and deaths are sad;
Duchesses now and again stoop low;
    Miss Belaney is bad.   20

{1959}

Time in a Public Ward

As life goes on to worse and worse
The bed beside me calls the nurse

And says, It's getting worse, I guess.
She makes the worse a little less
By needle. Soon along the wall
Another bed puts in a call.

After pills the lights go down;
The walls turn grey and pink and brown.
Time passes. All at once a jet
Of orange lights a cigarette   10
Within whose glow a caverned eye
Watches the cinder burn and die.

The walls go back to grey and pink
And brown again. One hears a sink
And low voices, rustling feet;
There's music somewhere, late and sweet.
Clocks in the town put by the night
Hour by hour, ticked and right.

{1959}

GOODRIDGE MACDONALD
1897–1967

The nephew of Confederation-period poet Charles G.D. Roberts, Goodridge MacDonald was born in Fredericton, New Brunswick, and attended school there and in Nelson, British Columbia. He began a career in civil service but resigned his position in 1916 in order to enlist in the Army Medical Corps, from which he was honourably discharged for medical reasons. He published a chapbook, *Armageddon, and Other Poems,* in 1917. Thereafter he lived as a free-lance writer and journalist; by 1925 he was working for the *Montreal Herald* and rose to become its associate editor. He published infrequently in Canadian literary periodicals, including a 1925 appearance in A.J.M. Smith's *McGill Fortnightly Review,* until *The Dying General* appeared as a Ryerson Poetry Chapbook in 1946. In four subsequent volumes, MacDonald commanded a terse, wry modernist style as current and pungent as that of any of the younger poets of the post-war period. Although R.G. Everson published his *Selected Poems* three years after his death, MacDonald's work, perhaps because it bridged literary generations as well as Aesthetic and modernist period styles, has largely been ignored.

EQUESTRIANS IN THE SPRING NIGHT

Horse and girl are one in flowing line:
Their lengthening shadow on the diminishing snow
Is a dark wave — a blue wind blowing.

Up the roadway ripple the other equestrians:
Throaty shout from a grey jacket;
From blonde crop uncovered, brief laughter,
Even the harshness of which is woven
Into the pattern of movement and horses,
And horsemen, above the diminishing snow.

From the snow in foreground flows   10
Unevenly, the sodden turf of spring.
The mountain is a background somnolence,
Its convention compromised only where the Cross
Glares unslumbering through unleafed branches.

In distant flurry of hoof-beats, men and girls,
Shaped to the horses, drift
Into the spring night, and diminishing snow,
Shadowless, gives back a mixture of street light
        and sky light.

[1951] {1955}

The Mocking

IN MEMORIAM, E.N.

On a March morning,
Poplars made grey smudge at street end;
Soiled cloud sheeted sky,
And each step woke
Idiot crackle of ice.

Then a cold knife was turned in the side;
The knife of the knowledge of death
(Yet blood did not flow.)
I knew that at Vence,
France, a friend had died.   10

The hand was stilled,
The eye, lidded; their indentures
To beauty, terminated.
Corruption closeted in a casket
Cancelled the artist's skill.

– All, then, all metaphors,
All epigrams;
Pleas, panegyrics and denunciations,
Addressed to the queller of breath, became meaningless,
In the sound of the closing of doors.   20

Then were Paul and Millay put to mock;
Donne and Stevens – all the bright expositors:
Mocked by the cold knife,
The wind with its pressure of grave mould,
And the dead, who walk and walk.

{1957}

FOR YOU ARE A LEGION

All these cars, my beloved, are on their way to your nuptials;
All these cars, freighted with fevered lovers.
With hymeneal chant of horns, and streamers
Of the new snow, they sweep gaily

Toward a thousand pledgings, and feastings, and a thousand
   ravishings.

A thousand of you, my love, being wooed and wedded,
There will remain, alone, unleashed, the you by me created.

All these cars, my love, bear the mourners from your obsequies
To the place of interment, and the spadeful of earth trickled on
   the caskets.
The cerements of January mist are about them,   10
And the blooms banked about these many hearses
Are as bright as the blossoms of the marriage day.

When bright limbs by thousands lie
Locked in the strait embrace of casketings,
Then will that you by me created follow its wild way
Along strange paths, and labyrinthian;
The passages of my innumerable hearts.

For you are a legion, my love, and I am an army; but only
The two of the many endure that I have created.

{1958}

JAY MACPHERSON

B.1931

Jay Macpherson was born in London, England, in 1931. She came to Newfoundland with her mother and brother at the age of nine, and in 1944 the family moved to Ottawa. When she was seventeen, some of her poems were published in *Contemporary Verse*, the Vancouver quarterly. She took her B.A. from Carleton College in Ottawa and an M.A. and Ph.D. in literature at the University of Toronto, both supervised by Northrop Frye. Robert Graves published her first collection, *Nineteen Poems*, in Mallorca in 1952. Macpherson published her second book, *O Earth Return!* with her own small press Emblem Books in 1954. From 1954 she taught at the University of Toronto; she was appointed Professor of English in 1973. In 1957 her best-known book, *The Boatman*, appeared; it incorporated both *O Earth Return!* and a suite of poems she had recently published in *Poetry*. The volume won the Governor General's Award and helped to establish the poetic sequence as a Canadian genre in the space between the poetry collection and the book-length long poem. It was reissued in 1968 as *The Boatman, and Other Poems*. *Welcoming Disaster: Poems, 1970–1974* was privately printed in 1974. The two collections were reissued together as *Poems Twice Told* in 1981; she has not published poetry since. Macpherson's scholarship focusses on pastoral romance, the Narcissus legend, and other classical myths, some of which she retold in 1962 as *Four Ages of Man: The Classical Myths*. She retired in 1996.

The Third Eye

Of three eyes, I would still give two for one.
The third eye clouds: its light is nearly gone.
The two saw green, saw sky, saw people pass:
The third eye saw through order like a glass
To concentrate, refine and rarify
And make a Cosmos of miscellany.
Sight, world and all to save alive that one
Fading so fast! Ah love, its light is done.

[1951] {1957}

The Anagogic Man

Noah walks with head bent down; —
For between his nape and crown
He carries, balancing with care,
A golden bubble round and rare.

Its gently shimmering sides surround
All us and our worlds, and bound
Art and life, and wit and sense,
Innocence and experience.

Forbear to startle him, lest some
Poor soul to its destruction come,
Slipped out of mind and past recall
As if it never was at all.

O you that pass, if still he seems
One absent-minded or in dreams,

10

Consider that your senses keep
A death far deeper than his sleep.

Angel, declare: what sways when Noah nods?
The sun, the stars, the figures of the gods.

{1957}

THE FISHERMAN

The world was first a private park
Until the angel, after dark,
Scattered afar to wests and easts
The lovers and the friendly beasts.

And later still a home-made boat
Contained Creation set afloat,
No rift nor leak that might betray
The creatures to a hostile day.

But now beside the midnight lake
One single fisher sits awake   10
And casts and fights and hauls to land
A myriad forms upon the sand.

Old Adam on the naming-day
Blessed each and let it slip away:
The fisher of the fallen mind
Sees no occasion to be kind,

But on his catch proceeds to sup;
Then bends, and at one slurp sucks up

The lake and all that therein is
To slake that hungry gut of his,

Then whistling makes for home and bed
As the last morning breaks in red;
But God the Lord with patient grin
Lets down his hook and hoicks him in.

{1957}

A GARDEN SHUT

A garden shut, a fountain sealed,
And all the shadowed mountains yield:
Dear Reader sits among the rocks
And fiddles at my seven locks.

How green my little world is grown
To entertain the man of stone!
The green man in the garden's lap
Draws his fill of vital sap,
But when the south wind blows is seen
Spineless as any other green.
The stone man with his burden on
Stands as stiff as Solomon,
Or wintry Herod made his heir –
Small comfort for my garden there.

The fishes in my garden's eye
Like thoughts, or thoughts like fish go by.
The crystal of the morning air
Leads up the daughters mild and fair

Closed in their bells of tinkling glass
Precious as ever Sheba was,   20
To gently promenade the place,
This circle of their earthly race;
Till from the shade in pride and scorn
Bursts the impetuous Unicorn,
Shatters the day and blacks the sun,
Spits rudely on his sexual thorn
The virgins one by shrieking one,
Crushes the green, and fells the stone,
Breaks fountain, wall, and so is gone.

Reader, here is no place for you.   30
Go wander as the wild birds do,
And never once, in peace reposed,
Wonder on whom my garden closed.

[1957] {1981}

No Man's Nightingale

Sir, no man's nightingale, your foolish bird,
I sing and thrive, by Angel finger fed,
And when I turn to rest, an Angel's word
Exalts an air of trees above my head,
Shrouds me in secret where no single thing
May envy no-man's-nightingale her spring.

{1957}

A LOST SOUL

Some are plain lucky – we ourselves among them:
Houses with books, with gardens, all we wanted,
Work we enjoy, with colleagues we feel close to –
        Love we have, even:

True love and candid, faithful, strong as gospel,
Patient, untiring, fond when we are fretful.
Having so much, how is it that we ache for
        Those darker others?

Some days for them we could let slip the whole damn
Soft bed we've made ourselves, our friends in Heaven   10
Let slip away, buy back with blood our ancient
        Vampires and demons.

First loves and oldest, what names shall I call you?
Older to me than language, old as breathing,
Born with me, in this flesh: by now I know you're
        Greed, pride and envy.

Too long I've shut you out, denied acquaintance,
Favoured less barefaced vices, hoped to pass for
Reasonable, rate with those who more inclined to
        Self-hurt than murder.   20

You were my soul: in arrogance I banned you.
Now I recant – return, possess me, take my
Hands, bind my eyes, infallibly restore my
        Share in perdition.

{1974}

OLD AGE OF THE TEDDY-BEAR

Ted getting shabby –
skull beneath skin?
No, but as matting,
bare patches, begin,
nameless maimed baby
peers out from within.

Once it was Tadwit,
now merely It:
old links with You and Him
no longer fit: 10
the melting snowman's slide,
leaving just grit?

Poor ted? no – frightening,
way it seems now:
angel that shielded me
gone soft like dough:
now to that damaged thing
what do I owe?

Something in both of us
never got born: 20
too late to hack it out,
or to unlearn
needed, familiar pain.
Come, little thorn.

{1974}

WHAT FALADA SAID

All I have left from home – the horse that brought me,
Dead, flayed, its head hung up, its power of speaking
Left, like an echo – gives its daily message
    In the dark entry:

"Daughter, betrayed and drudging here in exile,
Those who let these things happen were – believe me –
Foreigners, strangers, none of those who loved you:
    Not your true mother.

She if she knew would send someone to fetch you,
Carry you home, restore the past, again her   10
Child, joy from pain: at least, if she could know it
    She would be sorry."

So on my nursery floor my dolls consoled me.
No: there are four, not two: a constellation
Turning: maimed child, barbed mother – torn, rent open
    Womb, bladed baby.

{1974}

ANNE WILKINSON
1910–1961

Anne Gibbons was born in Toronto; she grew up there and in London, Ontario. Her mother was descended from the eminent Osler family, and Wilkinson would write an account of their history as *Lions in the Way: A Discursive History of the Oslers* (1956). After her father's death when Anne was nine, the family lived with her maternal grandfather in his Rosedale mansion, a setting she later identified as one of the "four corners of [her] world." She attended progressive schools in the United States and France. In 1932 she married Frederick Wilkinson, a surgeon; their marriage was dissolved in 1953. She wrote little before her early thirties, apart from a prize-winning childhood piece; her poems began to appear in periodicals only in the mid-1940s. She was the literary editor of the Toronto periodical *Here and Now* in 1949. Her first collection, *Counterpoint to Sleep,* was published in 1951, and *The Hangman Ties the Holly* in 1955. In 1956 she helped to found and generously endowed a new literary quarterly, the *Tamarack Review,* which would fill the gap left after 1953 by the cessation of *Contemporary Verse* in Vancouver and the imminent closure of John Sutherland's *Northern Review.* Wilkinson died of lung cancer in Toronto in 1961. A.J.M. Smith published her *Collected Poems of Anne Wilkinson and a Prose Memoir* in 1968. Dean Irvine edited *Heresies: The Complete Poems of Anne Wilkinson* in 2003.

O DON'T YOU HEAR THE WORM

"O don't you hear the worm
Turning the sod?"
"Softly, my silly,
The worm's on the rod."

"Turn away, blood's running
Down your poor head."
"Love, let the sunset
Reflect its own red."

"O move or you'll lie
On a row of spiked thorn."   10
"Hush, tis the green grass
Just newly shorn."

"Surely you taste my death
Sour on your tongue?"
"Not while your kisses
Are honey-bee hung."

"O can't you smell
The old rot of the dead?"
"My lovely, their bones
Will grow your rose bed."   20

"Now where do you go?
You nod off to sleep –"
"Why, where I am deaf
Though angels weep."

[1951] {2003}

In June and Gentle Oven

In June and gentle oven
Summer kingdoms simmer
As they come
And flower and leaf and love
Release
Their sweetest juice.

No wind at all
On the wide green world
Where fields go stroll-
Ing by
And in and out
An adder of a stream
Parts the daisies
On a small Ontario farm.

And where, in curve of meadow,
Lovers, touching, lie,
A church of grass stands up
And walls them, holy, in.

Fabulous the insects
Stud the air
Or walk on running water,
Klee-drawn saints
And bright as angels are.

Honeysuckle here
Is more than bees can bear
And time turns pale
And stops to catch its breath
And lovers slip their flesh

And light as pollen
Play on treble water   30
Till bodies reappear
And a shower of sun
To dry their languor.

Then two in one the lovers lie
And peel the skin of summer
With their teeth
And suck its marrow from a kiss
So charged with grace
The tongue, all knowing
Holds the sap of June   40
Aloof from seasons, flowing.

{1955}

LENS

I

The poet's daily chore
Is my long duty;
To keep and cherish my good lens
For love and war
And wasps about the lilies
and mutiny within.

My woman's eye is weak
And veiled with milk;
My working eye is muscled
With a curious tension,   10

Stretched and open
As the eyes of children;
Trusting in its vision
Even should it see
The holy holy spirit gambol
Counterheadwise,
Lithe and warm as any animal.

My woman's iris circles
A blind pupil;
The poet's eye is crystal,   20
Polished to accept the negative,
The contradictions in a proof
And the accidental
Candour of the shadows;

The shutter, oiled and smooth
Clicks on the grace of heroes
Or on some bestial act
When lit with radiance
The afterwords the actors speak
Give depths to violence,   30

Or if the bull is great
And the matador
And the sword
Itself the metaphor.

II

In my dark room the years
Lie in solution,
Develop film by film.

Slow at first and dim
Their shadows bite
On the fine white pulp of paper.   40

An early snap of fire
Licking the arms of air
I hold against the light, compare
The details with a prehistoric view
Of land and sea
And cradles of mud that rocked
The wet and sloth of infancy.

A stripe of tiger, curled
And sleeping on the ribs of reason
Prints as clear   50
As Eve and Adam, pearled
With sweat, staring at an apple core;

And death, in black and white
Or politic in green and Easter film,
Lands on steely points, a dancer
Disciplined to the foolscap stage,
The property of poets
Who command his robes, expose
His moving likeness on the page.

{1955}

On a Bench in the Park

On a bench in the park
Where I went walking
A boy and girl,

Their new hearts breaking
Sat side by side
And miles apart
And they wept most bitterly.

"Why do you mourn,"
I asked,
"You, who are barely born?"   10

"For gold that is gone,"
Said the girl,
"I weep distractedly."

I turned to the youth,
"And you?"
"For what I have not gained," he cried,
"Possessing her
I lost myself and died."

And so we sat, a trio
Turned to sobs,   20
And miles to go
And miles and miles apart

Till they, amazed
That one as old as I
Had juice enough for tears,
Dried their streaming eyes
To ask the cause of mine.

I told of the grit I'd found
In a grain of truth,
Mentioned an aching tooth   30
Decayed with fears

And the sum of all I'd lost
In the increased tax on years.

They yawned and rose
And walked away. I moved
To go but death sat down.
His cunning hand
Explored my skeleton.

1955

POEM IN THREE PARTS

I

Those behind me
Those about me
Millions crowding to come after me
Look over my shoulder.

Together we consider
The merit of stone
(I hold a stone in my hand for all to see)
A geologist tells the time it has endured
Endurance, a virtue in itself, we say,
Makes its own monument.   10

We pause, resent
The little span
A miser's rule
Inched out for man

But blood consoles us
Can be squeezed from us
Not from stone.

Saying this fools no one
A sudden bluster of words
Claims for human seed   20
A special dispensation
Foxes and flowers and other worthies
All excluded.

Immediately sixteen creeds
Cry out to be defended —
A state of emergency exists;
Flying buttresses
Revolving domes, a spire extended
By the spirit of
A new a startling growth of thorns   30

Skies in Asia catch
On uptilted wings of temples
In the Near East the talk is of stables.

II

Above-below the din
A few quiet men
Observe the cell's fragility

How Monday's child
Makes Tuesday's vegetable
And Wednesday petrifies
The leaf to mineral   40

While Friday sparks the whole in fire
And Sunday's elements disperse
And rise in air.

III

The stone in my hand
Is my hand
And stamped with tracings of
A once greenblooded frond,
Is here, is gone, will come,
Was fire, and green, and water,
Will be wind.   50

{1955}

THE RED AND THE GREEN

Here, where summer slips
Its sovereigns through my fingers
I put on my body and go forth
To seek my blood.

I walk the hollow subway
Of the ear; its tunnel
Clean of blare
Echoes the lost red syllable.

Free from cramp and chap of winter
Skin is minstrel, sings   10
Tall tales and shady
Of the kings of Nemi Wood.

I walk an ancient path
Wearing my warmth and singing
The notes of a Druid song
In the ear of Jack-in-the-Green.

But the quest turns round, the goal,
My human red centre
Goes whey in the wind,
Mislaid in the curd and why of memory.   20

Confused, I gather rosemary
And stitch the leaves
To green hearts on my sleeve;
My new green arteries

Fly streamers from the maypole of my arms,
From head to toe
My blood sings green,
From every heart a green amnesia rings.

{1955}

NATURE BE DAMNED

I

Pray where would lamb and lion be
If they lay down in amity?
Could lamb then nibble living grass?
Lamb and lion both must starve;
For none may live if all do love.

II

I go a new dry way, permit no weather
Here, on undertaker's false green sod
Where I sit down beneath my false tin tree.
There's too much danger in a cloud,
In wood or field, or close to moving water.   10
With my black blood – who can tell?
The dart of one mosquito might be fatal;

Or in the flitting dusk a bat
Might carry away my destiny,
Hang it upside down from a rafter
In a barn unknown to me.

I hide my skin within the barren city
Where artificial moons pull no man's tide,
And so escape my green love till the day
Vine breaks through brick and strangles me.   20

III

I was witch and I could be
Bird or leaf
Or branch and bark of tree.

In rain and two by two my powers left me;
Instead of curling down as root and worm
My feet walked on the surface of the earth,
And I remember a day of evil sun
When forty green leaves withered on my arm.

And so I damn the font where I was blessed,
Am unbeliever; was deluded lover; never   30

Bird or leaf or branch and bark of tree.
Each, separate as curds from whey,
Has signature to prove identity.

And yet we're kin in appetite;
Tree, bird in the tree and I.
We feed on dung, a fly, a lamb
And burst with seed
Of tree, of bird, of man,
Till tree is bare
And bird and I are bone   40
And feaster is reborn
The feast, and feasted on.

IV

I took my watch beside the rose;
I saw the worm move in;
And by the tail I yanked him out
And stamped him dead, for who would choose
To leave alive a sin?

The pale rose died of grief. My heel
Had killed its darling foe,
Worm that cuddles in the heart   50
To ravish it. If worm not tell
How should rose its fairness know?

V

Once a year in the smoking bush
A little west of where I sit
I burn my winter caul to a green ash.
This is an annual festival,

Nothing to stun or startle;
A coming together – water and sun
In summer's first communion.

Today again I burned my winter caul   60
Though senses nodded, dulled by ritual.

One hundred singing orioles
And five old angels wakened me;
Morning sky rained butterflies
And simple fish, bass and perch,
Leapt from the lake in salutation.
St. Francis, drunk among the daisies,
Opened his ecstatic eye.

Then roused from this reality I saw
Nothing, anywhere, but snow.   70

[1957] {1960}

VARIATIONS ON A THEME

A man needs only to be turned round once with his eyes shut in this world to be lost.
    — THOREAU

I

There is always a first flinging
Of the blood about in circles,
A falling down, a sickness ringing

In the ear, a swivelling eye
Uprooting tree whose tendrils flower
On sagging skin of sky.

Green blades cut, they spin so fast.
Round and round, a child on grass
Whose name in anagram is lost.

II

I turned round once; I shut my eyes;   10
I opened them on truth or lies.
And this is what I saw though
Cannot say: or false or true.

From arteries in graves, columns
Rose to soil the sky, and down
Their fluted sides the overflow
Slid to earth, unrolled and spread
On stalk and stone its plushy red.

Trees had shed their limbs, become
Mobile marble guards. Secret   20
Their manoeuvres in this land;
And while they marched a mad dog's tooth,
Rabid violet, tore half my hand.

The wind blew from the south
Before I turned, but here a north
Wind blew, and I was lost. It blew
A milch cow dry, a new moon down;
Then higher roared until it blew
Seven fuses of the sun.

III

We shut our eyes and turned once round   30
And were up borne by our down fall.
Such life was in us on the ground
That while we moved, earth ceased to roll,
And oceans lagged, and all the flames
Except our fire, and we were lost
In province that no settler names.

IV

I shut my eyes and turned once round;
I opened them on alien air;
Sea had shrunk to farmer's pond
And sky was pink and distance near.   40
A forest and its nights were now
Woodpile for an old man's fire;
And where above me one black crow
Had cawed my spring, two dirty doves
Sang daintily. I stoned the birds
But no stone hit, for of white gloves
My hands were made; I stole a stick
To break the sky; it did not crack;
I could not curse – though I was lost,
Had trespassed on some stranger's dream   50
Where swan forswears his lust,
The gull his scream.

V

I shut my eyes and turned twice round;
Once for death, once for love.

I fell down twice upon the ground
But what I saw I cannot prove.

Death turned me first. When he had done
Black rings moved about the sun;
Love turned me next. I fell to rest
In quicksand, and was quickly lost.   60

Death turned me first, will twirl me last
And throw me down beneath the grass
And strip me of this stuff, this dress
I am, although its form be lost.

{1957}

PHYLLIS WEBB

B.1927

Phyllis Webb was born in Victoria, British Columbia, and grew up there and in Vancouver. She studied with Roy Daniells and Earle Birney at the University of British Columbia. In the early 1950s she lived in Montreal, where she worked as a secretary at McGill University and completed a year of graduate study. Her first volume publication was in *Trio* (1954) with Eli Mandel and Gael Turnbull. *Even Your Right Eye,* her first solo collection, appeared in 1956. In 1957 she left for Paris, where she wrote for the CBC. After her return she taught in the English department at U.B.C. and published *The Sea Is Also a Garden* (1962). At the historic poetry conference at U.B.C. in 1963 she met American poets Charles Olson and Robert Creeley. She left academia to spend the subsequent year in San Francisco. Webb went to Toronto in 1964 as a CBC program organizer; with William Young she developed the long-running radio program *Ideas* (1966 to the present). In 1965 Webb published *Naked Poems,* with a revolutionary minimalism, dramatic exploitation of white space (which cannot be properly replicated below), and new uses of voice and line. Despite its impact, she published no new collections between *Naked Poems* and *Wilson's Bowl* (1980), although her *Selected Poems 1954-1965* appeared in 1971. When *Wilson's Bowl* was not even nominated for a Governor General's Award, a number of prominent Canadian writers raised funds for an award to Webb to express their great esteem for her work. In 1982 she published two collections of poetry, *Sunday Water: Thirteen Anti-Ghazals* and *The Vision Tree: Selected Poems,* the latter winning a Governor General's Award, as well as a selection of her essays and radio work, *Talking*. 1984's *Water and Light: Ghazals and Anti-Ghazals* extended her exemplary use of the arcane Persian verse form.

LEAR ON THE BEACH AT BREAK OF DAY

Down on the beach at break of day
observe Lear calmly observing the sea:
he tosses the buttons of his sanity
like aged pebbles into the bay;

cold, as his sexless daughters were,
the pebbles are round by a joyless war,
worn down on a troubled, courtly ground,
they drop in the sea without a sound;

and the sea repeats their logical sin,
shedding ring after ring of watery thin   10
wheels of misfortune of crises shorn
which spin to no end — and never turn.

And there Lear stands, alone.
The sun is rising and the cliffs aspire.
And there Lear stands, with dark small stones
in his crazed old hands. But farther and higher

he hurls them now, as if to free
himself with them. But only stones drop
sullenly, a hardened crop,
into the soft, irrational sea.   20

{1954}

MARVELL'S GARDEN

Marvell's garden, that place of solitude,
is not where I'd choose to live
yet is the fixed sundial
that turns me round
unwillingly
in a hot glade
as closer, closer I come to contradiction,
to the shade green within the green shade.

The garden where Marvell scorned love's solicitude —
that dream — and played instead an arcane solitaire,   10
shuffling his thoughts like shadowy chance
across the shrubs of ecstasy,
and cast the myths away to flowering hours
as yes, his mind, that sea, caught at green
thoughts shadowing a green infinity.

And yet Marvell's garden was not Plato's
garden — and yet — he *did* care more for the form
of things than for the thing itself —
ideas and visions,
resemblances and echoes,   20
things seeming and being
not quite what they were.

That was his garden, a kind of attitude
struck out of an earth too carefully attended,
wanting to be left alone.
And I don't blame him for that.
God knows, too many fences fence us out
and his garden closed in on Paradise.

On Paradise! When I think of his hymning
Puritans in the Bermudas, the bright oranges
lighting up that night! When I recall
his rustling tinsel hopes
beneath the cold decree of steel,
Oh, I have wept for some new convulsion
to tear together this world and his.

But then I saw his luminous plumèd Wings
prepared for flight,
and then I heard him singing glory
in a green tree,
and then I caught the vest he'd laid aside
all blest with fire.

And I have gone walking slowly in
his garden of necessity
leaving brothers, lovers, Christ
outside my walls
where they have wept without
and I within.

{1956}

SPROUTS THE BITTER GRAIN

Sprouts the bitter grain in my heart,
green and fervent it grows as all
this lush summer rises in heats about me,
calls along the vines of my wrath,
chokes and enchants my eyes.
Even the crows that nest in this valvular forest
scream and collect the glittering fires

of my hatreds, dispose this desperate love,
my fury, amid the sinister leaves.
Hot, the wind threatens my trees with weather,   10
rushes the crows to skies of their ancient glory,
vultures, and I watch, tormented by sun.
I am all land to this malignant grain, ambiguous,
it burgeons in a single season, like fear.
Like fear I have known it, a forest of green angels,
a threat of magnificent beasts. And Oh, I call,
Oh, to the gods of the temperate climes,
Praise me, destroy these criminal branches,
bring me – soft – the weather of meadows,
the seasons and gardens of children.   20

{1956}

PROPOSITIONS

I could divide a leaf
and give you half.

Or I could search for two leaves
sending you one.

Or I could walk to the river
and look across

and seeing you there,
or not there,

absence or presence,
would spring the balance to my day.   10

Or I could directly find you and take your hand
so that one hand would be given

and one kept, like a split leaf
or like two leaves separate.

These would be signs and offerings:
the just passion, just encountering.

Or we perhaps could speed four eyes,
the chariot horses of our dreams and visions,

in them direction and decision find.
The split leaf floating on the river,   20

the hand sketching in the air
a half-moon, its hidden wholeness there.

[1959] {1962}

BREAKING

Give us wholeness, for we are broken.
But who are we asking, and why do we ask?
Destructive element heaves close to home,
our years of work broken against a breakwater.

Shattered gods, self-iconoclasts,
it is with Lazarus unattended we belong
(the fall of the sparrow is unbroken song).
The crucifix has clattered to the ground,
the living Christ has spent a year in Paris,
travelled on the Metro, fallen in the Seine.   10

We would not raise our silly gods again.
Stigmata sting, they suddenly appear
on every blessed person everywhere.
If there is agitation there is cause.

Ophelia, Hamlet, Othello, Lear,
Kit Smart, William Blake, John Clare,
Van Gogh, Henry IV of Pirandello,
Gerard de Nerval, Antonin Artaud
bear a crown of darkness.
It is better so.   20

Responsible now each to his own attack,
we are bequeathed their ethos and our death.
Greek marble white and whiter grows
breaking into history of a west.
If we could stand so virtuously white
crumbling in the terrible Grecian light.

There is a justice in destruction.
It isn't "isn't fair."
A madhouse is designed for the insane,
a hospital for wounds that will re-open,   30
a war is architecture for aggression,
and Christ's stigmata body-minted token.
What are we whole or beautiful or good for but to be absolutely
    broken?

{1962}

MAKING

Quilted
patches, unlike the smooth silk loveliness
of the bought,
this made-ness out of self-madness
thrown across their bones to keep them warm.
It does.

Making
under the patches a smooth silk loveliness
of parts:
two bodies are better than one for this quilting,   10
throwing into the dark a this-ness that was not.
It does.

Fragments
of the splintered irrelevance of doubt, sharp
hopes, spear and splice into a nice consistency as once
under the pen, the brush, the sculptor's hand
music was made, arises now, blossom on fruit-tree bough.
It does.

Exercise,
exegesis of the will captures and lays   20
haloes around bright ankles of a saint.
Exemplary under the tree,
Buddha glows out now
making the intolerable, accidental sky
patch up its fugitive ecstasies.
It does.

It does,
and, all doing done, a child on the street runs

dirty from sun
to the warm infant born to soiled sheets   30
and stares at the patched external face.
It does.

From the making made and, made, now making
certain order – thus excellent despair
is laid, and in the room the patches of the quilt
seize light and throw it back upon the air.
A grace is made, a loveliness is caught
quilting a quiet blossom as a work.
It does.

And do you,   40
doubting, fractured, and untaught, St. John of the Cross,
come down and patch the particles and throw
across the mild unblessedness of day
lectures to the untranscended soul.
Then lotus-like you'll move upon the pond,
the one-in-many, the many-in-the-one,
making a numbered floral-essenced sun
resting upon the greening padded frond,
a patched, matched protection for Because.
And for our dubious value it will do.   50
It always does.

{1962}

POETICS AGAINST THE ANGEL OF DEATH

I am sorry to speak of death again
(some say I'll have a long life)
but last night Wordsworth's "Prelude"

suddenly made sense — I mean the measure,
the elevated tone, the attitude
of private Man speaking to public men.
Last night I thought I would not wake again
but now with this June morning I run ragged to elude
the Great Iambic Pentameter
who is the Hound of Heaven in our stress   10
because I want to die
writing Haiku
or, better,
long lines, clean and syllabic as knotted bamboo. Yes!

{1962}

NAKED POEMS SUITE 1

MOVING
to establish distance
between our houses.

It seems
I welcome you in.

Your mouth blesses me
all over.

There is room.

                              AND
                              here   10
                              and here and
                              here

and over   and
over   your mouth

TONIGHT
quietness. In me
and the room.

I am enclosed
by a thought

and some walls.

THE BRUISE   20

Again you have left
your mark.

Or we
have.

Skin shuddered
secretly.

FLIES

tonight
in this room

two flies   30
on the ceiling
are making

love
quietly. Or

so it seems
down here

YOUR BLOUSE

I people
this room
with things, a   40
chair,   a lamp,   a
fly   two books by
Marianne Moore.

I have thrown my
blouse on the floor.

Was it only
last night?

YOU
took

with so much   50
gentleness

my dark

[1963] {1965}

WILFRED WATSON

1911–1998

Known primarily as an experimental dramatist and the collaborator
of Marshall McLuhan on *From Cliché to Archetype* (1970), Wilfred
Watson was born in Rochester, England, and immigrated to
Duncan, British Columbia, with his family at the age of fifteen. He
was a sawmill worker for thirteen years. In 1940 he entered the
University of British Columbia, and in 1941 he married Sheila
Doherty. Sheila Watson would later publish experimental short
fiction and the great modernist novel *The Double Hook* in 1959.
Wilfred Watson enlisted in the Canadian navy in 1943. After the
end of the Second World War he took M.A. and Ph.D. degrees from
the University of Toronto; in 1954 he joined the English depart-
ment at the University of Alberta in Edmonton. His first volume of
poetry, *Friday's Child*, appeared with Faber and Faber in 1955.
Watson's plays began to be produced and published in the early
1960s. In his second volume of poetry, *The Sorrowful Canadians and
Other Poems* (1972), Watson began to experiment profoundly with
typography, numerology, and the white space of the printed page.
I Begin with Counting (1978) contains experimental concrete poems
arranging seventeen words on a stanza designed from a numerical
grid. From 1971 to 1978 he and his wife edited the little magazine
White Pelican at the University of Alberta. After his retirement in
1977 they lived in Nanaimo, British Columbia.

Graveyard on a Cliff of White Sand

By the unwashed beach
of the falling lake
there were three dead fish
collapsed in the belly;
and they were the walk
of ant and fly
who walked out of the cast and throw
of the mouldy wreath
when the gravedigger
hurried in the yellow   10
blow of the aspen leaf
and the tear shrank
into the mourner's eye

O mother grieving
the grief that is common and human
O woman wonderful
in your small miracle
of faith and loving –
quiet you, that another miracle
must come and the wind blow   20
into the troubles of the sky
the dust you place
on the upraised hand
of this high cliff – quiet you
that fence of rust
cannot keep, that ring
of cement cannot contain
when the gravedigger
spends his pay
and the wreaths moulder away   30

O love this world
if you can
where juniper
burns blue its cones
of seed and the whispering
weed candles and the moth
reshapes its figure
and the owl
owls it in the gully
and the hawk   40
hawks it and the cougar
pads out love's melancholy

this world, where
the bones shrink into
the grave and the cliff
whitens with birth
and the dead wave
is pierced by the living
reed, and love weeps
to fill the earth   50

Windermere Lake, B.C.

{1955}

O MY POOR DARLING

   O my poor darling
Legs arms and round backside
Flanks and thighs hotly eyed
Pawed at and then devoured

Chawed, masticated in
The fiery lion's inside
A sad end for a bride
   O my poor darling

   O my poor darling
I thought of Christian martyrs who   10
Were more disposed than you
To have the great beast spew
Them to eternity
And the later life anew
   O my poor darling

   O my poor darling
How could there be a joy
In such power to destroy?
How could such power employ
His glorious rage, to tooth?   20
How could such teeth annoy
   O my poor darling

   O my poor darling
What if the great beast seize
You with its gouty knees?
What if its great lungs wheeze?
What if its cruel gambols were
Age's senilities?
   O my poor darling

   O my poor darling   30
What is the bridegroom's song?
Lust? to lust in the young
Is to itch in the old man's dung –

Death and age in the genitals
Of youth creep like a worm along
    O my poor darling

    O my poor darling
How cruel that blazing face
How fierce was that grimace
That like an opening was ·
Yawning and grinning wide
Into a consuming furnace —
    O my poor darling

    O my poor darling
When the saints began to pray
The beast began to play;
When the saints began to play
It lifted up its paw to heaven
And brought it down to slay
    O my poor darling

    O my poor darling
How can an old, aged lion
Liver heart lungs reins stones
Nerve sinew bowels gone
Complete a martyrdom?
What has this bridegroom done?
O my poor darling —
    O my poor darling

{1955}

R.A.D. FORD
1915–1998

Robert Arthur Douglas Ford was born in Ottawa. He received a
B.A. from the University of Western Ontario and an M.A. in history
from Cornell University. He taught briefly at Cornell before joining
the Department of External Affairs in 1940. His distinguished
diplomatic career included postings to Colombia, Yugoslavia, and
Egypt, and culminated with his service as Ambassador to the Soviet
Union from 1968 to 1980. From 1980 to 1985 he was the federal gov-
ernment's special advisor on East-West relations. His first book of
poetry, *A Window on the North,* was published in 1956 and won the
Governor General's Award. It included his own poetry, marked by
his characteristic blend of formal precision and an historically and
geo-politically situated melancholy, as well as the first of his excep-
tionally able translations of Russian poetry, which he would gather
later as *Russian Poetry: A Personal Anthology* in 1984. In his second
collection, *The Solitary City* (1969), he translated as well from
Brazilian, Serbo-Croatian, and French poets. His *Coming from Afar:
Selected Poems 1940-1989* was published by McClelland and Stewart
in 1990. He died at Vichy, France.

A DELUSION OF REFERENCE

The arms of the sea are extended,
The hills, which are not really mountains,
Extinguished, and a delusion
Of reference sets in when you spread

Your hair to the light. It is a contagion
Like any other, and in all the cantons
Of the East there is no cure. Things
Unconnected seem in harmony, blazon
Before me, the shotgun becomes a decoration
On the wall, and pheasants' wings   10
Furnish the meadow. Until you turn away
Again negligently, and the reason
Of nature disappears while the universe
Settles into its usual disarray.

{1956}

ROADSIDE NEAR MOSCOW

Bent and heavy with rain,
Staggering in silence, profoundly
Occupied with the secret reconstruction
Of their balance, pine and tamarack
Trees, gathered in profane

Assembly to watch over the slow
Passing of the almost human-like
Column of prisoners, waiting for the snow
To fill in their tracks — strange
Judges of evil done   10

In many ways. Because I am not
Walking in chains, and am afraid
To look, lest by implication
Glance should be said guilty,
Unhappily turn my head

To the stale spectacle of the sun
Setting among the conifers.
And when it is gone, look down
For the column of men in vain –
In the thick arch of night 20

That has come suddenly,
Hobble my eyes to perceive
Nothing but the rain, turning
To snow – all that I wish to see.

{1956}

ELDON GRIER

1917–2001

Eldon Grier was born in London, England, while his father served with the Canadian army during the First World War. The family returned to Montreal in 1918. Grier left private school at the age of seventeen to become a painter. He studied under Goodridge Roberts and John Lyman in Montreal; *circa* 1945 he was apprenticed in Mexico to muralist Diego Rivera. Thereafter he taught at the Montreal Museum of Fine Art, under the supervision of Arthur Lismer. He contracted tuberculosis in 1950 and endured two and a half years of hospitalization. His second marriage, to painter Sylvia Tait in 1954, coincided with his taking up a career as a poet. The couple travelled widely; a substantial part of Grier's poetry was written in response to the scenes and persons he encountered. His first four books were privately printed. *The Ring of Ice* (1957) incorporated graphic work and watercolours by Tait. *A Friction of Lights* was published by the influential Contact Press in 1963. Subsequent volumes, including *Selected Poems 1955-1970* (1971), appeared with Louis Dudek's Delta Canada imprint. Grier's finest poems engage in overt or unspoken dialogue with the great artists of Modernism; his style and Dudek's invite comparison, especially in their travel poems. His *Collected Poems* appeared in 2000.

FROM *An Ecstasy*

This lively morning,

the young surveyors are warbling like Italians
and the first wasp moves spastically over
ashen winter grasses.

The great vista of the freight-yard is an enigma
I leave to my children.

Conspicuous for their absence are gondolas
In the crooks of the old canal.

Loving praise, a schoolgirl reads aloud beside
The bubblegum machine.   10
"His strong arms were about her.
'You shall not go back into the chest tonight!'"
(A perfect age for a traditionalist, I think.)

The blackbirds have peacock feathers on their backs.

Bright red burns carelessly at the foot of
a grave.

A bald man, surely walking for his health, asks
eagerly, "How far before I get a view?"

Bottle caps and shoelaces, things that have
survived the bottom of the white winter's well   20
receive my entire admiration.

    Paradox, and the world unstitched for a new lacing.

* * *

This morning I looked for a poem, "Saltimbanques."

It had disappeared

as so many things are soon to disappear.

If you hurry
          to Europe
you may be in time to give a handout to the last beggar,
to see a king on his charger.
You may find nomadic street-performers in
some out-of-the-way place; the thin sad acrobats
of Picasso,   10
          and gypsies,
facing extinction like a tribe of aborigines, as
slack and incorrigible as ever.
You may feel there is nothing more moving than
fishermen pushing off from the sand in their curving boats,

and these will be the last to go.

But go they must, like old trees coming down,
like music from the streets.

And for a while
there will be greyness   20
and confused improvisation.

We shall feel outrage and despair at the sight
of our lives

until we recognize a new beauty
growing up about us, something less harrowing
and ornate – more serene,
lighting up the streets
                              with clear slabs of colour.

But there is no need to explain.
It has its standards already,   30

you know what I'm talking about –

music, coming from the most unlikely places,
like new blood,

black and white, full of vitality.

{1957}

VIEW FROM THE HILL

Strangely taut,
held with ineffable poise,
the evening hangs for an instant
like your question,
               ready to slide exhausted
               down the windowpane,
to roll its glinting eye once and for all
               in a parody of death.

No one can argue
with such a time.   10
The air is eggshell thin

and time wears a piqued look
    like your lovely face.
      The factories underneath
the hill have lost their muscle of smoke,
    that acquisitive bulge.

This is perhaps how we
should live, uncommitted,
tight as string, spare as saints
between the two extremes.   20
    Smile if you like –
    but here is some of
the poet's wish; the fine edge of your profile,
    the abstract of my love.

{1957}

View from a Window – Mexico

The tenderness so hard to swallow
is partly the two flies settled in her hair.
Her mouth opens to the soothing air,
drool scabs curving down from its edges.

And her brother whom she holds shyly for me to admire . . .
the mess of mucous and the clinging feeding flies . . .
awake, a toxic film covers his eyes
shifting mechanically in patterns of escape.

Across the steeply climbing flat-faced street
at the six vertical ochre strips   10
her older sisters, short skirts flaring from the hips,
emerge and blow away buoyant as wasps.

Beauty complicates the average squalor,
carries the unpredictable like fallout
into the brutal levels, burns about
the ruin and the green vine with its yearning.

She hangs around; she says she's eight.
Her name is tuned for ceremonial complaint;
mine is, that dozy flies can travel here without restraint
in the gentlest of hatchures.   20

{1963}

AFTERWORD

By Brian Trehearne

The poets in this anthology, all of whom matured creatively between 1920 and 1960, considered it one of their primary obligations to modernize Canadian writing, to bring the country's poetry out of late Romantic stasis after the Great War into a fertile and combative response to the cultural, political, technological, philosophical, religious, and economic conditions of the modern era. To make it new, Ezra Pound's emblematic demand to the era's poets, was the constitutive literary ambition of the period of which this anthology offers a representation. No poet of significance emerging at the time failed to perceive this obligation, or failed in greater or lesser degree to fulfil it. That, in a word, is their modernism. It binds them, and it gives the period's poetry great consensual force. When we focus on each poet's other sensed obligations – for instance, to cultural nationalism; Communism; landscape mimesis; religious skepticism, or affirmation; introspection; gender skepticism; humanism; political evolution or revolution; engagement with global conflict – their shared energies may be dispersed, albeit into powerful visions. Individual poets may be defined and differentiated to points of such antipathy that it can be difficult to see any shared cultural consciousness at all: a Dorothy Livesay *versus* a Robert Finch, for example. But in their common reaction against Romanticism and its legatees, and in their commitments to modern poetry's possibilities of profound newness – for newness could be profound in and of itself in this period – they make up one great movement in Canada's cultural history.

This point of view gives rise, of course, to one of the anthology's principles of selection (see the Editorial Preface). There were prolific and/or highly popular poets active in the period who are not in this book: for instance, Annie

Charlotte Dalton, Katherine Hale, and Edna Jaques; or for that matter, Wilson MacDonald, Robert Norwood, and Arthur Stringer. They are absent because they did not feel that imperative of renewal and also because, in the editor's view, they did not publish any traditional poems worthy of renewed readership today. They certainly published poems of technical merit at times, in the terms of the late Romantic culture in which they were trained and to which they remained dedicated; but the merit of poems does not exist in a historical vacuum, and a competent Romantic poem written in the era of Mussolini or the Spanish Civil War or the Holocaust loses much of its merit to anachronism. The poets who did not perceive making it new as a radical obligation after the Great War were not responding fully or with compelling insight to the conditions of their time. Their merit, then, could *only* be technical and conservative; and in only one such case, that of Audrey Alexandra Brown, did technical merit in and of itself seem so compelling as to demand the poet's inclusion in the volume. She is the only poet here without any susceptibility to modernism or grasp of its inevitability in her chosen art; yet such a superb imitator of Keats deserves re-reading. She stands firm as the exception that proves the rule of the times.

As a principle of inclusion rather than exclusion, the shared will-to-modernize is clarifying of the historical situation of poets writing earlier in the period. E.J. Pratt has long been spoken of, by enough critics that we may call it a consensus, as a transitional figure, one who saw sufficiently beyond his Victorian cultural and moral education to grapple with some of the essential cruces of meaning in the modern world. It is certainly a worthwhile debate to ask whether Pratt is a modernist, and our multiple answers will of course depend on what we think essential or incidental to modernism. But no one will dispute that Pratt saw the need for a substantial renovation of poetic technique, embodied it in his own practice, and admirably championed others who went further in that line. His prodigious expansion of Canadian poetic diction alone is enough to tell us that a startling newness in poetry was an essential feature of his program for Canadian poetry. In addition, his determination to make the decasyllabic line susceptible of the vernacular rhythms of people of his time, and his inclusion in *The Titanic* of a multiplicity of voices and perspectives on the maritime tragedy, speak to his excitement at poetry's new technical liberty in the modern period. Was Pratt a modernist? I would say not, because I believe that the technical experiments are not allowed to generate multiple and conflictual notions of truth and because his individualism and humanism were shaken but not shattered by the century's events. But that he was *modern* for his times no one can reasonably deny. Other figures here we might also think transitional – for example, Louise Morey Bowman, Kenneth Leslie, Finch, Leo Kennedy – are in this same sense irrefutably modern, albeit for varying reasons of technique and understanding. Whatever the Victorian or Georgian echoes in their work, whatever their level of accomplishment in the project, they were all, ultimately, driven to be new.

Over the last thirty years or so the canon of modernist Canadian poetry has been considerably thinned out. Many poets once acclaimed at or near the centre of the canon – whether by critics, or anthologists, or the Governor General's Literary Awards committee – have been allowed to disappear from the field-defining anthologies of our time. Among these are Leslie, Finch, Charles Bruce, Anne Marriott, and Douglas LePan. A second group largely absent from contemporary critical discussion is composed of poets recognized in their own day as minor, but maintained within the canon's margins at the time by anthologists, editors, and critics: such figures as W.W.E. Ross, Raymond Knister, Kennedy, Kay Smith, George Johnston, Patrick Anderson, Miriam Waddington, and Elizabeth Brewster. A third group received little sustained recognition in their own day: for example, Bowman, Joe Wallace, Goodridge MacDonald, Floris Clark McLaren, and Eldon Grier. The fourth group is, of course, that of the major poets still too well established to be left out of any serious anthology: F.R. Scott, Earle Birney, Livesay, Irving Layton, Anne Wilkinson, and so on. In most cases, contemporary anthologies have significantly reduced the representation of these major poets' works relative to pre-1980 compendia. Only in the wholly deserving cases of A.M. Klein and P.K. Page has the typical representation of their poetry increased in recent years. All of these groups are included in the present anthology, in order to restore and extend as far as space permits our contemporary grasp on modern poetic activity in Canada. The period's poetry was deeper, broader, richer, and more various than we have recently wanted it to appear. The major figures remain in the foreground here, by quantity as by quality, but their works will be newly legible when backlit by Canadian modernist poetry's remarkable breadth and energy. Incidentally, that breadth is regional as well as canonical. The absence of poets from the prairies or from Canada's north is to be regretted, and it is dictated by the very low level of modernizing poetic activity in English specific to those places in the period in question; apart from these, the selection runs from Newfoundland to Vancouver Island.

The diversity of voices in the present anthology may encourage readers to renew or to rebut some of the prevailing critical assumptions about modernism and may suggest as yet unexplored means of reading the poets in literary-historical and biographical relation to one another. In preparing the anthology I have found it striking, for example, and discomfiting, how many good but critically forgotten poets were combatants in the Second World War. Birney's war poetry has remained reasonably well-known because of justified acclaim for the frequently anthologized "Road to Nijmegen" and because of his satirical novel of army life *Turvey* (1949), but fellow soldier-poets Johnston, LePan, George Whalley, and Bertram Warr are among those whose work anthologists have recently been readiest to set aside. All but Johnston wrote about their experiences, typically well after war's end (and Johnston may have done so elliptically in his satirically violent suburban portraits). The glimpse of war experience provided in this book invites new critical consideration of the poetry written by Canada's returning soldiers – and by one who did not return – and may serve as a useful counterweight to a canon largely centred on noncombatants. On a different front, it has been common since the literary contests of the 1940s to note the prevalence among Canadian poets of the academic profession; the identification is not typically complimentary, and it lurks as a subtext in a number of persistent critical narratives and judgments of Canadian modernism. The biographical headnotes in this book certainly affirm the demographic pattern, but it is to be hoped that fresh readers will at least want to verify the assumed link between the academic profession of a given poet and some well-defined academic quality in the verse. Meanwhile, such other professions as diplomacy, journalism, and social work were noticeably attractive to Canada's modern poets. Most readers of Page will be aware that her public service as the wife of a Canadian ambassador in a series of diplomatic postings played a part in the arc of her own creative life. Among their colleagues in Canada's diplomatic service in the 1950s were LePan and R.A.D. Ford. Poets making a significant part of their living from journalism, from hard-scrabble freelance writing to full employment at major Canadian news outlets, included Wallace, Leslie, MacDonald, Bruce, Ralph Gustafson, and Phyllis Webb. Employed at various periods of their lives as social workers were Livesay, Waddington, and Margaret Avison; the list suggests the attractiveness of the profession as one of the few in the period open to politicized women. I rehearse these professions of the Canadian modern poets for a number of reasons: to weaken the association we may still intuit between academia and Canadian modernist lives; to weaken, too, any presumption we may retain that modernist poets in Canada or else-where somehow remained aloof, in their poems or in their persons, from the historical conditions of their times; and to suggest, if only by association, the range of expertise, interest, and inspiration that their professions must have brought to their poetry and to hint at the kinds of rich historical contextualiza-tion that remain to be provided in the study of modern poetry in Canada.

The great cataclysmic events of the twentieth century directly engaged all of the poets in this book, although their responses vary widely, according above all to their judgment of poetry's role in public and political life (including the conviction, in a few cases, that it *has* none). The 1920s during which Canadian modernism in English emerged, in Toronto with the work of Bowman, Pratt, Knister, Ross, and Livesay, and in Montreal with A.J.M. Smith, Scott, Kennedy, and Klein, was fundamentally a post-war decade. Memories of unprecedented suffering in the Great War gave rise to a mood of cultural devastation and loss that coupled vitally but paradoxically with a fervent sense of moral liberation, a bubble of rapid economic expansion and profit, a new English-Canadian nationalist sentiment, and dramatic new art forms – mass photography, jazz, the talkies – that encouraged Canadian artists to slough off their post-Victorian educations and audiences. The Depression that followed the stock market crash of 1929 focussed poets' minds sharply in turn on the foundations of the capital-ist economy, on North American structures and experiences of class, and on social and economic reform. Most of the major poets of the decade aligned themselves with the politics of the left, with socialism the dominant affiliation (Scott, A.J.M. Smith, Kennedy, Leslie, Klein), while Livesay's Communism helped to cost her a place in Scott's mini-anthology *New Provinces: Poems of Several Authors* in 1936. Other Communist poets of the Depression did not in fact write poetry consistently or in their mature voices until after the decade's end: the briefly Stalinist Layton, the briefly Trotskyite Birney, and the life-long Leninist Wallace are examples.

The battle of the Canadian left against Fascism was in one sense lost, and in another won, when the Second World War began. Josef Stalin's agreement with Adolf Hitler on a pact of mutual non-aggression facilitated the Nazi leader's military ambitions for German expansion in Europe and severely disillusioned many on the left who had imagined the Soviet Union as a heartland of global resistance to the Fascist threat. On the other hand, the British and Canadian declarations of war with Germany (September 3 and 10, 1939 respectively) brought the long battle of the left against Fascism to its decisive moment and committed the Allied countries to a life or death struggle. The conflict gave rise in Canada, however, not immediately to a literature of war but to a home-front poetry with primarily social, economic, and psychological interests. A common periodical question of the day, "Where are the War Poets?," had as noted above a straightforward answer: they were fighting, and the poetry they wrote about their experiences of battle would either not be published or not be written until their service was completed. Nevertheless the remarkable poetic activity of the Canadian 1940s must be read against the backdrop of this unprecedented global conflict. A.J.M. Smith's "Ode: The Eumenides" incorporates an earlier poem entitled "On Seeing Pictures of the War Dead"; Page's "Stenographers" suffer in substantial part because of the absence of their "boyfriends of blood"; Layton's "The Swimmer" undergoes a symbolic initiation into the "act of war"; Klein's extraordinary representations of modern Montreal are partly generated by a desire – and, furtively, an inability – to look away from the "shaven heads" of his people in the concentration camps of Fortress Europe. Much critical work might be done on the crystallization in this home-front poetry of the psychological pressures of living and writing in a society at war.

The years after war's end raised new spectres of cataclysm as the industrial scale and atrocity of the Holocaust came gradually clear to those outside liberated Europe, and the little-understood power of the atom bomb that had forced Japan's surrender became iconic and psychologically searing with media coverage of the first hydrogen-bomb tests of the mid-1950s. A real grappling with the Cold War that took shape in the post-war years and dominated global politics in the 1950s would await major expression in poetry until the 1960s, following the apocalyptic brinksmanship of the Cuban missile crisis in 1962. By no means irrelevantly, Canadian poets of the 1950s were struggling, in a post-war era of Russian and American military and economic expansion, suburbanism and conformism, and renewed public moral hypocrisy, to affirm in various ways the right to individual consciousness and individual liberties. So, of course, was rock and roll. The new and maturing poetry voices of this period are notably more confessional than those of modernism's first twenty-five years, and this emphasis on a private language bridges the poetry of lyric self-assertion (that of Layton, Louis Dudek, Waddington, and Raymond Souster) with the intense psychological, satiric, and religious concerns of the newer impersonal poets (Johnston, Avison, James Reaney, Webb, Jay Macpherson). In most cases this inward turn was not a retreat so much as a determination to rediscover the grounds and stability of individual consciousness and belief in an era that rewarded a youth passed in wartime anxiety with bland new forms of collectivization and consumption.

Detailed historical contextualization of the writing of individual poets and of the collectives they formed makes up a relatively small proportion of critical activity on the period's literature. The major critical narratives of Canadian modernist poetry, when these have been sought, have instead been focussed on the developing doctrines and ideological contests of modernist poetic technique, broadly construed. A.J.M. Smith gave the modern Canadian poets their first major taxonomy when he distinguished "native" from "cosmopolitan" poets in his controversial introduction to *The Book of Canadian Poetry* in 1943. His preference for a cosmopolitan modernism was made clear by his inclusion of contemporary poets publishing in the Montreal little magazine *Preview* (1942–45), such as Anderson and Page, and his exclusion of the poets of *First Statement* (1942–45), such as Layton, Dudek, Waddington, and Souster. *First Statement* editor John Sutherland's rebuttal to Smith in his introduction to *Other Canadians: An Anthology of the New Poetry in Canada, 1940-1946* ridiculed Smith's own aestheticism and defended the *First Statement* group's phenomenological method and commitment to representations of the actual lived world in the increasingly Americanized vernacular of the day. Sutherland and the other editors of *First Statement* had also by this time propounded a critical distinction of some durability between poets who apparently took their example from British modern poetry (the *Preview* group, he suggested, and the earlier modernists) and others – who happened to publish in *First Statement* – who found American modernism more idiomatic in the Canadian reality. Related to these issues is another constitutive framework for the study of Canadian modernist poetry, that is, the prolonged debate within modernism in Canada, and in some cases within individual poetic careers, between the impersonalist orthodoxy descending from T.S. Eliot, Pound, and James Joyce *via* A.J.M. Smith to Canadian poetic theory, and the growing need to register subjective and engaged experience in lyric poetry, especially after the Second World War. The power of Smith's criticism, example, and anthology selections (not to mention the international prominence and weight of Eliot, Marianne Moore, and W.H. Auden) made the impersonal mode dominant in Canadian poetry to about 1950. Thereafter, the poets in the ascendant were increasingly lyric in orientation and intimate in subject matter: John Glassco, Layton, Dudek, Waddington, Grier, and Souster among those included here, Leonard Cohen and Al Purdy among those finding their characteristic voices in the 1960s (and on those grounds absent from the present selection). Intimate *lyric* is a notably male genre at the end of the modernist period; the new women poets of the 1950s, Avison, Webb, Wilkinson, and Macpherson, perhaps following the example of Page rather than of Livesay, must partly have determined on their rigorous impersonality of treatment as a means of making their mark in a literary culture in which Smith and men of his generation's views still held substantial editorial power.

Partly because of such strong disputes at mid-century, another set of useful critical narratives has relied on the emergence and editorial convictions of literary periodicals as a way of giving shape to the diverse poetic doctrines, practices, and communities of the period. The biographical headnotes in this anthology will make clear the poets' various affiliations with such periodicals as the *Canadian Forum* (Toronto, 1921–2000), the *McGill Fortnightly Review* (Montreal, 1925–27), *New Frontier* (Toronto, 1936–38), *Contemporary Verse* (Vancouver, 1941–53), *Preview, First Statement, Contact* (Toronto, 1952–54), and *Civ/n* (Montreal, 1953–55), most of which are good examples of the little magazine that typified the revolution in publishing that took place in modernist literary cultures. The successive foundation and cessation of these periodicals certainly provides a solid framework for the study of Canadian modern poetry from the 1920s through the 1950s, and a valid part of our literary history emerges from careful study of the editorial practices, group sensibilities, critical positions and postures, and poetry published in each magazine. Recent work in the field of the Canadian little magazine has emphasized the need to supersede the polemics and rivalries the magazines' contributors themselves propounded in their editorials and reviews in search of a polyphonic and inclusive narrative that reveals their common cultural work. In these efforts, the work of women poets and editors in the history of Canadian little magazines, almost entirely occluded, has become strikingly clear. The powerful role played by little magazines in Canadian modernist development is furthermore a needed and concrete reminder of these poets' close relations to the modernism of the United States and England and, to a lesser extent, of Europe. The situation of Canadian modernism within the broader modernist revolution in many of the world's literatures invites continued research today, partly because the period's story has been told within nationalist or post-nationalist critical dispensations that make it hard to perceive how strenuously and powerfully Canadian writers were interacting at the time with their global contemporaries.

That being said, it is entirely legitimate to ask whether Canadian modernism has any particular hallmarks that distinguish it from contemporary work in America, England, and Europe. One such distinctiveness may already be apparent: that Canadian poets of the era vigorously rejected the attraction of a few American and Anglo-Irish modernists to authoritarian forms of government and instead chose alignment with the politics of the left. As raucous and divisive as these could be in the 1930s, often pitting Communist against Socialist with as much vehemence as either directed towards capitalism, the poetry and its poets stood four-square against the rise of Fascism, especially after 1935, when the Soviet-promulgated Popular Front of Communist parties and other leftist political groups led to an electoral success in France and an eventual concentration of shared energies in Canada. Their distinctive politics must be due in part to Canadian modernism's coming of age in the Depression era of W.H. Auden, Stephen Spender, and Cecil Day Lewis, rather than in the prior period of William Butler Yeats's, T.S. Eliot's, and Ezra Pound's dominance. It would be pleasant of course, though utterly groundless, to speculate that the proclivity indicated something deep and widespread in the Canadian political consciousness as well.

Another striking feature of Canadian modernism, at least in the period between the wars, is its implicit cultural nationalism. This claim would be anathema to some of the poets of the time. A.J.M. Smith spent much of his critical energy defending, in common with major modernist theorists elsewhere, the principle of internationalism – in literary terms, cosmopolitanism – in the Canadian arts, that is, that Canadian art of all media must be understood and judged not only against other Canadian works but against the greatest works of the most powerful cultural traditions in the world. Smith's rejection of cultural nationalism must be understood, however, in the context of the 1920s, in which conservative literary forces allied themselves with the self-celebration of a war-tested and proven Canada. Smith's counter-nationalist rhetoric was determined by his rejection of what he saw as the cultural boosterism of such groups as the Canadian Authors Association. Yet it was a rhetoric that sought to impose the highest literary standards on Canada, and it was clearly predicated on the belief that Canada's modern culture should, could, and indeed would stand as an equal with the great cultures of the world: in short, a cultural nationalism written larger still. Until the Second World War Canadian poets were likelier to accept Smith's rhetoric of anti-nationalism than to endorse the underlying nationalism of his demands, and most saw themselves, whether cosmopolitan modernists, Communists of the International, or soldiers of the Allied nations, as participating (in Smith's words) in "the universal civilizing culture of ideas." But renewed nationalist ambition arose from the Second as it had from the First World War, and the sharp reaction to Smith's promulgation of cosmopolitan and native Canadian traditions suggests that the younger poets and critics had begun to re-imagine the Canadian cultural experience so as to emphasize and promote its individuation and uniqueness. One cultural narrative of the 1950s involves the various nationalist landmark events of the decade: the hearings of the Royal Commission on National Development in the Arts, Letters, and Sciences, familiarly known as the Massey Commission, culminating in its historic report of 1951; resulting from that report, the foundation of a National Library in 1953 and the Canada Council in 1957; the paradigm-shifting Canadian Writers

Conference at Queen's University, Kingston, in 1955, with its proceedings published as *Writing in Canada* in 1956; and the foundation of *Canadian Literature*, the first scholarly journal of Canadian writing, in 1959. While it is initially tempting to understand the pre- and post-World War Two cultural rhetorics as antithetical, they are more fruitfully conceived as period-specific emphases within a shared consciousness of Canada's literary and cultural independence, potential, and accomplishment.

A final example in the space of the present discussion of Canadian modernism's distinctiveness is the delay in Canada's concerted development of the modernist long poem. Readers seeking in the volume a Canadian accomplishment that is made more legible by reference to T.S. Eliot's *The Waste Land* or Ezra Pound's *Cantos* will be puzzled to see the long poem's absence as a prominent form until Louis Dudek's experiments of the 1950s. Important exceptions include, of course, Pratt's *The Titanic* of 1935, Livesay's "Day and Night" of 1936, Marriott's ground-breaking *The Wind Our Enemy* of 1939, and Klein's "Portrait of the Poet as Landscape" of 1945, all of which are included in the present volume. Yet none of these master-works of Canadian poetry succeeded in establishing a model for later poets or in making the long poem a durable and widespread Canadian genre. They are relatively isolated accomplishments, characteristic of the poet but not of his or her era, and the relation of each to modernism is fruitfully debatable: Klein's poem, for example, is scornful of modernist experimentalism and coterie culture. On the other hand, Dudek's private championing of the modern Canadian long poem in the course of the 1950s was of clearer modernist provenance – the influence of Pound was palpable, at least in *Europe* (1954) – and much broader impact. His influence on the *Tish* group's practice is well-documented, and the long poem became a definitive Canadian genre thereafter, although it would soon develop post-modern forms and anti-forms of structure and voice.

It was perhaps on such narrow grounds that Robert Kroetsch once remarked that Canadian literature "evolved directly from Victorian into Postmodern ... The country that invented Marshall McLuhan and Northrop Frye did so by not ever being Modern." Kroetsch's notorious remark bears repeating as exemplifying a critical attitude that vitiated Canadian modernist studies in the last two decades of the twentieth century. His prejudice has been exuberantly refuted in recent years by a new generation of modernist critics who are re-examining and re-editing the Canadian modernist canon, to remind us of the multitude of possible stories to be told about Canadian writing from the end of the Great War to the Canadian literary boom, self-celebration, and renaissance of the 1960s. The foundations of that centennial activity, and so many of its pre-occupations, will be found in the period of Canadian poetry represented in this book. It was in these years that Canadian poets first confronted global conflict on a world-destructive scale, and shaped a language of resistance; first raised questions of gender in economic, psychological, canonical, and ecological terms, and gave shape to feminist autobiography; first articulated Freudian and Jungian psychologies and recognized their inevitable impact on poetic voice and style; first took the death of God for granted, or struggled for faith among so many who thought God dead; first demanded and then forced a liberation of sexuality in poetic language and the popular imagination; first reconciled themselves to and found a way to live symbolically in modern urban space; first understood and represented the structures and human consequences of a class- and capital-based social contract; and first recognized that civilizations of the utmost apparent security may come to a sudden end, and insisted that poetry had a part to play in their necessary survival. They inherited and defended, too, many of the most forceful ideas of their Romantic predecessors: the defining power of transcendent and epiphanic vision; the unique nature, power, and above all perception of the poet; the tension of public and private selves; the continual renewal in poetic style of the vernacular; and the indisputable attractions of an intermittent withdrawal into the aesthetic realm. It is the editor's hope that the anthology will make possible a renewed audition of these weaving strands of voice and vision among the modern period's poets and encourage us to go on telling the history of these ideas in new and compelling ways.

SOURCES FOR COPY-TEXTS OF POEMS

Anderson, Patrick. "The Ball," "Drinker," "Winter in Montreal," "Rink," "Spiv Song" from *Return to Canada: Selected Poems* (Toronto: McClelland & Stewart, 1977). "Boy in a Russian Blouse" from *The White Centre* (Toronto: Ryerson Press, 1946).

Avison, Margaret. *Always Now: The Collected Poems*, vol. 1. Erin, Ontario: Porcupine's Quill, 2003. Poems reprinted from *Always Now* (in three volumes) by Margaret Avison by permission of The Porcupine's Quill. Copyright Margaret Avison, 2003.

Bailey, A. G. *Miramichi Lightning: The Collected Poems of Alfred Goldsworthy Bailey.* Fredericton: Fiddlehead Poetry Books, 1981.

Birney, Earle. *Collected Poems of Earle Birney.* Toronto: McClelland & Stewart, 1975.

Bowman, Louise Morey. "Sea Sand" from *Moonlight and Common Day* (Toronto: Macmillan, 1922). "The Old Fruit Garden" from *Dream Tapestries* (Toronto: Macmillan, 1924). "The Tea Kettle" from *Characters in Cadence* (Toronto: Macmillan, 1938).

Brewster, Elizabeth. "In the Library" from *East Coast* (Toronto: Ryerson Press, 1951). "If I Could Walk Out into the Cold Country," "Return of the Native" from *Collected Poems of Elizabeth Brewster*, vol. 1 (Ottawa: Oberon Press, 2003).

Brown, Audrey Alexandra. "Dante's Beatrice" from *A Dryad in Nanaimo*, 2nd ed. (Toronto: Macmillan, 1934). "Candles in the Glass" from *All Fools' Day* (Toronto: Ryerson Press, 1948). "To Chopin" from *Challenge to Time and Death* (Toronto: Macmillan, 1943).

Bruce, Charles. "Sea Sense" from *Wild Apples* (Sackville, New Brunswick: Tribune Press Ltd., 1927). "Tomorrow's Tide," "Armistice Day" from *Tomorrow's Tide* (Toronto: Macmillan, 1932).

Call, Frank Oliver. *Acanthus and Wild Grape*. Toronto: McClelland & Stewart, 1920.

Daniells, Roy. *Deeper into the Forest*. Toronto: McClelland & Stewart, 1948.

Dudek, Louis. "A Street in April" from *East of the City* (Toronto: Ryerson Press, 1946). "A White Paper," "On Poetry," "From *En Mexico*," "From *Atlantis*" from *Infinite Worlds* (Montreal: Vehicle Press, 1988). Some passages of "From *En Mexico*" corrected as in *The Poetry of Louis Dudek* (Ottawa: Golden Dog Press, 1998).

Finch, Robert. "The Statue," "Train Window," "The Smile," "Scroll-Section" from *Poems* (Toronto: Oxford University Press, 1946). "Window-Piece" from *The Strength of the Hills* (Toronto: McClelland & Stewart, 1948).

Ford, R.A.D. *Coming from Afar: Selected Poems 1940-89*. Toronto: McClelland & Stewart, 1990.

Glassco, John. *Selected Poems*. Toronto: Oxford University Press, 1971.

Grier, Eldon. *Selected Poems 1955–1970*. Montreal: Delta Canada, 1971.

Gustafson, Ralph. *Collected Poems* (in three volumes). Victoria: Sono Nis Press, 1987.

Johnston, George. *Endeared by Dark: Collected Poems*. Erin, Ontario: Porcupine's Quill, 1990. "War on the Periphery" and "Poor Edward" reprinted from *The Essential George Johnston* by permission of The Porcupine's Quill. Copyright George Johnston, 2007.

Kennedy, Leo. *The Shrouding*. Toronto: Macmillan, 1933.

Klein, A.M. *Complete Poems of A.M. Klein*. Toronto: University of Toronto Press, 1990. © University of Toronto Press Incorporated 1990. Reprinted with permission of the publisher.

Knister, Raymond. *Windfalls for Cider: The Poems of Raymond Knister*. Windsor: Black Moss Press, 1983.

Layton, Irving. Various poems from *A Wild Peculiar Joy: Selected Poems*. Copyright © 1982, 2004 by Irving Layton. Copyright © 2007 by the Estate of Irving Layton. Published by McClelland & Stewart Ltd. All poems reprinted with permission of the publisher and the author's estate.

LePan, Douglas. *Weathering It: Complete Poems 1948–1987*. Toronto: McClelland & Stewart, 1987.

Leslie, Kenneth. *O'Malley to the Reds and Other Poems*. Halifax: The Author, 1972.

Livesay, Dorothy. "On Looking into Henry Moore," "Green Rain," "Signature," "Lament," "The Touching," "Day and Night," "Bartok and the Geranium" from *The Self-Completing Tree: Selected Poems* (Vancouver: Porcepic, 1999). Poems reprinted with permission from Dundurn Press Ltd. Copyright 1999. "Testament," "Leda Again," Sea Sequence" reprinted from *Archive for our Times* (Vancouver: Arsenal Pulp Press, 1998) with permission of the publisher.

MacDonald, Goodridge. "Equestrians in the Spring Night" from *Compass Reading* (Toronto: Ryerson Press, 1955). "The Mocking," "For You are a Legion" from *Selected Poems* (Fredericton: Fiddlehead Poetry Books, 1970).

Mackay, L.A. *The Ill-Tempered Lover.* Toronto: Macmillan, 1948.

Macpherson, Jay. *Poems Twice Told: The Boatman and Welcoming Disaster.* Toronto: Oxford University Press, 1981.

Marriott, Anne. *Sandstone and Other Poems.* Toronto: Ryerson Press, 1945.

McLaren, Floris Clark. *Frozen Fire.* Toronto: Macmillan, 1937.

Page, P.K. *The Hidden Room: Collected Poems* (in two volumes). Erin, Ontario: Porcupine's Quill, 1997. Reprinted from *The Hidden Room* (in two volumes) by P.K. Page by permission of The Porcupine's Quill. Copyright P.K. Page, 1997.

Pratt, E.J. *Selected Poems.* Toronto: University of Toronto Press, 2000. © University of Toronto Press Incorporated 2000. Reprinted with permission of the publisher.

Reaney, James. "The Plum Tree," "Antichrist as a Child," "The Windyard," "Gifts" from *Poems* (Toronto: New Press, 1972). "April" from *A Suit of Nettles* (Toronto: Macmillan, 1958). Poems reprinted with permission from Dundurn Press Ltd. Copyright 1999.

Ross, W.W.E. *Shapes and Sounds: Poems of W.W.E. Ross.* Don Mills, Ontario: Longmans, 1968.

Scott, F.R. *Collected Poems of F.R. Scott.* Toronto: McClelland & Stewart, 1981.

Smith, A.J.M. *Complete Poems of A.J.M. Smith.* Edited by Brian Trehearne. London, Ontario: Canadian Poetry Press, 2007.

Smith, Kay. "Words for a Ballet" from *Footnote to the Lord's Prayer* (Montreal: First Statement Press, 1951). "You in the Feathery Grass," "When a Girl

Looks Down," "The One Stem" from *The Bright Particulars: Poems Selected and New* (Charlottetown: Ragweed Press, 1987).

Souster, Raymond. *Collected Poems of Raymond Souster*, vol. 1. Ottawa: Oberon Press, 1980.

Waddington, Miriam. *Collected Poems*. Toronto: Oxford University Press, 1986.

Wallace, Joe. *Poems*. Toronto: Progress Books, 1981.

Warr, Bertram. *Acknowledgement to Life: The Collected Poems of Bertram Warr*. Toronto: Ryerson Press, 1970.

Watson, Wilfred. "O My Poor Darling" from *Friday's Child* (New York: Farrar, Straus and Cudahy, 1955). "Graveyard on a Cliff of White Sand" from *Poems: Collected, Unpublished, New* (Edmonton: Longspoon / NeWest, 1986).

Webb, Phyllis. "Lear on the Beach at Break of Day," "Marvell's Garden," "Propositions," "Breaking," "Poetics Against the Angel of Death," "*Naked Poems* Suite 1" from *Selected Poems: The Vision Tree* (Vancouver: Talonbooks, 1982). "Sprouts the Bitter Grain," "Making" from *Selected Poems 1954–1965* (Vancouver: Talonbooks, 1971).

Whalley, George. *The Collected Poems of George Whalley*. Kingston, Ontario: Quarry Press, 1986.

Wilkinson, Anne. *Heresies: The Complete Poems of Anne Wilkinson, 1924–1961*. Edited by Dean Irvine. Montreal: Signal Editions, 2003.

The editor and publisher gratefully acknowledge the permission granted to reproduce the copyright material in this book. Every effort has been made to trace copyright holders and to obtain their permission for the use of copyright material. The publisher would be grateful to be notified of any corrections that should be incorporated in future reprints or editions of this book.

EDITORIAL EMENDATIONS TO COPY-TEXTS

The notes below indicate all changes made to indicated copy-texts. The word or phrase before the] is from the text of the poem as printed in this anthology; the word or phrase after the] is an error or other anomaly in the copy text.

page 4: Bowman, "Sea Sand"
LINE 20 rhythmical] rythmical

page 14: Knister, "Corn Husking VII"
LINE 38 on,"] on."

page 18: Wallace, "The Five Point Star"
LINE 20 pass] pass.

page 19: Wallace, "All My Brothers Are Beautiful"
LINE 16 buff] bluff

page 198: Finch, "Scroll-section"
LINE 1 practise] practice."

page 213: Marriott, *The Wind Our Enemy:*
LINE 136 "When I Grow Too Old to Dream"] "When I grow too Old to Dream"

page 240: Page, "If It Were You"
LINE 45: for a certain] for certain

page 343: Layton, "For My Sons, Max and David"
LINE 28 conquerors] conquerers

INDEX OF AUTHORS

INDEX OF TITLES AND FIRST LINES